Instant

CORBA

Robert Orfali • Dan Harkey • Jeri Edwards

WILEY COMPUTER PUBLISHING

JOHN WILEY & SONS, INC.

New York   Chichester   Weinheim   Brisbane   Singapore   Toronto

Publisher: Katherine Schowalter
Editor: Theresa Hudson
Managing Editor: Frank Grazioli
Text Design & Composition: Robert Orfali, Dan Harkey, and Jeri Edwards
Graphic Art: David Pacheco

This text is printed on acid-free paper.

The product descriptions are based on the best information available at the time of publication. Product prices are subject to change without notice.

Some illustrations incorporate clip art from Corel Systems Corporation's Corel Draw 5.0 clip art library.

All the views expressed in this book are solely the authors' and should not be attributed to IBM, BEA Systems, or any other IBM or BEA Systems employee. The three authors contributed equally to the production of this book.

Library of Congress Cataloging-in-Publication Data:

ISBN 0-471-18333-4

Foreword

Captain Zog

by Zog the Martian

Greetings, Earthlings! I'm Zog, the captain of the Martian team. My team and I have visited Earth several times to understand what distributed objects are all about. In our previous visits, we discovered **The Essential Distributed Objects Survival Guide**, and **Client/Server Programming with Java and CORBA**. These two books were absolutely vital in our mission to explore this new technology. We really like the concept of the *Object Web*; it has great potential for our Martian intergalactic network. So, we were very excited to hear about **Instant CORBA** by the same authors. We returned to Earth to pick up a copy of the book. We'll make sure everyone on Mars reads it to understand what CORBA is all about. If they're too busy, we'll tell them to take the Scenic Route. Yes, we will make sure that every Martian is CORBA-literate.

So what did I like about this book? It felt like it was talking directly to me and to my crew in a friendly voice. That's very important when you're from a foreign planet. The artwork is absolutely wonderful. I like to see pictures of myself in books (and especially on the cover). The ubiquitous scenarios show how objects really interact with each other. It's not that inert boring stuff you read in the textbooks. It makes objects come to life. As usual, the Soapboxes help us understand the issues and what the latest Earthling debates are all about. We like to hear strong opinions instead of just sterilized information.

Mars has adopted Java as its programming language and CORBA as its distributed objects infrastructure. So these "Martian books" are very helpful. They give us a jump-start on how to use distributed objects on our Intergalactic client/server webs. Hopefully, our CORBA objects will be able to talk to yours.

This book is very timely. I cannot recommend it enough to my fellow Martians. Through this foreword, I highly recommend this book to you Earthlings. If I can understand **Instant CORBA**, so can you. Through this foreword, I also want you to know that we're protesting the awful movie called *Mars Attacks*; it portrays Martians as war-like bullies. Nothing can be further from the truth. Martians are peace-loving beings. We use our distributed objects to improve Intergalactic communications and commerce, not to make war.

Preface

The next shift catalyzed by the Web will be the adoption of enterprise systems based on distributed objects and IIOP (Internet Inter-ORB Protocol). IIOP will manage the communication between the object components that power the system. Users will be pointing and clicking at objects available on IIOP-enabled servers.

The next version of Netscape Navigator and Netscape SuiteSpot Servers will be IIOP-compliant. IIOP will be integral to everything we do. Netscape Navigator will be able not only to browse content but also to browse objects. We expect to distribute 20 million IIOP clients over the next 12 months and millions of IIOP-based servers over the next couple of years. We'll put the platform out there so that people can start developing for it.

> — *Marc Andreessen,*
> *Netscape Cofounder*
> *(October, 1996)*

Marc Andreessen eloquently describes the *Object Web* or the morphing of distributed objects and the Web. The Object Web is the latest paradigmatic shift in the distributed software industry. It is redefining the way we develop, deploy, maintain, package, and sell our client/server applications. Objects break up the client and server sides of an application into smart components that can play together and roam across networks. The Web and Intranets provide the Intergalactic networks where these components live.

The Object Web is still under construction. It seems that everyone in the software business is building a piece of it today. The two foundation technologies of the Object Web are Java and CORBA/IIOP. Java provides the mobile code foundation; CORBA/IIOP provides the distributed object infrastructure.

CORBA and the Object Web

CORBA is a lot more than just an *Object Request Broker (ORB)*; it is also a complete distributed object platform. CORBA extends the reach of your applications across networks, languages, component boundaries, and operating systems. CORBA supplements Java with a rich set of distributed services that includes introspection, dynamic discovery, transactions, relationships, security, naming, and so on. CORBA provides the missing link between the Java mobile code environment and the world of intergalactic objects.

The major computing companies—including Sun, JavaSoft, IBM, Netscape, Apple, Oracle, BEA, and HP—have chosen CORBA/IIOP as their common way to connect distributed objects across the Internet and Intranets. Consequently, CORBA is about to become as ubiquitous as TCP/IP. In this book, we provide an instant guide to CORBA/IIOP; it's an introduction for people who are in a hurry.

What This Book Covers

Instant CORBA is a gentle guide to CORBA/IIOP. We start with the basic workings of a CORBA 2.0 ORB and the Object Web. Then we cover CORBA's 15 Object Services. Finally, we look at forthcoming CORBA attractions—the next-generation ORB. CORBA is a huge undertaking; it covers all aspects of distributed objects. Consequently, it is hard to do it justice in one short book. On the other hand, it's important that you understand the scope of this undertaking before you bury yourself in the details. In this book, we cover the big picture. But we also go into enough depth to give you an appreciation of how CORBA really works. If this is not enough, we include a bibliography and pointers on where to go for more information.

This book consists of four parts:

- **Part 1** starts with a gentle introduction to ORBs, IIOP, and the CORBA 2.0 infrastructure. Next, we look at the Object Web—the CORBA "killer app." This is not just another story of how an existing technology was adapted—via HTTP/CGI—to work with the World Wide Web. Instead, CORBA is replacing HTTP/CGI. The Web is bring recreated on top of a CORBA-based distributed object infrastructure. We explain what CORBA and Java do for each other. We also go over the Object Web's 3-tier client/server model. Finally, we cover the CORBA/Java ORBs. These are the newest and greatest ORBs written entirely in Java.

- **Part 2** explains the workings of a CORBA ORB in more detail. The ORB is the heart of CORBA. You must first master how it works before you can move on to more interesting things like distributed services and components. So we explain the ORB's static and dynamic invocations. The *Dynamic CORBA* lets you create very flexible systems where clients and servers discover each other at run time. We also explain CORBA's Interface Repository and introspection facilities. We show you how an object discovers its intergalactic universe. We also cover CORBA's activation services. An ORB must provide the illusion that all of its objects—and there can be millions of them—are up and running and active all the time, even though they are not.

- **Part 3** covers *all* 15 existing CORBA Services—OMG calls them collectively the *CORBAservices.* They include Naming, Events, Life Cycle, Persistence, Relationships, Externalization, Transactions, Concurrency Control, Licensing,

Query, Properties, Security, Time, Collections, and Trading Services. Object services are the basic building blocks for a distributed object infrastructure. They provide the next step up in the evolutionary chain toward creating distributed components—or what the OMG calls *business objects*. These services cover almost every aspect of distributed object computing.

■ **Part 4** is about the state of CORBA today and where it is going next. We first present a scorecard of the commercial ORBs. We tell you about the good, the bad, and the ugly in CORBA today. Then we cover CORBA, the next generation. We look at the near-term technologies that will most likely make it into CORBA 3.0 (due in mid-1997). The ORB itself will be enhanced with several new features—including messaging (MOM), multiple interfaces, and server-side portable frameworks. At a higher level, CORBA will be augmented with a Common Facility for *Mobile Agents* and a *Business Object Framework*. We conclude with the *Object Web II*—the final destination.

As you can see, we cover almost every aspect of CORBA in a very short space. To cover all this territory, we will keep this book moving at a fast pace.

How To Read This Book

As we recommend in all our books, it's best to ask your boss for a one-week, paid sabbatical to go sit on a beach and read this book. Tell him or her that it's the cheapest way to revitalize yourself technically and find out all there is to know about CORBA and the Object Web. If you have more important things to do on the beach (or little interest in the technical details), we suggest that you take the *Scenic Route*. It includes all the chapters in Parts 1 and 4. Look for the Scenic Route signs at the beginning of these chapters and in the Table of Contents. This will let you postpone reading the more technical chapters, but you will still have a solid overview of the Object Web and CORBA. The best news is that you should be able to complete the Scenic Route on a 5-hour plane ride. Consequently, this leaves you a lot more time for beach activities.

What the Boxes Are For

We use shaded boxes as a way to introduce concurrent threads in the presentation material. It's the book's version of multitasking. The *Soapboxes* introduce strong opinions or biases on some of the more controversial topics of distributed object computing. Because the discipline is so new and fuzzy, there's lots of room for interpretation and debate—so you'll get lots of Soapboxes that are just another opinion (ours). The *Briefing* boxes give you background or tutorial type informa-tion. You can safely skip over them if you're already familiar with a topic. The *Detail*

boxes cover some esoteric area of technology that may not be of interest to the general readership. Lastly, we use *Warning* boxes to let you know where danger lies.

Who Is This Book For?

CORBA is reshaping the Internet and client/server computing. By the end of 1997, CORBA and IIOP will become ubiquitous. This book is a quick guide to understanding CORBA, distributed objects, and the Object Web. It is for anybody who's associated with the computer industry and needs to understand where it's heading—this covers a very broad spectrum of readers. We wrote this book so that almost any computer-literate reader can take the Scenic Route; it will give you an "instant appreciation" of what the fuss is all about. The rest of the book gives you more details.

How Does This Book Compare With Our Other Books?

Your authors currently have 3 other books on the market that deal with CORBA and distributed objects in one way or another. And, they all have Martians on the cover. So, here's a guide to what these books cover (and how they compare):

- **Client/Server Programming with Java and CORBA** (Wiley, 1997) is about programming 3-tier client/server applications using CORBA and Java. We provide detailed code examples that use CORBA's rich programming features—including static and dynamic invocations, callbacks, introspection, the Interface Repository, and many others. We develop a framework for running CORBA server objects. We run benchmarks that compare CORBA/Java with the alternatives—DCOM, RMI, HTTP/CGI, and Sockets. We show how Java objects use CORBA to communicate with C++ objects, and vice versa. We develop a *Debit-Credit* benchmark for measuring the performance of database-centric 2-tier and 3-tier CORBA/Java applications. Finally, we develop a *Club Med* 3-tier client/server application using CORBA, Java, and JDBC. This book is for programmers.

- **The Essential Client/Server Survival Guide, Second Edition** (Wiley, 1996) provides an overview of the entire field of client/server computing—including NOSs, SQL databases, data warehouses, TP Monitors, groupware, the Internet, system management, tools, and distributed objects. The book also includes a 100-page introduction to the *Object Web*.

- **The Essential Distributed Objects Survival Guide** (Wiley, 1996) covers distributed objects in-depth—including CORBA, OpenDoc, DCOM/OLE, and ActiveX. The book also covers components, business objects, OpenStep, and Newi.

Instant CORBA is a standalone introduction to CORBA and the Object Web. To make this book stand on its own, we borrowed about 100 pages of relevant material from the two Survival Guides and the CORBA/Java programming book. We've consolidated everything you need to know about CORBA and the Object Web in one book. If you plan to write code, our CORBA/Java programming book starts out where this one leaves off.

A Personal Note

The common theme in all our books is that distributed objects and the Web are morphing into an *Object Web*. Each of our books provides one or more of the missing pieces. This book explains the CORBA underpinnings of the Object Web. We hope you enjoy the reading, the cartoons, and the Soapboxes. Drop us a line if you have something you want to "flame" about. We'll take compliments too. We're relying on word-of-mouth to let people know about the book, so if you enjoy it, please spread the word. You may also want to visit our Web site at *http://www.corbajava.engr.sjsu.edu*. Finally, we want to thank you, as well as our Martian friends, for trusting us to be your guides.

Acknowledgments

It's impossible to thank all the hundreds of people that helped us with this book. But, we'll give it a try:

- To Deans Don Kirk and Nabil Ibrahim of San Jose State University for providing Bob and Dan with a world-class CORBA/Java integration lab and for helping us set up a graduate research program around it. To IBM for giving Bob and Dan time to work on this CORBA/Java lab. To Microsoft for their generous donations to our lab—thank you, Jim Gray.

- To the BEA Tuxedo architects, field people, and large customers that have provided Jeri with tremendous insights on how ORBs and TP Monitors are currently being used in mission-critical environments.

- To Patty Dock, Ken Ausich, and their team of distributed object gurus for their ongoing support.

- To the technical people in different companies who helped us make some sense out of this difficult topic—including Marc Andreessen, Jeff Bauer, Tim Berners-Lee, Mark Betz, Jeff Bonar, Grady Booch, Ken Burgett, Rick Cattell, Dan Chang, Lee Chang, Ed Cobb, Alain Demour, Richard Finkelstein, Shel Finkelstein, Ira Forman, Bob Garnero, Pat Helland, Jim Gray, Gene Guglielmo, Pete Homan, Adam Ip, Ivar Jacobson, Ralph Johnson, Jeff Jones, Johannes Klein, Christina Lau, Charlie Kindel, Geoff Lewis, Marie Lenzi, Hal Lorin, Hari Madduri, Tom Mowbray, Ron Resnick, Mark Ryland, Chris Rygaard, Mary Rygaard, Annrai O'Toole, Kurt Piersol, Roger Sessions, Jon Siegel, Oliver Sims, Richard Soley, Dave Stodder, Chris Stone, John Tibbetts, Don Vines, Jon Udell, Walter Utz, Satya Vardharajan, Jonathan Wilcox, Jonathan Weedon, and Ron Zahavi.

- To the marketing directors and managers who fed us with up-to-the-minute information on their latest and greatest products—including Michael Barton, Lydia Bennett, Roger Bowman, Anthony Brown, Rick Berzle, Suresh Challa, Mala Chandra, Teri Dahlbeck, Bjorne Frogner, Barbara Hanscome, Scott Hebner, Jay Krackeler, Remy Malan, Cynthia McFall, John Parenica, Larry Perlstein, Cliff Reeves, and Nick Stier.

- To the Standish Group's Karen Boucher and Jim Johnson for making an early copy of their ORB report available to us.

- To our graduate students. Your energy was contagious.

- To Dave Pacheco for creating the wonderful technical illustrations in this book (the cartoons are still by Jeri).

- To our tireless copy editor, Larry Mackin.

- To the people at Wiley who had to deal with our pickiness—especially Terri Hudson, Frank Grazioli, Bob Ipsen, Moriah O'Brien, Ellen Reavis, and Katherine Schowalter.

- To the more than 300,000 readers of our previous books. Without your continued support we couldn't write these books.

Contents

Preface v

Foreword v

Part 1. CORBA: The Intergalactic Foundation 1

Chapter 1. Client/Server, CORBA-Style 3

Distributed Objects, CORBA-Style 4
   What Is a Distributed CORBA Object? 4
   Everything Is in IDL 5
   CORBA Components: From System Objects to Business Objects 6
OMG's Object Management Architecture 7
   The Object Request Broker (ORB) 7
   The Anatomy of a CORBA 2.0 ORB 10
CORBA 2.0: The Intergalactic ORB. 14
CORBAservices 17
   Object Services: Build-To-Order Middleware 19
CORBAfacilities 20
CORBA Business Objects 20
   Cooperating Business Objects 22
   The Anatomy of a CORBA Business Object. 23
   The Anatomy of a Client/Server Business Object. 24
   CORBA Component Nirvana 25
3-Tier Client/Server, Object-Style 27
Conclusion 28

Chapter 2. The Object Web: CORBA Meets Java 29

The Evolution of the Web 30
   CGI, The Protocol That Won't Go Away 31
   The 3-Tier Object Web 31
   Client/Server Interactions on the Object Web. 33
What CORBA Brings to Java 34

The Other Contenders 35
What Java Brings to CORBA 37
The Client/Server Object Web 38
Meet the Players 40
Conclusion 42

Chapter 3. Meet the CORBA/Java ORBs 43

Sun's Joe 44
NEO and Joe: A Short History 44
What Is Joe? 44
Iona's OrbixWeb 45
What Is OrbixWeb? 46
Visigenic's VisiBroker for Java 47
What Is VisiBroker for Java? 48
How Slow Are Java ORBs? 49
VisiBroker and Netscape ONE 49
Which Java ORB? 49
The Other CORBA ORBs 50
Conclusion 50

Part 2. ORB Fundamentals 51

Chapter 4. The Static CORBA 53

Static Versus Dynamic Methods 54
CORBA Static Method Invocations: From IDL to Interface Stubs 57
Conclusion 58

Chapter 5. The Dynamic CORBA 61

CORBA Dynamic Invocations 62
Dynamic Invocations: The Big Picture 62
The Dynamic Invocation Interfaces 64
Dynamic Invocation Scenarios 66
Dynamic Invocation: The Do-It-Yourself Scenario 66
Dynamic Invocation: The ORB-Can-Help Scenario 68
Dynamic Invocation: The Yet-Another-Way Scenario 69

Contents

The Price of Freedom 71
When To Use Dynamic 71
Conclusion 72

Chapter 6. The Existential CORBA 73

The CORBA 2.0 Initialization Interface 73
An Initialization Scenario 74
How You Find Your Other Objects 75
Who Activates My Objects? 76
The Server Side of CORBA 76
The CORBA::BOA Interface 76
BOA and Other Object Adapters 78
BOA Shared Server 79
BOA Unshared Server 80
BOA Server-per-Method 81
BOA Persistent Server 81
An Object Activation Scenario 82
Conclusion 84

Chapter 7. Metadata: Who Am I? 85

The CORBA IDL: A Closer Look 86
What Does an IDL Contract Cover? 87
The Structure of the CORBA IDL 87
An IDL Example 90
Type Codes: CORBA's Self-Describing Data 91
The CORBA 2.0 Interface Repository 92
What's an Interface Repository? 92
Why Is an Interface Repository Needed Anyway? 93
Interface Repository Classes: The Containment Hierarchy 93
The Interface Repository Class Hierarchy 94
Federated Interface Repositories 98
What Does a Global Repository ID Look Like? 99
CORBA IDL Without Pain 100
The Introspective CORBA Object 101
The CORBA Introspection Interface 101
Conclusion 102

Part 3. CORBA Services 103

Chapter 8. CORBA Services: Naming, Life Cycle, and Events. . . 105

The CORBA Object Naming Service 106
   Object Naming in a Nutshell 106
   What's in a CORBA Object Name? 107
   How Does It Work? 108
The CORBA Object Life Cycle Service 111
   A Compound Life Cycle Example 111
   The Life Cycle Interfaces 113
   The Compound Life Cycle Interfaces 114
The CORBA Event Service 115
   Suppliers and Consumers of Events 116
   Typed Events 118
   Point-to-Point Events 119
   Event Proxies 119
   The Push Event Interfaces 120
   A Push Event Scenario 122
Conclusion 124

Chapter 9. CORBA Services: Object Trader 125

Trading: The Big Picture 126
   Federated Traders 127
   Policies, Constraints, and Preferences 128
   The Core Trader Interfaces 129
   The Trader Administration Interfaces 131
   A Trader Scenario 132
Conclusion 134

Chapter 10. CORBA Services: Transactions and Concurrency . . 135

The CORBA Object Transaction Service 136
   What Is a Transaction? 136
   Object Transaction Service: Features 139
   The Elements of the Object Transaction Service 140
   The OTS Interfaces 141
   An Object Transaction Scenario 144
The CORBA Concurrency Control Service 146

The Concurrency Control Service and Transactions 146

Locks 147

Locksets 147

Nested Transactions and Locking 147

The Concurrency Control Interfaces 148

Conclusion 149

Chapter 11. CORBA Services: Object Security 151

Are Distributed Objects Less Secure? 152

CORBA Security: The Key Features 153

Authentication: Are You Who You Claim to Be? 154

Privilege Delegation: Whose Credentials Are These Anyway? 156

Authorization: Are You Allowed to Use This Resource? 158

Audit Trails: Where Have You Been? 160

Non-Repudiation: Can You Prove It in Court? 161

Non-Tampering and Encryption 163

Security Domains 163

Managing Security Policies 165

The Security Interfaces 166

The Security Extensions to the CORBA Object Model 166

Scenario: How You Manipulate Secure Objects 168

Interfaces for Security-Aware Applications 169

Scenario: Do-It-Yourself Access Control 171

Scenario: Do-It-Yourself Delegation 172

Scenario: Do-It-Yourself Audits 173

A Non-Repudiation Scenario 174

Interfaces for Security Administration 175

Out-of-the-Box Security: Common Secure IIOP 177

Conclusion 177

Chapter 12. CORBA Services: Persistence and Externalization . . 179

The CORBA Persistent Object Service (POS) 180

What Is POS? 180

Single-Level Stores Versus Two-Level Stores 182

POS: The Client's View 182

POS: The Persistent Object's View 183

The Elements of POS 183

POS Protocols: The Object-PDS Conspiracy 185

The POS Interfaces 186

The POS CLI Interfaces 187

The CORBA Externalization Service. 189

Stream Power. 190

Externalization Service: The Base Interfaces. 190

A Stream Scenario 192

Object Databases 194

What's an ODBMS Good For? 195

ODMG-93 and CORBA 198

Chapter 13. CORBA Services: Query and Collections 205

The CORBA Query Service. 205

Federated Queries 206

Collections for Manipulating Query Results 207

Query Service: The Collection Interfaces 207

Query Service: The Query Interfaces 208

A Simple Query Scenario 209

A More Complex Query Scenario 210

The CORBA Collection Service 212

Collection Basics 213

The CORBA Core Collection Types 213

Restricted-Access Collections 217

Conclusion 218

Chapter 14. CORBA Services: Object Relationships and Time . . 219

The CORBA Relationship Service 219

Why a Relationship Service? 220

What Exactly Is a Relationship? 220

Levels of Relationship Service 222

Relationship Service: The Base Interfaces 223

Relationship Service: Graphs of Related Objects 224

Relationship Service: The Containment and Reference Relationships 226

The CORBA Object Time Service 228

UTC Time 230

The Time Service Interfaces 230

A Timer-Based Event Trigger Scenario 232

Conclusion 234

Chapter 15. CORBA Services: Licensing and Properties **235**

The CORBA Object Licensing Service. 235
   What Does the Licensing Service Do? 236
   Licensing Service Interfaces 237
   A Licensing Scenario 238
The CORBA Object Property Service 239
   Property Service Interfaces 240
   Conclusion. 241

Part 4. CORBA: What's Next? **243**

Chapter 16. CORBA ORBs: The State of the Union **245**

The Vendor Scorecard 245
CORBA ORBs: The Good, the Bad, and the Ugly 247
   CORBA ORBs: The Good 247
   CORBA ORBs: The Bad 249
   CORBA ORBs: The Ugly 249
TP Monitors Meet ORBs 250
Is CORBA Ready for Client/Sever Prime Time? 253

Chapter 17. CORBA: The Next Generation **255**

CORBA 3.0: The Next-Generation ORB 256
CORBA 3.0 Messaging: ORB Meets MOM 256
   What Does CORBA Do for MOM? 257
   What Does MOM Do for CORBA? 257
   When to Use CORBA, MOM-Style 260
   How Will CORBA Do MOM? 261
CORBA 3.0: The Portable Server 262
   Is It Goodbye BOA? 263
   What Is POA? 263
   What Are SFAs? 264
CORBA 3.0: Multiple Interfaces and Versioning. 264
   The Composite Object 265
   Interface Versioning 266
CORBA 3.0: Pass-By-Value 267

Common Facilities: Compound Documents and Mobile Agents 268
    CORBA Mobile Agents. 268
    What Does a CORBA Agent Look Like? 268
    The Agent Execution Environment. 269
    CORBA Meets Compound Documents 270
    What Is OpenDoc? 274
    OpenDoc's Constituent Technologies 274
    Client/Server, OpenDoc-Style. 275
The CORBA Business Object Framework. 276
    The Elements of BOF. 277
    The Component Assembly Line. 279
Conclusion 279

Chapter 18. The Object Web II Vision 281

Compound Documents as Open Web Browsers 281
The Desktop Is the Browser 282
Compound Documents as Portable Component Stores. 283
What Is a Shippable Place? 284
The Future Web Client 285
The Object Web II 286
It's Time To Say Good-Bye. 288

Where to Go for More Information 289
Index 293

Part 1
CORBA: The Intergalactic Foundation

An Introduction to Part 1

We start Part 1 with a tour of the CORBA intergalactic foundation. We provide a gentle introduction to ORBs, IIOP, and the CORBA 2.0 infrastructure. Next, we look at the Object Web—the CORBA "killer app." This is not just another story of how an existing technology was adapted—via HTTP/CGI—to work with the World Wide Web. Instead, CORBA is replacing HTTP/CGI. The Web is bring recreated on top of a CORBA-based distributed objects infrastructure. We call this marriage of distributed objects and the Internet the *Object Web*.

The major computing companies—including Sun, JavaSoft, IBM/Lotus, Netscape, Apple, Oracle, BEA, and HP—have chosen the CORBA Object Web as their intergalactic component infrastructure. CORBA IIOP provides the common way to connect distributed objects across the Internet and Intranets. Consequently, CORBA could become almost as ubiquitous as TCP/IP. The Object Web will create a mass market for components that run on top of CORBA middleware. But, we're getting ahead of our story. To get the real scoop, read Part 1.

Here's what we will be covering in Part 1:

- **Chapter 1** provides a birds' eye tour of CORBA 2.0. It's the world's fastest introduction to CORBA for people that are *really* in a hurry. This is how you become an "Instant CORBA guru" in two hours or less. Of course, you must really be strapped for time to take this shortcut. For the rest of our readers, this chapter gives you the top-level view of CORBA—the forest. The trees are in Parts 2 and 3. By the end of this chapter, you'll know all about the ORB, IIOP, CORBAservices, CORBAfacilities, and CORBA business objects. You will also get a dose of 3-tier intergalactic client/server computing, CORBA-style.

- **Chapter 2** is about the Object Web—CORBA's killer app. We first tell you how CORBA does the Web. Then we tell you what CORBA does for Java, and vice versa. We explain how the Java and CORBA object models complement each other. Next, we compare CORBA with its competitors—including HTTP/CGI, DCOM/Java, Java RMI, and straight Sockets. Finally, we use a shopping mall analogy to introduce the CORBA Object Web players. It's quite a crowd.

- **Chapter 3** is about CORBA/Java ORBs. These are the newest and greatest ORBs, written entirely in Java. Consequently, they are also mobile ORBs—or *ORBlets*. Yes, you can now ship CORBA ORBs around the intergalactic network as part of a Java applet. ORBs will also be embedded in browsers so that you don't have to ship them around.

We hope that you'll enjoy this big-picture tour, even if you're into details. Part 1 provides the setting that you'll need to understand the rest of this book. If you're on the fast track, we suggest that you read all of Part 1 before jumping directly into Part 4. This may be all the CORBA you ever need.

Chapter 1

Client/Server, CORBA-Style

The *Common Object Request Broker Architecture (CORBA)* is the most important (and ambitious) middleware project ever undertaken by our industry. It is the product of a consortium—called the Object Management Group (OMG)—that includes over 700+ companies, representing the entire spectrum of the computer industry. The notable exception is Microsoft, which has its own competing object broker called the *Distributed Component Object Model (DCOM)*. For the rest of our industry, the next generation of middleware is CORBA. The CORBA object bus defines the shape of the components that live within it and how they interoperate. Consequently, by choosing an open object bus, the industry is also choosing to create an open playing field for components.

What makes CORBA so important is that it defines middleware that has the potential of subsuming every other form of existing client/server middleware. In other words, CORBA uses objects as a unifying metaphor for bringing existing applications to the bus. At the same time, it provides a solid foundation for a component-based future. The magic of CORBA is that the entire system is self-describing. In addition, the specification of a service is always separated from the implementation. This lets you incorporate existing systems within the bus.

CORBA was designed to allow intelligent components to discover each other and interoperate on an object bus. However, CORBA goes beyond just interoperability.

It also specifies an extensive set of bus-related services for creating and deleting objects, accessing them by name, storing them in persistent stores, externalizing their states, and defining ad hoc relationships between them.

CORBA lets you create an ordinary object and then make it transactional, secure, lockable, and persistent by making the object multiply-inherit from the appropriate services. This means that you can design an ordinary component to provide its regular function, and then insert the right middleware mix when you build it or create it at run time. So, welcome to the age of flexible "made to order" middleware. There is nothing like it for any other form of client/server computing.

This chapter is about the CORBA object bus and the object system services that extend the bus. We start with an overview of CORBA and what it does for intelligent components. We then cover the CORBA object model and the architecture that ties it all together. Finally, we will put the whole thing in a familiar client/server perspective. As you will see, some key distributed object pieces are still lacking. In Part 4, we will look at what's brewing in the upcoming OMG specifications.

DISTRIBUTED OBJECTS, CORBA-STYLE

Perhaps the secret to OMG's success is that it creates interface specifications, not code. The interfaces it specifies are always derived from demonstrated technology submitted by member companies. The specifications are written in a neutral *Interface Definition Language (IDL)* that defines a component's boundaries— that is, its contractual interfaces with potential clients. Components written to IDL should be accessible across languages, tools, operating systems, and networks. And with the adoption of the CORBA 2.0 specification in December 1994, these components should be able to interoperate across multivendor CORBA object brokers.

What Is a Distributed CORBA Object?

CORBA objects are blobs of intelligence that can live anywhere on a network. They are packaged as binary components that remote clients can access via method invocations. Both the language and compiler used to create server objects are totally transparent to clients. Clients don't need to know where the distributed object resides or what operating system it executes on. It can be in the same process or on a machine that sits across an intergalactic network. In addition, clients don't need to know how the server object is implemented. For example, a server object could be implemented as a set of C++ classes, or it could be implemented with a million lines of existing COBOL code—the client doesn't know the difference. What the client needs to know is the interface its server object publishes. This interface serves as a binding contract between clients and servers.

Everything Is in IDL

As we said earlier, CORBA uses IDL contracts to specify a component's boundaries and its contractual interfaces with potential clients. The CORBA IDL is purely declarative. This means that it provides no implementation details. You can use IDL to define APIs concisely, and it covers important issues such as error handling. IDL-specified methods can be written in and invoked from any language that provides CORBA bindings—currently, C, C++, Ada, and Smalltalk (COBOL, Java, and Objective C are in the works). Programmers deal with CORBA objects using native language constructs. IDL provides operating system and programming language independent interfaces to all the services and components that reside on a CORBA bus. It allows client and server objects written in different languages to interoperate (see Figure 1-1).

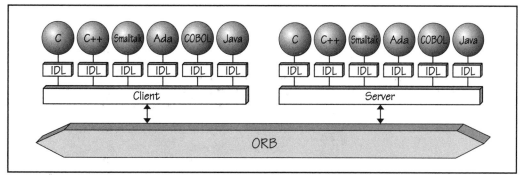

Figure 1-1. CORBA IDL Language Bindings Provide Client/Server Interoperability.

You can use the OMG IDL to specify a component's attributes, the parent classes it inherits from, the exceptions it raises, the typed events it emits, and the methods its interface supports—including the input and output parameters and their data types. The IDL grammar is a subset of C++ with additional keywords to support distributed concepts; it also fully supports standard C++ preprocessing features and pragmas.

The ambitious goal of CORBA is to "IDL-ize" all client/server middleware and all components that live on an ORB. OMG hopes to achieve this goal by following two steps: 1) it will turn everything into nails, and 2) it will give everyone a hammer.

■ The "nail" is the CORBA IDL. It allows component providers to specify in a standard definition language the interface and structure of the objects they provide. An IDL-defined contract binds the providers of distributed object services to their clients. For one object to request something from another object, it must know the target object's interface. The CORBA *Interface Repository* contains the definitions of all these interfaces. It contains the *metadata* that lets components discover each other dynamically at run time. This makes CORBA a self-describing system.

■   The "hammer" includes the set of distributed services OMG providers will supply. These services will determine which objects are on the network, which methods they provide, and which object interface adapters they support. The location of the object should be transparent to the client. It should not matter whether the object is in the same process or across the world.

Does this all sound familiar? It should. We're describing the "object wave" of client/server computing; this time it's between cooperating objects as opposed to cooperating processes. The goal of this new wave is to create multivendor, multiOS, multilanguage "Legoware" using objects. Vendors such as Oracle, Sun, HP, IBM, Digital, Apple, Netscape, Tandem, and NCR are all using CORBA as their standard IDL-defined interface into the object highway. The IDL is the contract that brings it all together.

CORBA Components: From System Objects to Business Objects

Notice that we've been using the terms "components" and "distributed objects" interchangeably. CORBA distributed objects are, by definition, components because of the way they are packaged. In distributed object systems, the unit of work and distribution is a component. The CORBA distributed object infrastructure makes it easier for components to be more autonomous, self-managing, and collaborative. This undertaking is much more ambitious than anything attempted by competing forms of middleware. CORBA's distributed object technology allows us to put together complex client/server information systems by simply assembling and extending components. You can modify objects without affecting the rest of the components in the system or how they interact. A client/server application becomes a collection of collaborating components.

The ultimate "Nirvana" in the client/server components business are supersmart components that do more than just interoperate—they collaborate at the semantic level to get a job done. Programmers can easily get things to collaborate by writing code for the two sides of the collaboration. The trick, however, is to get components that have no previous knowledge of each other to do the same. To get to that point, you need standards that set the rules of engagement for different component interaction boundaries.

OMG'S OBJECT MANAGEMENT ARCHITECTURE

In the fall of 1990, the OMG first published the *Object Management Architecture Guide (OMA Guide)*. It was revised in September 1992. The details of the Common Facilities were added in January 1995. Figure 1-2 shows the four main elements of the architecture: 1) *Object Request Broker (ORB)* defines the CORBA object bus; 2) *CORBAservices* define the system-level object frameworks that extend the bus; 3) *CORBAfacilities* define horizontal and vertical application frameworks that are used directly by business objects; and 4) *Application Objects* are the business objects and applications—they are the ultimate consumers of the CORBA infrastructure. This section provides a top-level view of the four elements that make up the CORBA infrastructure.

The Object Request Broker (ORB)

The *Object Request Broker (ORB)* is the object bus. It lets objects transparently make requests to—and receive responses from—other objects located locally or remotely. The client is not aware of the mechanisms used to communicate with, activate, or store the server objects. The CORBA 1.1 specifications—introduced in 1991—only specified the IDL, language bindings, and APIs for interfacing to the ORB. So, you could write portable programs that could run on top of the dozen CORBA-compliant ORBs on the market (especially on the client side). CORBA 2.0 specifies interoperability across vendor ORBs.

A CORBA ORB provides a wide variety of distributed middleware services. The ORB lets objects discover each other at run time and invoke each other's services. An

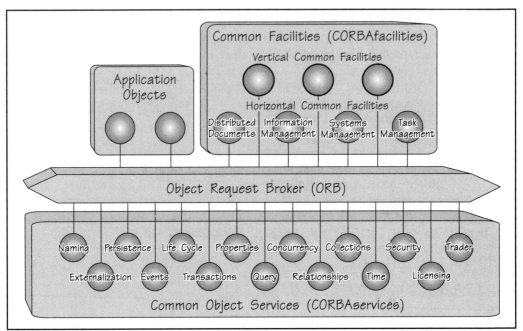

Figure 1-2. The OMG Object Management Architecture.

ORB is much more sophisticated than alternative forms of client/server middleware—including traditional Remote Procedure Calls (RPCs), Message-Oriented Middleware (MOM), database stored procedures, and peer-to-peer services. In theory, CORBA is the best client/server middleware ever defined. In practice, CORBA is only as good as the products that implement it.

To give you an idea of why CORBA ORBs make such great client/server middleware, we offer the following "short" list of benefits that every CORBA ORB provides:

- ■ **Static and dynamic method invocations**. A CORBA ORB either lets you statically define your method invocations at compile time, or it lets you dynamically discover them at run time. So you get either strong type checking at compile time or maximum flexibility associated with late (or run-time) binding. Most other forms of middleware only support static bindings.

- ■ **High-level language bindings**. A CORBA ORB lets you invoke methods on server objects using your high-level language of choice. It doesn't matter what language server objects are written in. CORBA separates interface from implementation and provides language-neutral data types that make it possible to call objects across language and operating system boundaries. In contrast, other types of middleware typically provide low-level, language-specific, API libraries. And they don't separate implementation from specification—the API is tightly bound to the implementation, which makes it very sensitive to changes.

- **Self-describing system**. CORBA provides run-time metadata for describing every server interface known to the system. Every CORBA ORB must support an *Interface Repository* that contains real-time information describing the functions a server provides and their parameters. The clients use metadata to discover how to invoke services at run time. It also helps tools generate code "on-the-fly." The metadata is generated automatically either by an IDL-language precompiler or by compilers that know how to generate IDL directly from an OO language. For example, the MetaWare C++ compiler generates IDL directly from C++ class definitions; Visigenic/Netscape's *Caffeine* generates IDL directly from Java bytecodes. To the best of our knowledge, no other form of client/server middleware provides this type of run-time metadata and language-independent definitions of all its services. As you will discover later in this book, business objects and components require all the late-binding flexibility they can get.

- **Local/remote transparency**. An ORB can run in standalone mode on a laptop, or it can be interconnected to every other ORB in the universe using CORBA 2.0's *Internet Inter-ORB Protocol (IIOP)* services. An ORB can broker inter-object calls within a single process, multiple processes running within the same machine, or multiple processes running across networks and operating systems. This is completely transparent to your objects. Note that the ORB can broker among fine-grained objects—like C++ classes—as well as more coarse-grained objects. In general, a CORBA client/server programmer does not have to be concerned with transports, server locations, object activation, byte ordering across dissimilar platforms, or target operating systems—CORBA makes it all transparent.

- **Built-in security and transactions**. The ORB includes context information in its messages to handle security and transactions across machine and ORB boundaries.

- **Polymorphic messaging**. In contrast to other forms of middleware, an ORB does not simply invoke a remote function—it invokes a function on a target object. This means that the same function call will have different effects, depending on the object that receives it. For example, a *configure_yourself* method invocation behaves differently when applied to a database object versus a printer object (also see the following Briefing box).

- **Coexistence with existing systems**. CORBA's separation of an object's definition from its implementation is perfect for encapsulating existing applications. Using CORBA IDL, you can make your existing code look like an object on the ORB, even if it's implemented in stored procedures, CICS, IMS, or COBOL. This makes CORBA an evolutionary solution. You can write your new applications as pure objects and encapsulate existing applications with IDL wrappers.

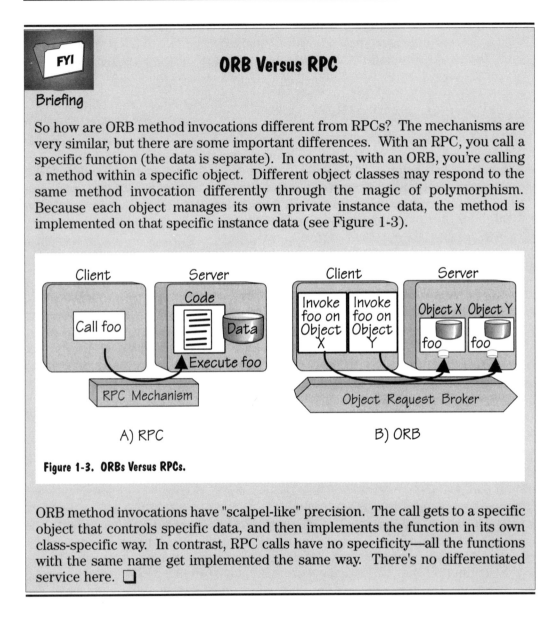

FYI   **ORB Versus RPC**

Briefing

So how are ORB method invocations different from RPCs? The mechanisms are very similar, but there are some important differences. With an RPC, you call a specific function (the data is separate). In contrast, with an ORB, you're calling a method within a specific object. Different object classes may respond to the same method invocation differently through the magic of polymorphism. Because each object manages its own private instance data, the method is implemented on that specific instance data (see Figure 1-3).

Figure 1-3. ORBs Versus RPCs.

ORB method invocations have "scalpel-like" precision. The call gets to a specific object that controls specific data, and then implements the function in its own class-specific way. In contrast, RPC calls have no specificity—all the functions with the same name get implemented the same way. There's no differentiated service here. ❑

The Anatomy of a CORBA 2.0 ORB

A CORBA 2.0 *Object Request Broker (ORB)* is the middleware that establishes the client/server relationship between objects. Using an ORB, a client object can transparently invoke a method on a server object that can be on the same machine or across a network. The ORB intercepts the call and is responsible for finding an object that can implement the request, pass it the parameters, invoke its method, and return the results. The client does not have to be aware of where the object is located, its programming language, its operating system, or any other system aspects that are not part of an object's interface. It is very important to note that the client/server roles are only used to coordinate the interactions between two objects. Objects on the ORB can act as either client or server, depending on the occasion.

Figure 1-4 shows the client and server sides of a CORBA ORB. The light areas are new to CORBA 2.0. Even though there are many boxes, it's not as complicated as it appears to be. The key is to understand that CORBA, like SQL, provides both static and dynamic interfaces to its services. This happened because the OMG received two strong submissions to its original ORB *Request For Proposal (RFP)*: one from HyperDesk and Digital based on a dynamic API, and one from Sun and HP based on static APIs. The OMG told the two groups to come back with a single RFP that combined both features. The result was CORBA. The "Common" in CORBA stands for this two-API proposal, which makes a lot of sense because it gives us both static and dynamic APIs.

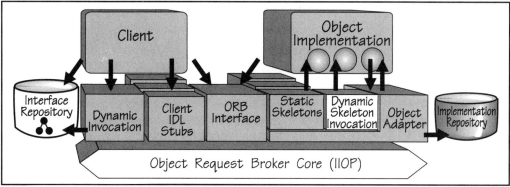

Figure 1-4. The Structure of a CORBA 2.0 ORB.

Let's first go over what CORBA does on the client side:

■ ***The Client IDL Stubs*** provide the static interfaces to object services. These precompiled stubs define how clients invoke corresponding services on the servers. From a client's perspective, the stub acts like a local call—it is a local *proxy* for a remote server object. The services are defined using IDL, and both client and server stubs are generated by the IDL compiler. A client must have an IDL stub for each interface it uses on the server. The stub includes code to perform *marshaling*. This means that it encodes and decodes the operation and its parameters into flattened message formats that it can send to the server. It also includes header files that enable you to invoke the method on the server from a higher-level language like C, C++, Java, or Smalltalk without worrying about the underlying protocols or issues such as data marshaling. You simply invoke a method from within your program to obtain a remote service.

- *The Dynamic Invocation Interface (DII)* lets you discover methods to be invoked at run time. CORBA defines standard APIs for looking up the metadata that defines the server interface, generating the parameters, issuing the remote call, and getting back the results.

- *The Interface Repository APIs* allow you to obtain and modify the descriptions of all the registered component interfaces, the methods they support, and the parameters they require. CORBA calls these descriptions *method signatures*. The *Interface Repository* is a run-time distributed database that contains machine-readable versions of the IDL-defined interfaces. Think of it as a dynamic metadata repository for ORBs. The APIs allow components to dynamically access, store, and update metadata information. This pervasive use of metadata allows every component that lives on the ORB to have self-describing interfaces. The ORB itself is a self-describing bus (see the next Briefing box).

- *The ORB Interface* consists of a few APIs to local services that may be of interest to an application. For example, CORBA provides APIs to convert an object reference to a string, and vice versa. These calls can be very useful if you need to store and communicate object references.

CORBA 2.0 Global Repository IDs

Briefing

With CORBA 2.0, ORBs provide global identifiers—called *Repository IDs*—to uniquely and globally identify a component and its interface across multivendor ORBs and repositories. The Repository IDs are system-generated, unique strings that are used to maintain consistency in the naming conventions used across repositories—no name collisions are allowed. Repository IDs are generated via *pragmas* in IDL. The pragma specifies whether to generate them via DCE *Universal Unique Identifiers (UUIDs)* or via a user-supplied, unique prefix appended to IDL-scoped names. The Repository ID itself is a string consisting of a three-level name hierarchy. ❏

The support for both static and dynamic client/server invocations—as well as the Interface Repository—gives CORBA a leg up over competing middleware. Static invocations are easier to program, faster, and self-documenting. Dynamic invocations provide maximum flexibility, but they are difficult to program; they are very useful for tools that discover services at run time.

The server side cannot tell the difference between a static or dynamic invocation; they both have the same message semantics. In both cases, the ORB locates a server object adapter, transmits the parameters, and transfers control to the object implementation through the server IDL stub (or skeleton). Here's what CORBA elements do on the server side of Figure 1-4:

■ The **Server IDL Stubs** (OMG calls them *skeletons*) provide static interfaces to each service exported by the server. These stubs, like the ones on the client, are created using an IDL compiler.

■ The **Dynamic Skeleton Interface (DSI)**—introduced in CORBA 2.0—provides a run-time binding mechanism for servers that need to handle incoming method calls for components that do not have IDL-based compiled skeletons (or stubs). The Dynamic Skeleton looks at parameter values in an incoming message to figure out who it's for—that is, the target object and method. In contrast, normal compiled skeletons are defined for a particular object class and expect a method implementation for each IDL-defined method. Dynamic Skeletons are very useful for implementing generic bridges between ORBs. They can also be used by interpreters and scripting languages to dynamically generate object implementations. The DSI is the server equivalent of a DII. It can receive either static or dynamic client invocations.

■ The **Object Adapter** sits on top of the ORB's core communication services and accepts requests for service on behalf of the server's objects. It provides the run-time environment for instantiating server objects, passing requests to them, and assigning them object IDs—CORBA calls the IDs *object references*. The Object Adapter also registers the classes it supports and their run-time instances (i.e., objects) with the *Implementation Repository*. CORBA specifies that each ORB must support a standard adapter called the *Basic Object Adapter (BOA)*. Servers may support more than one object adapter.

■ The **Implementation Repository** provides a run-time repository of information about the classes a server supports, the objects that are instantiated, and their IDs. It also serves as a common place to store additional information associated with the implementation of ORBs. Examples include trace information, audit trails, security, and other administrative data.

■ The **ORB Interface** consists of a few APIs to local services that are identical to those provided on the client side.

This concludes our panoramic overview of the ORB components and their interfaces.

CORBA 2.0: THE INTERGALACTIC ORB

CORBA 1.1 was only concerned with creating portable object applications; the implementation of the ORB core was left as an exercise for the vendors. The result was some level of component portability, but not interoperability. CORBA 2.0 added interoperability by specifying a mandatory *Internet Inter-ORB Protocol (IIOP)*. The IIOP is basically TCP/IP with some CORBA-defined message exchanges that serve as a common backbone protocol. Every ORB that calls itself CORBA-compliant must either implement IIOP natively or provide a *half-bridge* to it. Note that it's called a half-bridge because IIOP is the "standard" CORBA backbone. So any proprietary ORB can connect with the universe of ORBs by translating requests to and from the IIOP backbone.

In addition to IIOP, CORBA supports *Environment-Specific Inter-ORB Protocols (ESIOPs)* for "out-of-the-box" interoperation over specific networks. CORBA 2.0 specifies DCE as the first of many optional ESIOPs (pronounced "E-SOPs"). The DCE ESIOP provides a robust environment for mission-critical ORBs. The DCE ESIOP is supported in HP's *ORB Plus* and Digital's *ObjectBroker.*

You can use inter-ORB bridges and IIOP to create very flexible topologies via federations of ORBs. Figure 1-5 shows an IIOP backbone with various proprietary ORBs feeding into it via half-bridges. Note the presence of the DCE ESIOP. You can segment ORBs into domains based on administrative needs, vendor ORB implementations, network protocols, traffic loads, types of service, and security concerns. Policies on either side of the fence may conflict, so you can create firewalls around

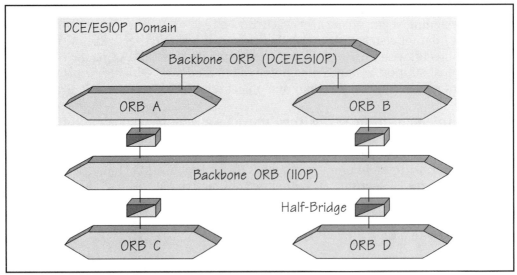

Figure 1-5. An Intergalactic Federation of Multivendor ORBs.

the backbone ORB via half-bridges. CORBA 2.0 promotes diversity and gives you total mix-and-match flexibility, as long as you use IIOP for your global backbone.

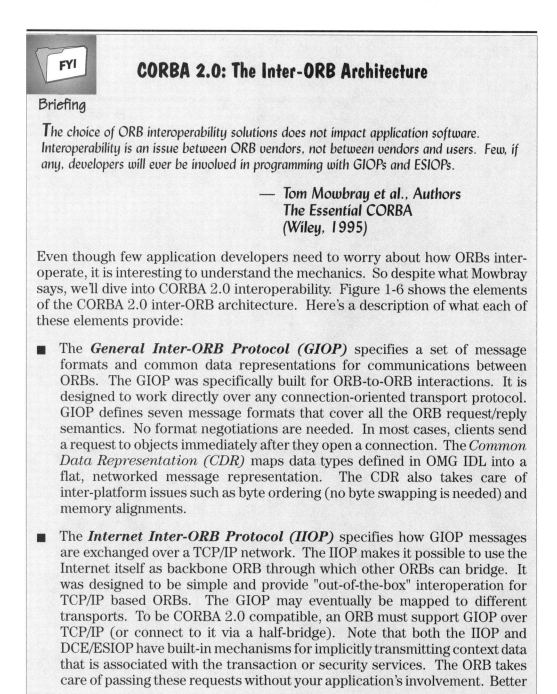

FYI

CORBA 2.0: The Inter-ORB Architecture

Briefing

The choice of ORB interoperability solutions does not impact application software. Interoperability is an issue between ORB vendors, not between vendors and users. Few, if any, developers will ever be involved in programming with GIOPs and ESIOPs.

— *Tom Mowbray et al., Authors*
The Essential CORBA
(Wiley, 1995)

Even though few application developers need to worry about how ORBs interoperate, it is interesting to understand the mechanics. So despite what Mowbray says, we'll dive into CORBA 2.0 interoperability. Figure 1-6 shows the elements of the CORBA 2.0 inter-ORB architecture. Here's a description of what each of these elements provide:

- The ***General Inter-ORB Protocol (GIOP)*** specifies a set of message formats and common data representations for communications between ORBs. The GIOP was specifically built for ORB-to-ORB interactions. It is designed to work directly over any connection-oriented transport protocol. GIOP defines seven message formats that cover all the ORB request/reply semantics. No format negotiations are needed. In most cases, clients send a request to objects immediately after they open a connection. The *Common Data Representation (CDR)* maps data types defined in OMG IDL into a flat, networked message representation. The CDR also takes care of inter-platform issues such as byte ordering (no byte swapping is needed) and memory alignments.

- The ***Internet Inter-ORB Protocol (IIOP)*** specifies how GIOP messages are exchanged over a TCP/IP network. The IIOP makes it possible to use the Internet itself as backbone ORB through which other ORBs can bridge. It was designed to be simple and provide "out-of-the-box" interoperation for TCP/IP based ORBs. The GIOP may eventually be mapped to different transports. To be CORBA 2.0 compatible, an ORB must support GIOP over TCP/IP (or connect to it via a half-bridge). Note that both the IIOP and DCE/ESIOP have built-in mechanisms for implicitly transmitting context data that is associated with the transaction or security services. The ORB takes care of passing these requests without your application's involvement. Better

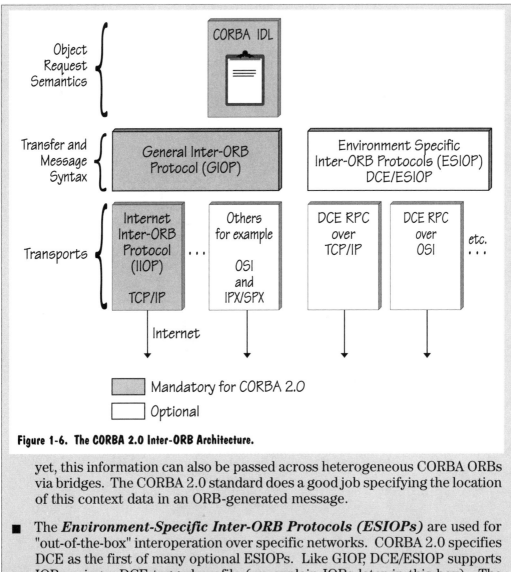

Figure 1-6. The CORBA 2.0 Inter-ORB Architecture.

yet, this information can also be passed across heterogeneous CORBA ORBs via bridges. The CORBA 2.0 standard does a good job specifying the location of this context data in an ORB-generated message.

■ The ***Environment-Specific Inter-ORB Protocols (ESIOPs)*** are used for "out-of-the-box" interoperation over specific networks. CORBA 2.0 specifies DCE as the first of many optional ESIOPs. Like GIOP, DCE/ESIOP supports IORs using a DCE tagged profile (we explain IORs later in this box). The DCE/ESIOP uses the GIOP CDR to represent OMG IDL data types over the DCE RPC. This means that DCE IDL is not required. Instead, OMG IDL and CDR types are mapped directly into DCE's native *Network Data Representation (NDR)*. The DCE ESIOP currently provides a robust environment for mission-critical ORBs. It includes advanced features such as Kerberos security, cell and global directories, distributed time, and authenticated RPC. DCE also lets you transmit large amounts of data efficiently, and it supports multiple underlying transport protocols, including TCP/IP. Finally, with DCE

> you can use both connection and connectionless protocols for your ORB communications.
>
> GIOP also defines a format for *Interoperable Object References (IORs)*. An ORB must create an IOR (from an object reference) whenever an object reference is passed across ORBs. IORs associate a collection of *tagged profiles* with object references. The profiles describe the same object, but they each describe how to contact the object using a particular ORB's mechanism. More precisely, a profile provides self-describing data that identifies the ORB domain to which a reference is associated and the protocols it supports. ❑

CORBAservices

CORBAservices are collections of system-level services packaged with IDL-specified interfaces. You can think of object services as augmenting and complementing the functionality of the ORB. You use them to create a component, name it, and introduce it into the environment. OMG has published standards for fifteen object services:

■ The **Life Cycle Service** defines operations for creating, copying, moving, and deleting components on the bus.

■ The **Persistence Service** provides a single interface for storing components persistently on a variety of storage servers—including Object Databases (ODBMSs), Relational Databases (RDBMSs), and simple files.

■ The **Naming Service** allows components on the bus to locate other components by name; it also supports federated naming contexts. The service also allows objects to be bound to existing network directories or naming contexts—including ISO's *X.500*, OSF's *DCE*, Sun's *NIS+*, Novell's *NDS*, and the Internet's *LDAP*.

■ The **Event Service** allows components on the bus to dynamically register or unregister their interest in specific events. The service defines a well-known object called an *event channel* that collects and distributes events among components that know nothing of each other.

■ The **Concurrency Control Service** provides a lock manager that can obtain locks on behalf of either transactions or threads.

■ The **Transaction Service** provides two-phase commit coordination among recoverable components using either flat or nested transactions.

- The ***Relationship Service*** provides a way to create dynamic associations (or links) between components that know nothing of each other. It also provides mechanisms for traversing the links that group these components. You can use the service to enforce referential integrity constraints, track containment relationships, and for any type of linkage among components.

- The ***Externalization Service*** provides a standard way for getting data into and out of a component using a stream-like mechanism.

- The ***Query Service*** provides query operations for objects. It's a superset of SQL. It is based on the upcoming SQL3 specification and the Object Database Management Group's (ODMG) *Object Query Language (OQL)*.

- The ***Licensing Service*** provides operations for metering the use of components to ensure fair compensation for their use. The service supports any model of usage control at any point in a component's life cycle. It supports charging per session, per node, per instance creation, and per site.

- The ***Properties Service*** provides operations that let you associate named values (or properties) with any component. Using this service, you can dynamically associate properties with a component's state—for example, a title or a date.

- The ***Time Service*** provides interfaces for synchronizing time in a distributed object environment. It also provides operations for defining and managing time-triggered events.

- The ***Security Service*** provides a complete framework for distributed object security. It supports authentication, access control lists, confidentiality, and non-repudiation. It also manages the delegation of credentials between objects.

- The ***Trader Service*** provides a "Yellow Pages" for objects; it allows objects to publicize their services and bid for jobs.

- The ***Collection Service*** provides CORBA interfaces to generically create and manipulate the most common collections.

All these services enrich a distributed component's behavior and provide the robust environment in which it can safely live and play.

Figure 1-7 shows the *Request For Proposal (RFP)* schedules that OMG is using to develop the object service specifications. OMG RFPs are requests for a technology. They result in responses from members on how to implement a particular standard. Members must base their responses on existing products or products that are in development (some proof of concept is needed). Usually an RFP is met by merging the responses obtained from several organizations. From the time the OMG issues an RFP, it takes about 12 to 16 months to obtain a working standard. As you can see, the OMG has almost completed the work on its object services. The action is

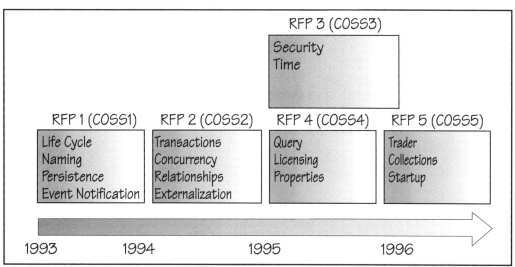

Figure 1-7. The OMG Road Map for Delivering Object Services.

now shifting to the CORBAfacilities and Business Objects. In addition, there's quite a bit of work being done at the ORB level. We cover CORBA 3.0 in Part 4.

Object Services: Build-To-Order Middleware

CORBA object services provide a unique approach for creating *build-to-order* middleware. It's unlike anything classical client/server systems provide today. With CORBA, component providers can develop their objects without any concern for system services. Then, depending on what the customer's needs are, the developer (or system integrator) can mix the original component with any combination of CORBA services to create the needed function. They do this by subclassing the original class, and then mixing it with the required object service classes via multiple inheritance. For example, you may develop a component called "car" and create a concurrent, persistent, and transactional version of car by multiply inheriting from the corresponding services. You can also use some of these services via delegation.

In addition, some ORB vendors will take advantage of their metaclass CORBA extensions to let you create your mixins at object-creation time. A *metaclass* is a class that is also a run-time object. This means that you can create and customize new classes at run time. Object factories can use these metaclass facilities to compose a class at run time based on a client's request. You can create made-to-order classes by multiply inheriting from existing object services. For example, the factory can take an ordinary component such as a "car" and make it transactional, lockable, and secure by multiply inheriting from existing object service classes. This approach is the ultimate form of made-to-order middleware.

The beauty is that the original component provider may have known nothing about transactions, security, or locking. These services are dynamically added to the component at factory creation time based on the client's requirements.

If you don't like multiple inheritance, some ORB implementations let you add methods "on-the-fly" to existing classes. In particular, you can add *before* and *after* callbacks that are triggered before and after any ordinary method executes. You can use these before and after calls to call any of the existing CORBA services—or, for that matter, anything that lives on an ORB. You can even attach scripts to before/after triggers. For example, you can use a *before* trigger to obtain a lock from the concurrency service; you use the *after* trigger to release the lock.

By combining metaclass technology with CORBA services, you will be able to create last-minute, customized middleware environments for running particular components. It demonstrates the ultimate flexibility of objects. Most component developers will probably take a more conservative approach and create their mixins at compile time or via a tool at build time. In either case, it's still a lot more flexible than anything you can do with today's client/server middleware.

CORBAfacilities

CORBAfacilities are collections of IDL-defined frameworks that provide services of direct use to application objects. Think of them as the next step up in the semantic hierarchy. The two categories of common facilities—*horizontal* and *vertical*—define rules of engagement that business components need to effectively collaborate. To give you a feel for where things stand, in October 1994 the OMG issued the Common Facilities *Request for Proposal 1 (RFP1)* to obtain technology submissions for compound documents. In March 1996, OMG adopted OpenDoc as its compound document technology. It calls it the *Distributed Document Component Facility (DDCF)*. DDCF specifies presentation services for components and a document interchange standard based on OpenDoc's Bento.

The Common Facilities that are currently under construction include mobile agents, data interchange, business object frameworks, and internationalization. Like the highway system, Common Facilities are an unending project. The work will continue until CORBA defines IDL interfaces for every distributed service we know of today, as well as ones that are yet to be invented. When this happens, CORBA will provide IDL interfaces for virtually every networked service (many will be IDL-ized versions of existing middleware).

CORBA BUSINESS OBJECTS

Business objects provide a natural way for describing application-independent concepts such as customer, order, competitor, money, payment, car, and patient.

They encourage a view of software that transcends tools, applications, databases, and other system concepts. The ultimate promise of object technology and components is to provide these medium-grained components that behave more like the real world does. Of course, somebody must first define the rules of engagement for these components to play, which is where the OMG comes into the picture.

According to OMG's *Business Object Task Force*, a business object is an application-level component you can use in unpredictable combinations. A business object is, by definition, independent of any single application. Post-monolithic applications will consist of suites of business objects—the application simply provides the environment to execute these business objects. In other words, a business object is a component that represents a "recognizable" everyday life entity. In contrast,

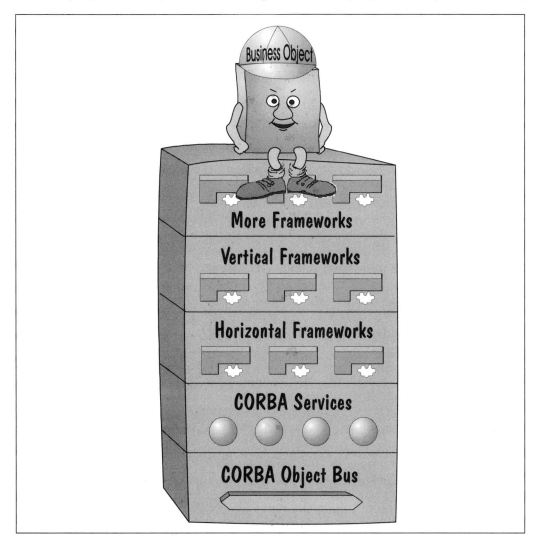

system-level objects represent entities that make sense only to information systems and programmers—they're not something an end user recognizes.

In a high-rise building, everyone's ceiling is someone else's floor until you get to the penthouse. Then the sky is your ceiling. You may think of the business object as the penthouse of components. According to the OMG definition, these top-level objects are recognizable to the end user of a system. The size of the object maps to "business" things like cars or tax forms. The word business is used in a very loose sense. A business object is a self-contained *deliverable* that has a user interface, state, and knows how to cooperate with other separately developed business objects to perform a desired task.

Cooperating Business Objects

Business objects will be used to design systems that mimic the business processes they support. In the real world, business events are seldom isolated to a single business object. Instead, they typically involve clusters of objects. To mimic their real-world counterparts, business objects must be able to communicate with each other at a semantic level. You can capture and describe these object interactions using most of the popular design methodology tools—including Ivar Jacobson's *use cases*, Ian Graham's *task scripts*, Grady Booch's *interaction diagrams*, and Jim Rumbaugh's *event traces*. All these methodologies use some form of scenario diagrams to show who does what to whom and when. These scenarios can document the full impact of specific business events.

Business objects must have late and flexible binding—and well-defined interfaces—so that they can be implemented independently. A business object must be capable of recognizing events in its environment, changing its attributes, and interacting with other business objects. Like any CORBA object, a business object exposes its interfaces to its clients via IDL and communicates with other objects using the ORB.

Figure 1-8 shows a suite of four business objects that are part of a car reservation system: *customer, invoice, car,* and *car lot*. Note that *car lot* is a business object that contains other business objects—cars. Clearly, these four business objects have some agreed-upon semantics for communicating with each other to perform business transactions. Under the covers, they could use the CORBA *Object Transaction Service* to synchronize their actions. They also know how to share a single window to display their views seamlessly.

So how is this different from a traditional application? With very little work, you can reuse some of these business objects in another application context. For example, a car sales program could reuse most of these objects, especially if they were designed to work with more than one semantic suite. For example, the car, customer, and invoice objects could support multiple views to handle different

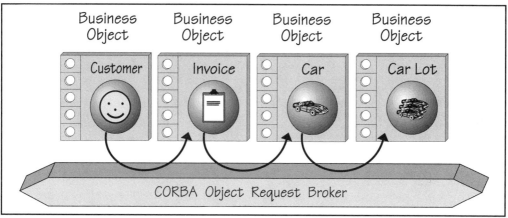

Figure 1-8. A Car Reservation System Using Cooperating Business Objects.

business situations. In the extreme, the business objects could be specialized through inheritance to take into account the particularities of the car sales business. As you'll see in the next section, a business object is not a monolithic entity. It is factored internally into a set of cooperating objects that can react to different business situations. Business objects are highly flexible.

The Anatomy of a CORBA Business Object

A CORBA business object is a variation of the *Model/View/Controller (MVC)* paradigm. MVC is an object design pattern used to build interfaces in Smalltalk and in almost every GUI class library. MVC consists of three kinds of objects. The *model* represents the application object and its encapsulated data. The *view* represents the object visually on the screen. And the *controller* defines the way the user interface reacts to user input and GUI events.

In the CORBA model, a business object also consists of three kinds of objects (see Figure 1-9):

■ *Business objects* encapsulate the storage, metadata, concurrency, and business rules associated with an active business entity. They also define how the object reacts to changes in the views or model.

■ *Business process objects* encapsulate the business logic at the enterprise level. In traditional MVC systems, the controller is in charge of the process. In the CORBA model, short-lived process functions are handled by the business object. Long-lived processes that involve other business objects are handled by the business process object—it's a specialization of the business object that handles long-lived processes and the environment at large. For example, it knows how to handle a workflow or long-lived transaction. The process object

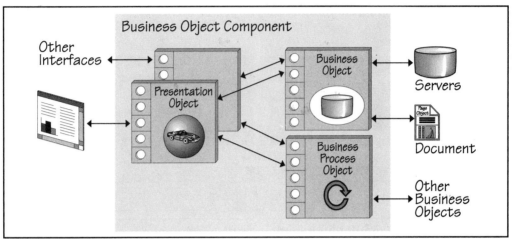

Figure 1-9. The Anatomy of a Business Object.

typically acts as the glue that unites the other objects. For example, it defines how the object reacts to a change in the environment. This type of change may be caused by the execution of a business transaction or by an incoming message from another business object. Note that some business objects may be entirely process-oriented and not associated with specific data or presentations.

■ ***Presentation objects*** represent the object visually to the user. Each business object can have multiple presentations for multiple purposes. The presentations communicate directly with the business object to display data on the screen. And sometimes they communicate directly with the process object. The OMG also recognizes that there are non-visual interfaces to business objects.

A typical business object component consists of a business object, one or more presentation objects, and a process object. Note that these entities act as a body. The underlying division of labor between the various objects is transparent to the users and clients of the business object. A business object also interacts with other servers and system-level objects but, again, in a totally encapsulated manner. The user only sees the aggregate business object. And clients of the object only deal with IDL-defined interfaces that are exposed by the aggregate business object. The OMG has issued an RFP for *Common Business Objects* and a *Business Object Facility*. The facility will provide a framework for business objects to exchange semantic information and agree on the rules of engagement. We expect this framework to be fleshed out by mid-1997 (more on this in Part 4).

The Anatomy of a Client/Server Business Object

Typically, a business object—like a car—may have different presentation objects spread across multiple clients. The business object and the process object may reside in one or more servers. The beauty of a CORBA-based architecture is that all the constituent objects have IDL-defined interfaces and can run on ORBs (see Figure 1-10). So it does not matter if the constituent objects run on the same machine or on different machines (ORBs provide local/remote transparency). As far as clients are concerned, they're still dealing with a single business object component, even though it may be factored into objects running in different machines. A well-designed business object builds on the CORBA services. For example, you can use the concurrency and transaction services to maintain the integrity of the business object's state. The ORB gives you these services for free, so you might as well use them.

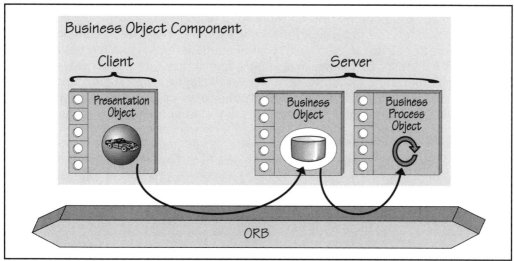

Figure 1-10. The Anatomy of a Client/Server Business Object.

CORBA Component Nirvana

Cooperative Business Objects (CBOs) are real things. Like other real things, they can be mixed and matched to suit user requirements—with no developer intervention necessary. You take an entity-like thing such as a customer and that's what you deliver—a customer object all by itself. You get a whole customer and nothing but the customer ready to run and use!

> — *Oliver Sims, Author*
> *Business Objects*
> *(McGraw-Hill, 1994)*

At the most basic level, a component infrastructure provides an object bus—the *Object Request Broker (ORB)*—that lets components interoperate across address spaces, languages, operating systems, and networks. The bus also provides mechanisms that let components exchange metadata and discover each other. At the next level, the infrastructure augments the bus with add-on *system-level services* that help you create supersmart components. Examples of these services include licensing, security, version control, persistence, suite negotiation, semantic messaging, scripting, and transactions.

The ultimate goal is to let you create components that behave like *business objects*. These are components that model their real-world counterparts in some application-level domain. They typically perform specific business functions—for example, a customer, car, or hotel. You can group these business objects into visual suites that sit on a desktop but have underlying client/server webs.

So the ultimate Nirvana in the client/server components business are supersmart business object components that do more than just interoperate—they collaborate at the semantic level to get a job done. For example, roaming agents on a global network must be able to collaborate to conduct negotiations with their fellow agents. Agents are examples of business objects. The infrastructure provides application-level collaboration standards in the form of *application frameworks* (OMG calls them *domain frameworks*). These frameworks enforce the rules of engagement between independent components. They also allow them to collaborate in suites.

Figure 1-11 shows the evolution of components from interoperability to collaboration. This evolution corresponds to the service boundaries of the component infrastructure. The component bus gives you simple interoperability, the system services give you supersmart components, and the application frameworks provide the application-level semantics for components to collaborate in suites.

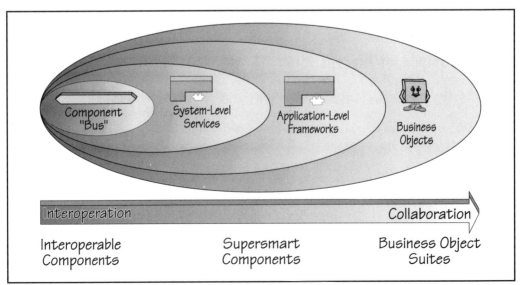

Figure 1-11. Component Evolution and Infrastructure Boundaries.

3-TIER CLIENT/SERVER, OBJECT-STYLE

Business objects are ideal for creating scalable 3-tier client/server solutions because they are inherently decomposable. A business object is not a monolithic piece of code. Instead, it is more like a Lego of cooperating parts that you break apart and then reassemble along 3-tier client/server lines (see Figure 1-12). The first tier represents the visual aspects of the business object—one or more visual objects may each provide a different view. These visual objects typically live on the client. In the middle tier are server objects that represent the persistent data and the business logic functions. In the third tier are existing databases and legacy server applications. The partitioning of business objects is very dynamic. You should be able to decide where to host the different parts at run time.

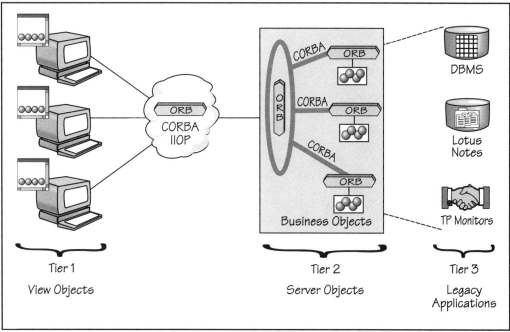

Figure 1-12. 3-Tiered Client/Server, Object-Style.

Middle-tier server objects interact with their clients (the view objects) and implement the logic of the business object. They can extract their persistent state from multiple data sources—for example, SQL databases, HTML files, Lotus Notes, and TP Monitors. The server object provides an integrated model of the disparate data sources and back-end applications. Clients interact with business objects that naturally correspond to domain entities. They do not have to concern themselves with the hodgepodge of functions, stored procedures, and databases that live in the third tier. The business object hides all this nastiness.

The server object can cache the data it extracts on a local object database for fast subsequent access; or it may choose to directly update the third-tier data sources with fresh views from the object state. Clients must never directly interact with third-tier data sources. These sources must be totally encapsulated and abstracted by the middle-tier server objects. For example, you should be able to swap one database for another without impacting the clients.

The clients typically interact with the middle-tier server objects via an ORB. In addition, middle-tier objects can communicate with each other via a server ORB that they can use to balance loads, orchestrate distributed transactions, and exchange business events. This makes ORB-based business objects very scalable. Finally, server objects communicate with the third tier using traditional middleware. We will have a lot more to say about business objects in Part 4.

CONCLUSION

> *Everybody can resonate with objects—managers, 3 year olds, and superprogrammers. Object-oriented technology appeals to all these different camps.*
>
> **— Jim Gray**

Distributed CORBA objects—modelled as business objects—are an excellent fit for 3-tier client/server architectures. They provide scalable and flexible solutions for intergalactic client/server environments and for the Internet and Intranets. Business objects can be naturally decomposed and split across multiple tiers to meet an application's needs. They are self-describing and self-managing blobs of intelligence that you can move around and execute where it makes the most sense. Most importantly, business objects are evolutionary—they don't force you to throw away your existing server applications and start from scratch. You can encapsulate what you already have and incrementally add new intelligence, one component at a time.

Chapter 2

The Object Web: CORBA Meets Java

CORBA objects may have finally found their "killer app." It's called the *Object Web*—or the marriage of distributed objects and the World Wide Web. The major computing companies—including Sun, JavaSoft, IBM, Netscape, Apple, Oracle, BEA, and HP—have chosen CORBA IIOP as the common way to connect distributed objects across the Internet and Intranets. Consequently, CORBA may become almost as ubiquitous as TCP/IP by the end of 1997. This will create a mass market for components that run on top of CORBA middleware.

This is good news for those of us who are in the market for a great heterogeneous component infrastructure based on distributed objects. In the last few years, many of us discovered that a distributed object standard—even if it is supported by over 700 companies—is not enough to create a successful component infrastructure. Commercial CORBA ORB offerings from the major software vendors were not enough either. Even great technology was not enough! Components also require a thriving ecosystem to be commercially viable. In the Microsoft world, the ecosystem for ActiveX is provided by OLE killer apps such as Visual Basic, Word, Access, and Excel. Until the advent of the Object Web, the CORBA world had great technology but no thriving ecosystem. No one got rich writing CORBA components. But this is about to change.

The Evolution of the Web

Figure 2-1 shows the progression of Web technologies. In 1994, the Web was mainly a giant—and very trendy—unidirectional medium for publishing and broadcasting electronic documents. In late 1995, the Web became a more interactive client/server application platform; the *Common Gateway Interface (CGI)* is now being used to access every known server environment.

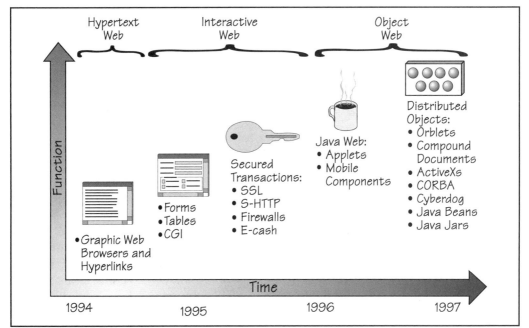

Figure 2-1. The Evolution of Web Technologies.

In 1996, the Web finally discovered objects. Java is the first step toward creating a client/server *Object Web*. Is there life after Java? This may come as a surprise, but the answer is yes. Java is a necessary but not sufficient step toward creating an Object Web. The next step requires even more object caffeine. We're talking about blending Java with a distributed object infrastructure; your cup of Java will soon include CORBA ORBlets, OLE COMlets, and compound document frameworks such as ActiveX, OpenDoc, and Java Beans. We hope you like your coffee strong.

Java offers tremendous flexibility for distributed application development, but it currently does not support a client/server paradigm. To do this, Java needs to be augmented with a distributed object infrastructure, which is where OMG's CORBA comes into the picture. CORBA provides the missing link between the Java portable application environment and the world of intergalactic back-end services. The intersection of Java and CORBA object technologies is the natural next step in the evolution of the Object Web.

CGI, The Protocol That Won't Go Away

The predominant 3-tier client/server model for the Internet today is the *Common Gateway Interface (CGI)*. But CGI over HTTP is a slow, cumbersome, and stateless protocol. CGI is not a good match for object-oriented Java clients. In a sense, the Web server lives in the middle ages, while the clients are postmodern. Some server vendors are trying to extend CGI with proprietary server APIs. Examples of such attempts include Netscape's *NSAPI*, Microsoft's *ISAPI*, NeXT's *WebObjects Framework*, and Oracle's *WebServer API*. This closed trend is a dead end; it leads to a totally non-standard server Web.

Netscape's *Open Network Environment (ONE)*, JavaSoft's *Enterprise Java*, Oracle's *Network Computing Architecture*, and the new generation of Java ORBs are reversing this closed trend. The idea is to create an open Web server environment based on CORBA. This makes a lot of sense because CORBA is a distributed object bus built with open standards; it was designed from the start to support intergalactic client/server systems.

The 3-Tier Object Web

As a result of all this work, a new Object Web model is starting to emerge along the lines shown in Figure 2-2, which shows a 3-tier client/server application model. As usual, the first tier belongs to the client. In this case, the client belongs to browsers, Java client applications, and shippable applets. The second tier is provided by any server that can service both HTTP and CORBA clients. The third tier belongs to traditional servers.

The middle-tier CORBA/HTTP combination is supported on almost every server platform—including Unixes, NT, OS/2, NetWare, MacOS, OS/400, MVS, and Tandem NonStop Kernel. CORBA objects act as middle-tier application servers; they encapsulate the business logic. They interact with client components via a Java ORBlet or any regular CORBA ORB that can run IIOP over the Internet. Of course, the CORBA objects on the server can interact with each other using a CORBA ORB. They can also talk to existing server applications in the third tier using SQL or any other form of middleware.

The second tier must also provide a server-side component coordinator (or Object TP Monitor). We know of two major projects that are creating CORBA-based TP Monitors: IBM's *Business Object Server Solution (BOSS)* and BEA Systems'

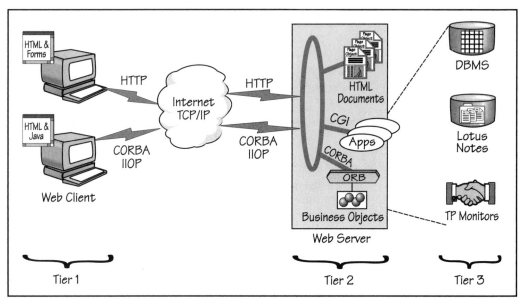

Figure 2-2. An Object Web Model Based on Java Clients and CORBA ORBs.

Tuxedo-based *ObjectWare*. But, what is a *server-side component*? It's a CORBA server object that also implements a minimum set of component services. A good example of this is Oracle's *Cartridges*. These are named CORBA objects that are also transactional, secure, and capable of emitting events.

A server component must also be *buildable*. This means that it must provide a build interface that lets you assemble it using visual tools. For example, the object can provide an icon that represents it to the tool. When you click on the icon, the object will display the methods it supports and the CORBA events it emits (this is all done via introspection).   So you will be able to wire object ensembles by connecting output events to input methods.

The third tier is almost anything a CORBA object can access.   This includes procedural TP Monitors, MOMs, DBMSs, ODBMSs, Lotus Notes, and e-mail. So the CORBA business objects replace CGI applications in the middle tier, which is good.

In addition, the Java client can directly communicate with a CORBA object using the Java ORB. This means that CORBA replaces the HTTP/CGI as the middleware layer for object-to-object communications, which is also very good. Like HTTP, CORBA's IIOP uses the Internet as its backbone. This means that both IIOP and HTTP can run on the same networks. HTTP is used to download Web pages, applets, and images; CORBA is used for Java client-to-server communications.

Client/Server Interactions on the Object Web

Figure 2-3 shows how a typical Web-based client interacts with its server on the Object Web:

1. ***Web browser downloads HTML page.*** In this case, the page includes references to embedded Java applets.

2. ***Web browser retrieves Java applet from HTTP server.*** The HTTP server retrieves the applet and downloads it to the browser in the form of bytecodes.

3. ***Web browser loads applet.*** The applet is first run through the Java run-time security gauntlet and then loaded into memory.

4. ***Applet invokes CORBA server objects.*** The Java applet can include IDL-generated client stubs, which let it invoke objects on the ORB server. Alternatively, the applet can use the CORBA *Dynamic Invocation Interface* to generate server requests "on-the-fly." The session between the Java applet and the CORBA server objects will persist until either side decides to disconnect.

In the example, the Java client is a downloadable applet. Of course, the client can also be a regular Java application. The difference is that you do not have to download a Java application over the Internet, which removes the overhead of the HTTP download. But then you would give up the benefit of being able to dynami-

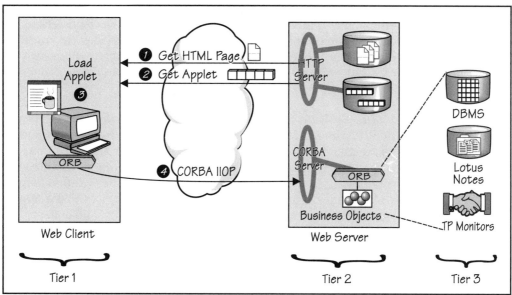

Figure 2-3. How HTTP, CORBA, and Java Play Together.

cally load a client on demand. Today's Java ORBs support either approach. So we have an evolutionary solution that does not disrupt existing Web applications.

What CORBA Brings to Java

Augmenting the Web infrastructure with CORBA provides three immediate benefits: 1) it gets rid of the CGI bottleneck on the server; 2) it provides a scalable and robust server-to-server Web infrastructure; and 3) it extends Java with a distributed object infrastructure. We briefly explain what this means:

■ ***CORBA avoids the CGI bottleneck.*** It allows clients to directly invoke methods on a server. The client passes the parameters directly using precompiled stubs, or it generates them "on-the-fly" using CORBA's dynamic invocation services. In either case, the server receives the call directly via a precompiled skeleton. You can invoke any IDL-defined method on the server, not just the ones defined by HTTP. In addition, you can pass any typed parameter instead of just strings. This means there's very little client/server overhead, especially when compared with HTTP/CGI. With CGI, you must start a new instance of a program every time an applet invokes a method on a server; with CORBA, you don't. In addition, CGI does not maintain state between client invocations; CORBA does.

■ ***CORBA provides a scalable server-to-server infrastructure.*** Pools of server business objects can communicate using the CORBA ORB. These objects can run on multiple servers to provide load-balancing for incoming client requests. The ORB can dispatch the request to the first available object and add more objects as the demand increases. CORBA allows the server objects to act in unison using transaction boundaries and related CORBA services. In contrast, a CGI application is a bottleneck because it must respond to thousands of incoming requests; it has no way to distribute the load across multiple processes or processors.

■ ***CORBA extends Java with a distributed object infrastructure.*** Currently, Java applets cannot communicate across address spaces using remote method invocations. This means that there is no easy way for a Java applet to invoke a method on a remote object. CORBA allows Java applets to communicate with other objects written in different languages across address spaces and networks. In addition, CORBA provides a rich set of distributed object services that augment Java—including metadata, transactions, security, naming, trader, and collections.

With CORBA, Java clients and applets can invoke a wide variety of IDL-defined operations on the server. In contrast, HTTP clients are restricted to a limited set of operations. Server-side applications are regular CORBA objects. Consequently, they are available on a permanent basis. There is no need to go through the overhead of spawning a CGI script for every invocation.

Table 2-1 summarizes the differences between today's Java-to-CGI client/server approach and a solution based on CORBA's IIOP protocol. CORBA was designed from the start to provide powerful 3-tier client/server solutions. In contrast, client/server interactions were wedged into HTTP and CGI; it's more of an after-thought. CORBA naturally extends Java's object model for distributed environments. CORBA also makes it easier to split Java applets into components that can be distributed along client/server lines. This means that the client side of the applet can remain small, which reduces the download time.

Table 2-1. Java Clients With CORBA IIOP Versus HTTP-CGI.

Feature	Java With CORBA ORB	Java With HTTP-CGI
State preservation across invocations	Yes	No
IDL and Interface Repository	Yes	No
Metadata support	Yes	No
Dynamic invocations	Yes	No
Transactions	Yes	No
Security	Yes	Yes
Rich object services	Yes	No
Callbacks	Yes	No
Server/server infrastructure	Yes	No
Server scalability	Yes	No
IDL-defined methods	Yes	No

This highly uneven comparison clearly demonstrates why the Java Web needs CORBA. However, CORBA is not the only middleware infrastructure to extend the Web. There are at least three other serious contenders—Sockets, OLE's *DCOM with ActiveX*, and Java's *RMI*.

The Other Contenders

In Part 4 of our book, **Client/Server Programming with Java and CORBA** (Wiley, 1997), we cover the top five competing infrastructures for building the Object Web—including streamed Sockets, HTTP/CGI, Java RMI, CORBA/IIOP with Caffeine, and DCOM/ActiveX. We wrote the same client/server application using each of the competing technologies. We then put together a report card that compares the following aspects of each system: 1) the client/server development process, 2) the Java integration facilities, 3) installation and deployment, 4) Ping performance, and 5) intergalactic reach. Table 2-2 shows our Michelin rating of the five contending Object Web technologies. Four stars is the highest rating. A hollow star is the worst rating; it means the function is not there.

Table 2-2. Comparing Java/CORBA ORBs and Their Competition.

Feature	CORBA/IIOP	DCOM	RMI	HTTP/CGI	Sockets
Abstraction level	★★★★	★★★★	★★★★	★★	★
Seamless Java integration	★★★★	★★★	★★★★	★★	★★
OS platform support	★★★★	★★	★★★★	★★★★	★★★★
All-Java implementation	★★★★	★	★★★★	★★★★	★★★★
Typed parameter support	★★★★	★★★★	★★★★	★	★
Ease of configuration	★★★	☆	★★★	★★★	★★★
Distributed method invocations	★★★★	★★★	★★★	☆	☆
State across invocations	★★★★	★★★	★★★	☆	★★
Dynamic discovery and metadata support	★★★★	★★★	☆	☆	☆
Dynamic invocation	★★★★	★★★★	★	☆	☆
Performance (remote Pings)	★★★★ 3.3 msecs	★★★ 3.9 msecs	★★★ 5.5 msecs (extrapolated)	☆ 603.8 msecs	★★★★ 2.0 msecs
Wire-level security	★★★★	★★★★	★★★	★★★	★★★
Wire-level transactions	★★★★	★★★	☆	☆	☆
Persistent object references	★★★★	★	☆	☆	☆
URL-based naming	★★★	★	★★	★★★★	★★★
Multilingual object invocations	★★★★	★★★	☆	★★★	★★★★
Language-neutral wire protocol	★★★★	★★★★	☆	★★★★	☆
Intergalactic scaling	★★★★	★	★	★★	★★★★
Open standard	★★★★	★★	★★	★★★★	★★★★

Yes, CORBA is inevitable. Why? Table 2-2 says it all (the details are in our programming book). CORBA's only real competition is DCOM. RMI is a niche ORB; it's not going anywhere on the enterprise. Sockets is just a low-level protocol. And HTTP/CGI just doesn't cut it. So, it's CORBA versus DCOM. It appears CORBA won the first round. But the battle will continue for the remainder of the century.

What Java Brings to CORBA

In a sense, the Java infrastructure starts where CORBA ends. CORBA provides a distributed object infrastructure that lets applications extend their reach across networks, languages, component boundaries, and operating systems. Java provides a portable object infrastructure that works on every major operating system. CORBA deals with network transparency, while Java deals with implementation transparency. Here's a short list of what Java does for CORBA:

■ *Java allows CORBA to move intelligent behavior around.* Java's mobile code facilities let you dynamically move intelligence across the intergalactic CORBA infrastructure to where you need it most. This allows both clients and servers to dynamically gain intelligence. You can partition an application at run time to run on clients and servers without recompiling.

■ *Java complements the CORBA Life Cycle and Externalization Services.* It makes it possible for a CORBA ORB to move around an object's behavior as well as its state.

■ *Java is making CORBA ubiquitous on the Web.* The Object Web may be the CORBA killer app. For example, Netscape is bundling Visigenic's *VisiBroker for Java*—a CORBA-compliant Java ORB—in all its future browsers and servers. This makes CORBA IIOP the distributed object model for both the Internet and Java. The Netscape browser may be the most popular client application in existence, with over 40 million users.

■ *Java simplifies code distribution in large CORBA systems.* Java code can be deployed and managed centrally from the server. You update your code once on the server and then let the clients receive it when and where they need it. In theory, this should make it easier for you to manage large client/server Intranet installations; it doesn't require that you manually update each individual desktop or laptop.

■ *Java complements CORBA's agenting infrastructure.* CORBA is defining an agenting framework for distributed objects. This framework will let *roaming objects* move from node to node based on rules you define. A roaming object typically carries its state, itinerary, and behavior in its travels. Java bytecodes are ideal for shipping behavior around. Java is becoming ubiquitous; consequently, the agents can safely assume that a Java Virtual Machine will be present on every node they visit. But, you should note that Java applets are currently stateless. So, they need to be augmented with an agenting infrastructure—like CORBA's—that lets them carry their state along with their behavior.

■ *Java complements CORBA's component services.* CORBA's compound document service—based on OpenDoc—defines visual containers for components as well as mobile storage containers. Java will provide the portable "Beans" that visually play in these containers. CORBA's mobile container structure—based on OpenDoc's Bento—is ideal for moving around collections of Java Beans and other components. In theory, Bento can also be used as a portable store for moving around Java agents.

■ *Java is a great language for writing CORBA objects.* Java is almost the ideal language for writing both client and server objects. Java's built-in multithreading, garbage collection, and error management make it easier to write robust networked objects. Java's object model complements CORBA's; they both use the concept of interfaces to separate an object's definition from its implementation.

In the past, OMG has kept its distance from implementation and language issues (except for bindings). Consequently, CORBA is a language-independent object model, which is good. However, Java solves some thorny problems that have stood in the way of developing a truly portable distributed object market. This is especially true in the area of components and roaming agents. Without turning this into a Soapbox, we feel that OMG should treat Java as an extension of the CORBA project for object portability. Java is more than just another object language with CORBA bindings; it is also a portable object platform.

The Client/Server Object Web

The bottom line is that Java is primarily a mobile code system, while CORBA is a distributed object infrastructure. Java lets you write portable applications that can run on any machine in the galaxy. CORBA provides an intergalactic distributed object infrastructure over the Internet. CORBA lets Java objects communicate with any other object, anywhere. So the two projects are very complementary.

Currently, most Java applications have been stand-alone demos, but the real value of Java is when you build portable clients to much larger transactional systems. This is where CORBA comes into the picture. You can use CORBA and Java today to create some dynamite client/server applications. The relationship between CORBA and Java will only grow in time to provide more varied services for the *Object Web*.

As we explain in our other books, the Object Web must also be augmented with a compound document framework that lets you distribute, cache, and seamlessly display groups of related components. We call this technology *Shippable Places*. You will hear more about this in Part 4.

The good news is that once the Object Web technology takes off, it will subsume all other forms of client/server computing—including TP Monitors, Database, and Groupware. Distributed objects and the Web can do it all, and better. Objects will help us break large monolithic applications into more manageable multivendor components that can live and coexist on intergalactic networks. They are also our only hope for managing and distributing the millions of software entities that will live on these intergalactic networks. The Java Object Web is the killer application that will bring CORBA to the masses of Intranet and Internet programmers.

In our previous books, we offer Figure 2-4 as our answer to the question: Which way client/server? The Ethernet era of client/server saw a file-centric application wave (the NetWare wave) followed by a database-centric wave (the Oracle wave); TP Monitors and Groupware generated minor ripples. The Object Web is the next big wave.

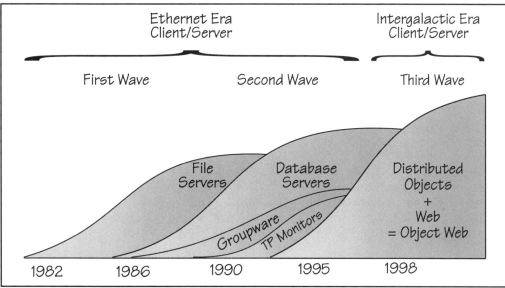

Figure 2-4. The Waves of Client/Server.

This new threshold marks the beginning of a transition from *Ethernet* client/server to *intergalactic* client/server that will result in the irrelevance of proximity. The center of gravity is shifting from single-server, 2-tier, LAN-based departmental client/server to a post-scarcity form of client/server. Here, every machine on the global "information highway" can be both a client and a server. Table 2-3 contrasts these two eras of client/server computing.

Table 2-3. Web Client/Server Versus Traditional Client/Server.

Application Characteristic	Intergalactic Era Client/Server	Ethernet Era Client/Server
Number of clients per application	Millions	Fewer than 100
Number of servers per application	100,000+	1 or 2
Geography	Global	Campus-based
Server-to-server interactions	Yes	No
Middleware	ORBs on top of Internet	SQL and stored procedures
Client/server architecture	3-tier (or n-tier)	2-tier
Transactional updates	Pervasive	Very infrequent
Multimedia content	High	Low
Mobile agents	Yes	No
Client front-ends	OOUIs, compound documents, and shippable places	GUI
Timeframe	1997-2000	1985 till present

Meet the Players

In a sense, the Object Web will be a gigantic showcase for CORBA technology. To use a shopping mall analogy, the anchor stores of the CORBA Object Web are Netscape, Oracle, JavaSoft, and IBM/Lotus. This mall is also populated with hundreds of software vendors that provide the boutiques and specialty stores—including specialized ORBs, tools, components, and services. There should be enough critical mass to attract the shoppers with the dollars—ISVs, IT shops, and consumers of software. Let's take a quick look at what each of these players provide:

■ **Netscape** is making CORBA ubiquitous on the client. It is bundling the *VisiBroker for Java* ORB with every browser. Netscape is also using CORBA for its server-to-server infrastructure. Potentially, Netscape can distribute over 20 million CORBA ORBs on the client and over a million CORBA ORBs on the server. CORBA also allows Netscape servers to play with other servers on the enterprise.

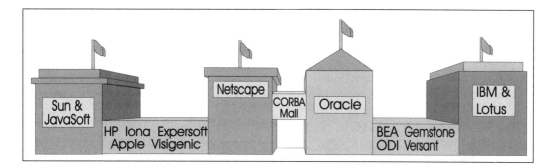

■ **Oracle** sells $4 billion worth of software—mostly on the server. Oracle has adopted CORBA as the platform for its *Network Computing Architecture*. Oracle's entire software line, from the database engines to stored procedures, tools, and the Internet, will be built on a CORBA object bus. For example, the database engine will be componentized using CORBA. Third parties will be able extend the database using CORBA components called *Cartridges*. All the Oracle tools—including *Developer 2000* and *Sedona*—will target CORBA on the client and on the server. Oracle is building most of the CORBA Services on top of the Visigenic IIOP ORB. This ORB will first appear in *Oracle Web Server 3.0*; it will serve as the foundation for Oracle's Internet products. The ORB will seamlessly communicate with other CORBA-compliant IIOP ORBs on both the client and the server.

■ **JavaSoft** is building Enterprise Java on top of a CORBA/IIOP foundation. The *Java Transaction Service* is based on CORBA transactions and will be built into the *Joe* ORB. Eventually, a CORBA ORB will be distributed with the Enterprise Java JDK. In addition, SunSoft is building its Internet server strategy around CORBA using its *NEO* ORB and *Solstic*e.

■ **IBM/Lotus** is building its cross-platform network computing infrastructure on CORBA/Java. In addition to the *SOM 4.0* CORBA ORB, IBM intends to bundle a Java runtime with all its OS platforms. The IBM *VisualAge* tool will target CORBA/Java objects on both clients and servers across all the IBM platforms. Finally, IBM is developing a scalable server-side component coordinator—called BOSS—for managing middle-tier CORBA/Java objects.

■ **The boutiques** come in all shapes. They include long-standing CORBA players like Apple, HP, SunSoft, Iona, Tandem, Digital, Novell, and Expersoft. This camp also includes the ODBMS vendors—for example, ODI, GemStone, and Versant. In addition, TP Monitor vendors are now morphing ORBs with traditional TP Monitors—for example, BEA is building a scalable CORBA-based TP Monitor on top of Tuxedo. On the client side, Apple and CI Labs are building OpenDoc-based frameworks on top of CORBA. The boutiques also include tool vendors—such as Symantec and Borland—and some major IT shops. Finally, the boutiques include the major ISVs that gravitate in the Netscape, IBM, JavaSoft, and Oracle orbits. So there will be quite a crowd.

In summary, this new CORBA coalition is building around a killer app called the Object Web. The Web transforms CORBA from a set of standards to a set of products that fulfill an intergalactic need. CORBA becomes a powerful architecture that ties together products that form the Object Web. For example, ORBs running in Netscape browsers can talk to middle-tier Oracle *Cartridges* that also happen to be CORBA business objects. *Object Transaction Coordinators*—from IBM, BEA, and Hitachi—can coordinate these server-side business objects because they too sit on the CORBA bus. Components and Beans from Apple, CI Labs, JavaSoft, IBM, Oracle, Netscape, and others can also play on the CORBA bus. The CORBA bus is the foundation technology that brings together all these disparate pieces of software from multiple vendors. The CORBA/Java Object Web will eventually draw in thousands of smaller software developers that will create specialized components that service this huge market.

In parallel, Microsoft is building its own rendition of the Object Web; it is based on DCOM and ActiveX. Viper is the DCOM Component Coordinator; it is Microsoft's secret weapon for winning the Object Web. Currently, the Microsoft Web appears to be a single-anchor mall with tons of boutiques. So, let the games begin.

CONCLUSION

Java is the first step toward creating an Object Web, but it is still not enough. Java offers tremendous flexibility for distributed application development, but it currently does not support a client/server paradigm. To do this, Java needs to be augmented with a distributed object infrastructure, which is where OMG's CORBA comes into the picture. CORBA provides the missing link between the Java portable application environment and the world of intergalactic back-end services. The intersection of Java and CORBA object technologies is the natural next step in the evolution of the Object Web. The Web—with Java and CORBA—provides a ubiquitous platform for network-centric computing.

Chapter 3

Meet the CORBA/Java ORBs

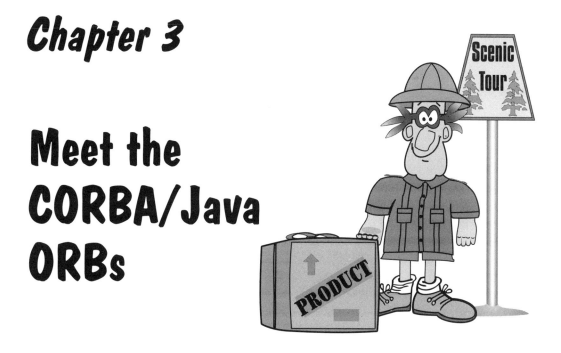

CORBA/Java ORBs are popping up everywhere. In their rush, vendors are bringing their ORBs to market without even waiting for the official OMG Java bindings for CORBA to gel. These vendors seem to be working on Java time. So what exactly is a CORBA/Java ORB? It's a CORBA IIOP ORB that's written entirely in Java for portability. The ORB must be able to generate Java language bindings from CORBA IDL. In addition, any code generated by the IDL compiler must be in pure Java; you should be able to download that code and run it on any machine hosting a Java run-time environment.

With a Java ORB, an ordinary Java applet can directly invoke methods on CORBA objects using the IIOP protocol over the Internet. The applet totally bypasses CGI and HTTP; the client and the server establish a direct communication link using the ORB. You can load the client-side, CORBA-enabled applet into any commercial Java-enabled browser, and then execute it. These downloadable Java ORBs are also called *ORBlets*.

So where can you get one of these CORBA/Java ORBs? As we go to press, we know of three ORBs that more or less fit the bill: Sun's *Joe*, Iona's *OrbixWeb*, and Visigenic/Netscape's *VisiBroker for Java* (previously known as *Black Widow*). In this chapter, we go over the main features of these three ORBs. We will also briefly introduce some of the key non-Java CORBA ORBs. We anticipate that over the next year all the major CORBA vendors will introduce Java ORBs on top of IIOP. So you may want to know who these vendors are.

SUN'S JOE

Sun—the creator of Java—was one of the six founding members of OMG. Consequently, Sun's client/server vision has always been "distributed objects everywhere." As you would expect, the integration of CORBA and Java is high on Sun's agenda. In Sun's view, you can use the Object Web for all client/server application development—including departments, Intranets, and the Internet. In this section, we first give you a quick history of Sun's CORBA/Java integration efforts. Then we look at Joe's features.

NEO and Joe: A Short History

In September 1995, Sun announced *NEO*—a 3-tier client/server architecture that brings together Java, CORBA objects, and the Web. The NEO acronym does not stand for anything in particular. The NEO product includes: 1) the *NEOnet* CORBA ORB (previously known as DOE), 2) the Java and OpenStep client environments, 3) the *Solstice* distributed systems management framework, and 4) client/server development tools and programmer workbenches.

In January 1996, Sun first introduced CORBA IDL bindings for Java at the OMG meeting in San Diego; it also announced a Java ORB called *Joe*. In May 1996, Sun—or JavaSoft—announced that Joe was now part of *Enterprise Java*—a core Java framework. This means that Joe will be incorporated into a future Java run time. In July 1996, JavaSoft shipped the first widely available beta of Joe. In November 1996, JavaSoft declared Joe to be the "official" Java ORB for the enterprise. In December 1996, JavaSoft announced Java Transactions based on the CORBA Object Transaction Service.

What Is Joe?

Joe is primarily a client-side Java ORB. This means that you can download a Joe ORBlet along with your applet, and then use it to invoke server objects on a NEO ORB (see Figure 3-1). Of course, you can also permanently install the Joe code on your machine to avoid downloading it with every applet. Joe and NEO currently communicate using two proprietary Sun protocols: NEO ORB and Door (from project Spring). By the time you read this, Sun should have implemented the IIOP protocol on both Joe and NEO.

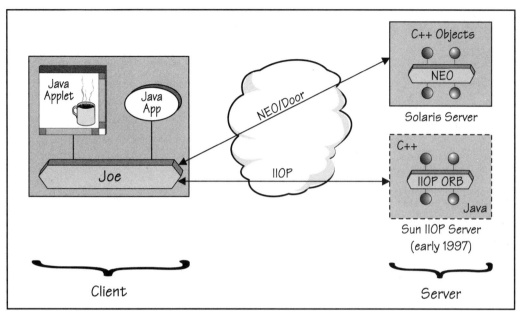

Figure 3-1. Joe and NEO: The Client and Server Story.

Joe clients can receive asynchronous calls from a server via a *callback* service (see the next Details box). To receive callbacks, the Java applet must: 1) define the CORBA object via IDL, 2) create an instance of that object, and 3) export the object reference to a server. The remote server can communicate with the applet by simply invoking an operation on that object reference. The invocation is then delivered to the Joe client as an ordinary Java method invocation.

Joe also includes an *IDL-to-Java* compiler that automatically generates Java client class stubs from standard CORBA IDL files. Currently, server-side objects must be written for the NEO ORB platform. As we go to press, Joe clients can only talk to NEO objects. This is obviously a limitation because NEO only runs on Sun's Solaris. In addition, NEO only supports server objects written in C or C++. So there is no server-side Java. Of course, the IIOP version of Joe—expected in early 1997—will be able to speak to any Java CORBA ORB that supports IIOP.

IONA'S ORBIXWEB

Iona is the leading provider of CORBA technology. Its C++ Orbix ORB now runs on 20 operating systems—including 12 Unix variants, OS/2, NT, Windows 95, Macintosh System 7.5, OpenVMS, and MVS. Iona ORBs support both IIOP and the proprietary Orbix protocol. In July 1996, Iona released *OrbixWeb V1*.

Callbacks

Details

So what's a callback? It's a call from a server to a client. A callback reverses the client and server roles; it allows a client to become a server. Typically, a CORBA ORB is both a client and a server. Consequently, any client can automatically receive callbacks. Any server that has an object reference for the client's callback object can remotely invoke it.

Once you get the hang of it, you'll find that callbacks are extremely versatile. They let you create very dynamic client/server environments that fully complement Java. Callbacks extend the client's event-driven architecture to include messages from their servers. In general, servers invoke callbacks whenever they have something urgent to tell you. Callbacks from servers will soon magically pop up inside your applets or Java client applications (see Figure 3-2). Yes, we're moving to a brave new world where every client is also a server. ☐

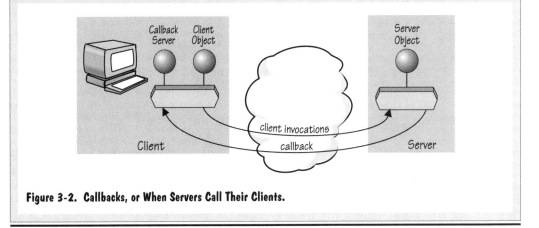

Figure 3-2. Callbacks, or When Servers Call Their Clients.

What Is OrbixWeb?

OrbixWeb V1 is a client-side Java implementation of Iona's Orbix CORBA ORB. It's a lightweight ORB that can be shipped over the Internet in the form of bytecodes. OrbixWeb allows Java applets and client applications to communicate with an Orbix server using either the CORBA IIOP protocol or the older Iona Orbix protocol. Clients can issue both static and dynamic invocations. OrbixWeb is IIOP-based. Consequently, you should be able to talk to server objects on any ORB that supports IIOP.

Currently, you must write your Orbix server objects in C++ (see Figure 3-3). However, *OrbixWeb V2* should be available by the time you read this; it went into beta in November 1996. This new version provides a complete server-side Java implementation. It also supports callbacks on the clients.

The OrbixWeb IDL-to-Java compiler is similar to Sun's, but with some differences. Iona intends to fully comply with the OMG CORBA binding for Java as soon as it is finalized.

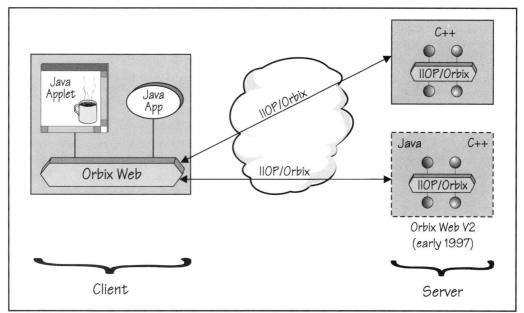

Figure 3-3. OrbixWeb: The Client and Server Story.

VISIGENIC'S VISIBROKER FOR JAVA

VisiBroker started life as PostModern's *Black Widow* ORB. It was the first CORBA ORB to support both client and server Java objects. The ORB is written entirely in Java, which makes it a downloadable ORBlet. In early 1996, PostModern was acquired by Visigenic—a leading vendor of database middleware. In July 1996, Visigenic changed the name of Black Widow to *VisiBroker for Java*; PostModern's C++ *Orbeline* ORB is now called *VisiBroker for C++*. In late July 1996, Netscape announced that its *Netscape ONE* initiative will use VisiBroker for Java as its ORB. Netscape will incorporate VisiBroker in all its future browsers and servers. Finally, in February 1997, Oracle announced it will use VisiBroker as its ORB; it will be the foundation for NCA.

What Is VisiBroker for Java?

VisiBroker for Java is a CORBA client and server ORB written entirely in Java (see Figure 3-4). All Visigenic ORBs fully implement the IIOP protocol, which makes it easy for C++ objects to invoke methods on Java objects, and vice versa. VisiBroker for Java supports both static and dynamic CORBA method invocations. Methods on a server can be invoked by Java client applications or by applets within a browser. If the browser supports it, the applets can use Secure Sockets.

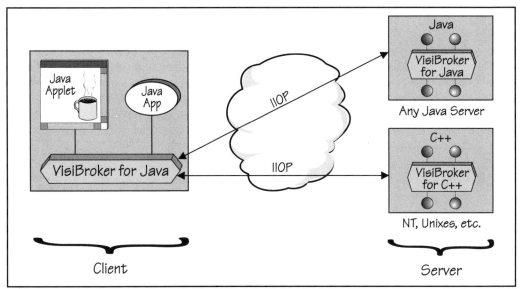

Figure 3-4. VisiBroker: The Client and Server Story.

VisiBroker for Java includes a full CORBA Interface Repository written in Java. Visigenic intends to fully comply with the OMG CORBA binding for Java as soon as it is finalized. The VisiBroker IDL compiler generates skeleton code for the server objects in C++ or Java; it also generates Java stubs for the client side.

VisiBroker for Java comes with a fault-tolerant object naming service called the *OSAgent*. Multiple OSAgents running in the same network locate each other and automatically partition the namespace among themselves. This lets you replicate and load-balance objects on different server machines. In the case of a crash, the ORB automatically re-routes the client calls to one of the replicas. The VisiBroker for Java ORB is implemented in less than 100 KBytes of Java bytecodes. Consequently, you can easily download it to the client machine if it's not already there. The ORB supports both client and server functions, which means any client can implement callbacks. By the time you read this, VisiBroker will support Java versions of the CORBA Naming, Event, and Transaction Services. VisiBroker also supports *Caffeine*—a pure Java development environment on top of CORBA/IIOP.

Caffeine makes CORBA transparent to Java programmers. Your Java objects can invoke other objects over a CORBA IIOP ORB without requiring that you write IDL.

How Slow Are Java ORBs?

We keep hearing that C++ is much faster than Java. So how slow are these all-Java ORBs? In our book **Client/Server Programming with Java and CORBA** (Wiley, 1997), we ran the same Ping benchmark against two ORBs: *VisiBroker for Java* and *VisiBroker for C++*. The latter is one of the fastest and most seasoned C++ ORBs. The big surprise was that the JIT-compiled Java ORB performed remote Pings as well as its C++ counterpart—they both clocked 3.2 msec response times.

VisiBroker and Netscape ONE

The Netscape *Open Network Environment (ONE)* is a standards-based platform (and tools) for creating a new generation of distributed client/server applications for the Internet. The distributed object model for this new platform is CORBA IIOP. CORBA will be used to integrate Java clients, servers, and tools.

According to Netscape, "IIOP unlocks the power of network applications by providing an open, platform-independent protocol for connecting network-centric applications. Through IIOP, corporations can gradually expose and interconnect their business applications, not only behind the corporate firewall, but also through the *Extranet* to electronic markets, consumers, and other companies. Netscape ONE applications will be able to use the underlying IIOP protocol to gain access to CORBA services and IIOP-compliant enterprise applications, such as business objects, EDI, and transaction services."[1]

The Netscape *Internet Foundation Classes* will provide platform-independent services for Netscape ONE applications written in Java and JavaScript. You should be able to invoke any CORBA object via JavaScript. The idea is to create your high-performance client and server applications in Java and then use JavaScript for casual scripting. Any IDL-defined CORBA object should be Java-scriptable.

WHICH JAVA ORB?

Table 3-1 compares the Java ORBs. All these ORBs have strong backers: Joe will be included with every Java Development Kit; VisiBroker will be included with every Netscape browser and Oracle server; and OrbixWeb is sold by Iona—the leading ORB vendor.

---

[1] Source: *The Netscape ONE Development Environment Vision and Product Roadmap* (July 29, 1996).

Table 3-1. A Comparison of Java CORBA ORBs, Circa Late 1996.

CORBA Feature	OrbixWeb	Joe	VisiBroker for Java
Client-side Java	Yes	Yes	Yes
Static method invocations	Yes	Yes	Yes
Dynamic method invocations	Yes	No	Yes
Interface Repository	Yes (in Version 2)	No	Yes
Server callbacks	Yes (in Version 2)	Yes	Yes
Native Java over IIOP	No	No	Yes (Caffeine)
Server-side Java	Yes (in Version 2)	No	Yes
Wide market support	Yes	Yes	Yes

THE OTHER CORBA ORBS

The Java CORBA market is still in its infancy. Currently, most of the CORBA vendors are busy upgrading their ORBs to CORBA 2.0 and IIOP. They haven't got to Java yet. Some vendors are waiting for the OMG Java CORBA bindings to firm up before delivering Java ORBs to the market. By the end of 1996, most of the major ORB vendors introduced CORBA 2.0 versions of their ORBs. We expect most of these vendors to provide Java ORBs and services shortly after. So it may still be too early to pick a winner. The CORBA ORB vendors fall into two camps: the major system vendors and innovative software startups.

ORBs from major system vendors include Digital's *ObjectBroker*, IBM's *SOM*, Sun's *NEO/Joe*, Oracle's *Web Request Broker*, ICL's *DAIS*, and HP's *ORB Plus*. ORBs from innovative software startups include Expersoft's *PowerBroker*, Iona's *Orbix*, and Visigenic's *VisiBroker*. This list is by no means complete. In addition, the CORBA world also includes literally hundreds of products that build on top of ORB middleware—including client/server tools, publish-and-subscribe systems, component repositories, ODBMSs, and system management platforms.

Conclusion

The nice thing about CORBA is that you'll always have more than one ORB to choose from. It's a very competitive market. We've now completed the big picture tour. Yes, it's time to jump into some of the details. If you're on the Scenic Tour, you should skip to Part 4.

Part 2
ORB
Fundamentals

An Introduction to Part 2

In Part 2, we dive a little deeper into CORBA and explain the workings of the ORB in more detail. The ORB is the heart of CORBA. You must first master how it works before you can move on to more interesting things like distributed services and components. After six years of standardization, ORBs are becoming almost commodity-like. You should be able to switch from one vendor ORB to the next without too much disruption.

So how are ORB vendors differentiating their products? As you will see in the next few chapters, the action is now moving to the server side of the ORB. This is an area where vendors still face serious challenges. In addition, vendors can differentiate their products by the CORBA Object Services they support. We cover CORBA Services in Part 3.

Here's what we will be covering in Part 2:

- *Chapter 4* is about CORBA *static* method invocations. Why start with static invocations? Because it's the bedrock of CORBA programming. This familiar programming model lets you invoke methods on remote CORBA server objects just like you would on any ordinary language object. It is a simple and efficient model that hides all the nastiness of distributed object programming behind a familiar language facade. In this chapter, we also tell you about the magic of CORBA object references.

- *Chapter 5* starts our exploration of the dynamic CORBA. We cover CORBA's *Dynamic Invocation Interface (DII)* in detail. With CORBA's dynamic invocations, any client can construct a remote method call "on-the-fly," and then invoke it. The DII lets you create very flexible systems where clients and servers discover each other at run time. Servers offer new services and interfaces whenever they become available. We're talking about a brave new world where discovery and serendipity become the norm. These are two very important requirements for the Object Web.

- *Chapter 6* is about how you bootstrap yourself into the CORBA world. You must first find your ORB, and then use it to discover the universe of CORBA objects. We also cover how server objects conspire with their ORBs to create the illusion that all objects are up and running all the time. This conspiracy benefits the clients. It's part of the CORBA philosophy to keep the client side simple. Server objects must appear to be always actively waiting on the client to invoke their methods.

- *Chapter 7* is about metadata—or self-describing objects. We explain the CORBA IDL in detail. We then cover the Interface Repository. We tell you how it stores IDL-generated metadata and how you can retrieve it. Finally, we cover the CORBA *introspection* services. You will discover that CORBA objects are supersmart. They can tell you quite a bit about themselves.

CORBA lets you create very flexible and extensible systems. Part 2 explains the foundations of this self-describing and highly dynamic infrastructure.

Chapter 4

The Static CORBA

In this chapter, we start our detailed exploration of CORBA by going over static method invocations. For many of us, static invocations are all we need from an ORB. It's the most basic function that we must all master. By now, all the ORBs do a stellar job with static invocations. Of course, it took three generations of ORBs to perfect this process. The client code you write to perform static invocations is also highly portable across multivendor ORBs. You write your client code using your high-level language of choice and then let the ORB take care of all the messy details involved with delivering the invocations to the server.

If you come from the world of client/server, static invocations on the surface appear to be like RPCs. If you come from the world of Java, C++, or Smalltalk, a static invocation will appear to be like any ordinary method invocation, except that it is remote. Ideally, you should not be able to tell the difference between a local object invocation and a remote one. The ORB provides language bindings that make it all transparent. In practice, some distributed object semantics may always surface. For example, you must first obtain a reference to a CORBA object before you can invoke its methods. However, it's these object references that make CORBA much more powerful than RPCs or ordinary language objects. Here's why.

A CORBA *object reference* is a very powerful unit of distributed service negotiation. It points to an object interface—i.e., a set of related methods that operate on an individual object. In contrast, an RPC only returns a reference to a single function. Furthermore, you can aggregate CORBA interfaces via multiple-inheritance. In addition, CORBA objects are polymorphic—the same call behaves differently depending on the object type that receives it. Of course, RPCs don't support inheritance, polymorphism, or unique objects with state. The bottom line is that a CORBA object reference provides scalpel-like precision; it lets you invoke a set of methods on a specific object. Unique object references are the most efficient way to obtain remote services on the intergalactic network.

Static Versus Dynamic Methods

Figure 4-1 shows the two types of client/server invocations that are supported by a CORBA ORB: static and dynamic. In both cases, the client performs a request by having access to an object reference (i.e., object ID) and invoking the method that performs the service (see the following Details box). The server can't tell the difference between static and dynamic invocations.

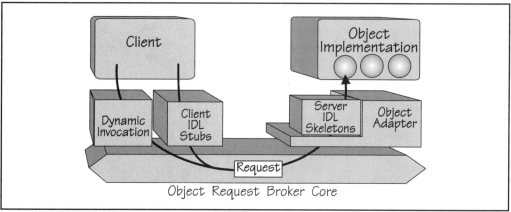

Figure 4-1. CORBA's Static and Dynamic Method Invocations.

Clients see the object interfaces through the perspective of a *language mapping*—or *binding*—that brings the ORB right up to the programmer's level. Client programs should be able to work without any source changes on any ORB that supports the language binding. They should be able to call any object instance that implements the interface. The implementation of the object, its object adapter, and the ORB used to access it is totally transparent to both static and dynamic clients.

The *static interface* is directly generated in the form of stubs by the IDL precompiler. It is perfect for programs that know at compile time the particulars of the operations they will need to invoke. The static stub interface is bound at compile time and provides the following advantages over the dynamic method invocation:

- ***It is easier to program***—you call the remote method by simply invoking it by name and passing it the parameters. It's a very natural form of programming.

- ***It provides more robust type checking***—the checking is enforced by the compiler at build time.

- ***It performs well***—a single API call is issued to the stub, which takes it from there. In our programming book, we ran some benchmarks that show dynamic invocations to be about 40 times slower than their static counterparts. Most of the overhead is in the preparation of the dynamic message.[1]

- ***It is self-documenting***—you can tell what's going on by reading the code.

In contrast, the *dynamic* method invocation provides a more flexible environment. It allows you to add new classes to the system without requiring changes in the client code. It's very useful for tools that discover what services are provided at run time. You can write some very generic code with dynamic APIs. However, most applications don't require this level of flexibility and are better off with static stub implementations.

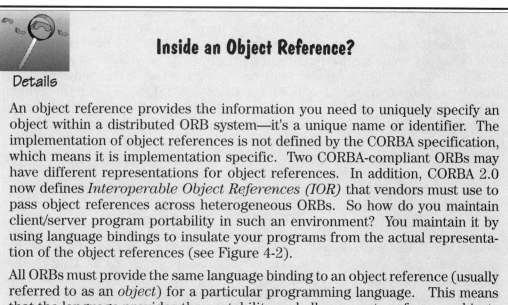

Inside an Object Reference?

Details

An object reference provides the information you need to uniquely specify an object within a distributed ORB system—it's a unique name or identifier. The implementation of object references is not defined by the CORBA specification, which means it is implementation specific. Two CORBA-compliant ORBs may have different representations for object references. In addition, CORBA 2.0 now defines *Interoperable Object References (IOR)* that vendors must use to pass object references across heterogeneous ORBs. So how do you maintain client/server program portability in such an environment? You maintain it by using language bindings to insulate your programs from the actual representation of the object references (see Figure 4-2).

All ORBs must provide the same language binding to an object reference (usually referred to as an *object*) for a particular programming language. This means that the language provides the portability and allows you to reference objects that run on different ORBs from within your programs. What happens if your program is accessing object references on two different ORBs? According to CORBA, your programs should still work fine; it is up to the vendors to resolve—

---

[1] Source: Orfali and Harkey, **Client/Server Programming with Java and CORBA** (Wiley, 1997).

via the IORs—any object reference conflicts that may be encountered by the client code.

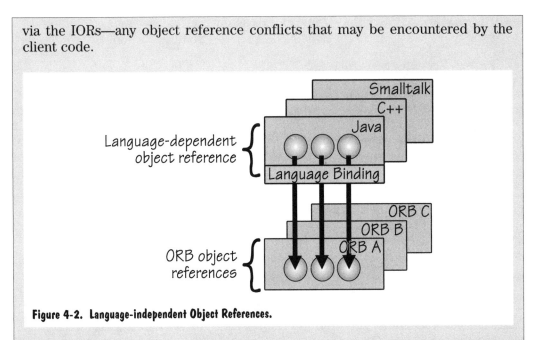

Figure 4-2. Language-independent Object References.

How do the client programs obtain object references? They usually receive them from directories or invocations on other objects to which they have references. You can convert an object reference to a string-name that you can store in files. The string-name can be preserved or communicated by different means, and then turned back into an object reference by the ORB that produced the string. CORBA defines two ORB interface functions—*object_to_string* and *string_to_object*—to help store, communicate, and retrieve object references. Client programs can use these two functions to obtain a string-name and convert it to an object reference, and vice versa.

We also expect the OMG to get into the business of allocating "well-known object references." The CORBA 2.0 Initialization specification already includes a few well-known objects. We cover ORB initialization in Chapter 6.

Finally, the ORB interface defines some operations that you can invoke on any object reference. These operations are directly implemented by the ORB on the object reference. This means that they're not passed to the object implementation. You can invoke the ORB method *get_interface* on any object reference to obtain an Interface Repository object that provides type and metadata information for that object. You can invoke the ORB method *get_implementation* on any object reference to obtain an *Implementation Repository* object that describes the implementation of that object. You can invoke the ORB method *is_nil* on any object reference to test if an object exists. You'll see examples of how the **CORBA::ORB** interface is used in Chapter 5 and in Part 3. ❑

CORBA Static Method Invocations: From IDL to Interface Stubs

Figure 4-3 shows the steps you go through to create your server classes, provide interface stubs for them, store their definitions in the Interface Repository, instantiate the objects at run time, and record their presence with the Implementation Repository. Let's go through these steps one-by-one and see what's involved:

1. *Define your object classes using Interface Definition Language (IDL)*. The IDL is the means by which objects tell their potential clients what operations are available and how they should be invoked. The IDL definition language defines the types of objects, their attributes, the methods they export, and the method parameters.

2. *Run the IDL file through a language precompiler*. A typical CORBA-compliant precompiler processes the IDL files and produces language *skeletons* for the implementation server classes.

3. *Add the implementation code to the skeletons*. You must supply the code that implements the methods in the skeletons. In other words, you must create your server classes.

4. *Compile the code*. A CORBA-compliant compiler is typically capable of generating at least three types of output files: 1) *import files* that describe the objects to an Interface Repository; 2) *client stubs* for the IDL-defined methods—these stubs are invoked by a client program that needs to statically access IDL-defined services via the ORB; and 3) *server skeletons* that call the methods on the server—they're also called *up-call interfaces*. You must provide the code that implements the server classes. The automatic generation of stubs frees developers from having to write them, and frees applications from dependencies on a particular ORB implementation.

5. *Bind the class definitions to the Interface Repository*. Typically, you use a utility to bind—or, if you prefer, load—the IDL information in an Interface Repository that programs can access at run time.

6. *Register the run-time objects with the Implementation Repository*. The Object Adapter records in the *Implementation Repository* the object reference and type of any object it instantiates on the server. The Implementation Repository also knows which object classes are supported on a particular server. The ORB uses this information to locate active objects or to request the activation of objects on a particular server.

7. *Instantiate the objects on the server*. At startup time, a server *Object Adapter* may instantiate server objects that service remote client method invocations. These run-time objects are instances of the server application

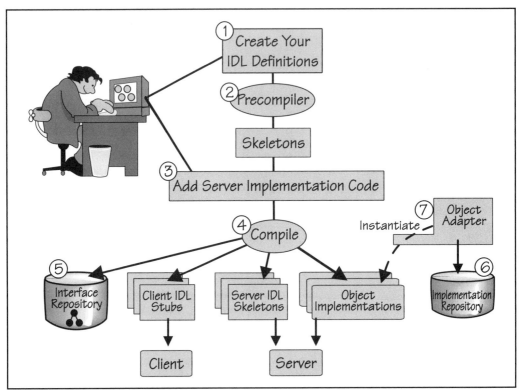

Figure 4-3. Defining Services: From IDL To Interface Stubs.

classes. CORBA specifies different Object Adapter strategies that are used to create and manage the run-time objects (more on this in Chapter 6).

The seven steps we just outlined are typical of most CORBA implementations. CORBA, of course, allows deviations. For example, it is not a requirement for IDL source code to be available, as long as the interface information is available in stub form or in an Interface Repository. You don't have to implement the server objects as classes as long as they're encapsulated by IDL stubs. The separation of the interface from the implementation enables you to incorporate existing legacy systems within an ORB environment.

CONCLUSION

This chapter was short and sweet. Static method invocations are really quite simple. Most of the work is done for you by the ORB. You must write IDL to describe the interfaces the server exports to its clients. However, even this can be simplified by letting the language compiler directly generate the IDL from native class definitions. For example, Netscape/Visigenic's *Caffeine* automatically generates CORBA stubs and skeletons by post-processing Java bytecodes; it can also optionally generate CORBA IDL.

The last remaining headache for static CORBA invocations is the management of stubs. Remember, the client must possess both a stub and an object reference before it can invoke methods on a server object. It's easy to pass an object reference, but how do we get that stub to the client? It's typically part of the client code. However, Java is making it easier to download stubs as Java bytecodes. The new CORBA Java bindings even specify a portable stub format; it lets stubs work with multiple ORBs. For example, you should be able to download an Orbix-generated stub from the server, and then use it to statically invoke methods via VisiBroker on the client. Yes, static CORBA is becoming very dynamic.

Chapter 5

The Dynamic CORBA

In this chapter, we introduce a stubless run-time binding approach—the CORBA *Dynamic Invocation Interface (DII)*. CORBA's DII lets a client pick any target object at run time and then dynamically invoke its methods. Your client can invoke any operation on any object without requiring precompiled stubs. This means that your client discovers interface-related information at invocation time; it requires no compile-time knowledge.

In the client/server world, the DII is the closest thing we have to absolute freedom. Servers offer new services and interfaces whenever they become available. Clients will discover these interfaces at run time and know how to call them. It's all part of the CORBA magic. The DII provides a very dynamic environment that allows your systems to remain flexible and extensible. This is a very desirable feature, especially in intergalactic environments like the Internet.

But how do clients first discover these remote objects? They do this using a variety of mechanisms. In the simplest approach, you can provide the client with a "stringified" object reference. The client can then convert the string into a live object reference and make the connection. Clients can also look up objects by name using the CORBA *Naming Service*. Or, they can discover these objects via CORBA's Yellow Pages—the *Trader Service*.

In an Object Web environment, objects will be dynamically discovered by spiders, crawlers, bots, search engines, publish-and-subscribe services, and agents of all types. The Traders will keep them up-to-date with the latest and greatest. It's becoming a very dynamic world out there. Once clients discover these objects, they will need the CORBA DII to invoke their operations. The alternative is to download a Java applet with a prebuilt client for a particular service. There is room for both approaches.

CORBA DYNAMIC INVOCATIONS

Before you can dynamically invoke a method on an object, you must first find the object and obtain its reference. Once you have the object reference, you can use it to retrieve the object's interface and dynamically construct the request. You must specify in the request the method you want to execute and its parameters. You typically obtain this information from an *Interface Repository (IR)*. A *Trader Service* can augment the IR. For example, it can specify the range of values a server expects.

Dynamic Invocations: The Big Picture

Let's assume that you acquired—by whatever means—a reference for the object you want to dynamically invoke. Here's a very high-level description of how you invoke a remote method on this object (see Figure 5-1):

1. ***Obtain the interface name***. In our scenario, we have a reference for the server object. CORBA objects are introspective; they can provide you with quite a bit of information about themselves. Consequently, we can ask this object for the name of its interface by invoking the object's *get_interface* method. This call returns a reference to **InterfaceDef** object. This is an object inside an Interface Repository that describes this interface. We cover the Interface Repository in Chapter 6.

2. ***Obtain the method description from the Interface Repository.*** We can use the **InterfaceDef** as an entry-point for navigating the Interface Repository. We can obtain all kinds of detailed information about the interface and the methods it supports. CORBA specifies about ten calls for navigating the Interface Repository and describing the objects it contains. In our example, the client issues a *lookup_name* to find the method it wants to invoke. It then issues a *describe* call to obtain the method's full IDL definition. Or you can issue a *describe_interface* to obtain a full description of the interface and find the method you want to invoke.

3. ***Create the argument list***. CORBA specifies a self-defining data structure for passing parameters, which it calls the *Named Value List*. You implement this

list using an **NVList** pseudo-object. You create the list by invoking *create_list* and as many *add_item* calls as it takes to add each argument to the list. Alternatively, you can let the ORB create the list for you by invoking *create_operation_list* on a **CORBA::ORB** object. You must pass it the name of the operation for which it returns a list.

4. ***Create the request***. A request is a CORBA pseudo-object that contains the name of the method, the argument list, and the return value. You create a request by invoking *create_request*. You must pass it the name of the method to invoke, the **NVList**, and a pointer to the return value. Alternatively, you can create a short version of the request by invoking *_request* and passing it the name of the method you want to invoke. You use the short version to invoke methods that do not require parameters.

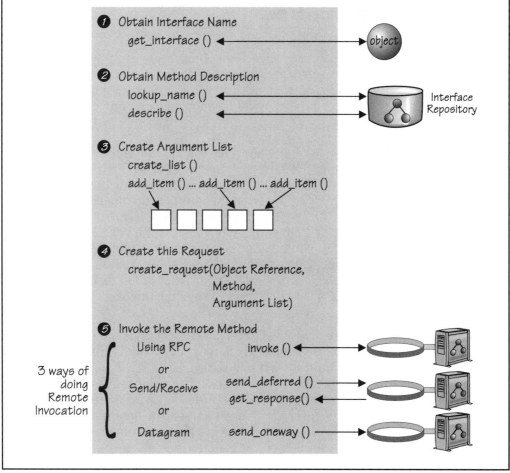

Figure 5-1. The CORBA Dynamic Invocation Process.

5. **Invoke the request**. You can invoke a request in one of three ways: 1) the *invoke* call sends the request and obtains the results; 2) the *send_deferred* call returns control to the program, which must then poll for the response by issuing *poll_response* or *get_response*; and 3) the send call can be defined to be a datagram by issuing *send_oneway*—in this case, no response is needed. These three invocation styles are sometimes referred to as synchronous, deferred synchronous, and one-way.

As you can see, it takes quite a bit of effort to dynamically invoke a method. Actually, invoking the method is easy—the hard part is constructing the request. This task is made even more complicated by the different ways you can construct and invoke a remote method. As usual, you're trading off complexity and performance for added flexibility.

The Dynamic Invocation Interfaces

The services you need to dynamically invoke an object are part of the CORBA core. Unfortunately, the methods are dispersed across four interfaces in the CORBA module (see methods with light buttons in Figure 5-2). Here's a quick overview of the methods in these four interfaces that you use for dynamic invocation:

■ **CORBA::Object** is a pseudo-object interface that defines operations that every CORBA object must support.[1] It's the root interface for all CORBA objects. This interface includes three methods that you can use to construct dynamic invocations. You invoke *get_interface* to obtain the interface an object supports. The call returns a reference to an **InterfaceDef**, which is an object inside an Interface Repository that describes this interface. You invoke *create_request* to create a **Request** object; you must pass it the method name and parameters for the remote invocation. Or, you can create a short version of the request object by invoking *_request*; you simply pass it the name of the method (or operation in CORBA-speak) that you want to remotely invoke.

■ **CORBA::Request** is a pseudo-object interface that defines the operations on a remote object. The *add_arg* method incrementally adds arguments to the request. The *invoke* method does a call/return. The *send_deferred* method returns control to your program after transmitting the request. You invoke *poll_response* to find out if there's any returned message. Then you invoke *get_response* to read the message. You can send a datagram by invoking *send_oneway*. You invoke *delete* to delete the **Request** object from memory.

---

[1] These operations are performed by the ORB. You simply inherit them when you create your object.

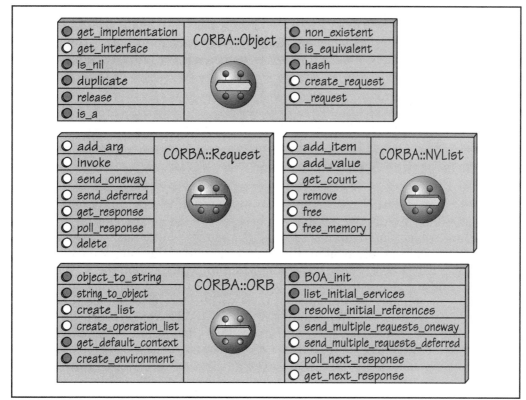

Figure 5-2. The Dynamic Invocation Interfaces.

■ **CORBA::NVList** is a pseudo-object interface that helps you construct parameter lists. An **NVList** object maintains a list of self-describing data items called NamedValues. The **NVList** interface defines operations that let you manipulate a list. You invoke *add_item* to add a parameter to the list. You can set its value by invoking *add_value*. You invoke *get_count* to obtain the total number of items allocated for this list. You can remove an item from the list by invoking *remove*. You invoke *free_memory* to free any dynamically allocated out-arg memory associated with the list. And you invoke *free* to free the list structure itself; it will call *free_memory* on your behalf.

■ **CORBA::ORB** is a pseudo-object interface that defines general-purpose ORB methods. You can invoke these methods on an ORB pseudo-object from either a client or server implementation. Six of these methods are specific to the construction of a dynamic request. You invoke *create_list* to create an empty **NVList** pseudo-object that you must then populate. If you want the ORB to do the work for you, call *create_operation_list* instead. This method will create an **NVList** and automatically populate it with the descriptions of the arguments for the remote operation you specify. The **ORB** provides four operations for sending and receiving multiple requests. You invoke *send_multiple-_requests_oneway* to send a multiple datagrams. You invoke *send_multiple-_requests_deferred* to send multiple request/reply messages. You poll for replies by invoking *poll_next_response*; you invoke *get_next_response* to read the next response.

In addition to these four interfaces, you also use Interface Repository objects to construct a remote invocation. It's quite an undertaking.

Dynamic Invocation Scenarios

Are you getting overwhelmed by all these interfaces? If you are, don't feel bad. You're not alone. We discovered that the best way to decipher this stuff is to walk through three object interaction scenarios that show how the pieces play together. Why three? Because there is more than one way to skin this cat. We call the first scenario "Do-It-Yourself." It shows how to do a remote invocation the hard way. We call the second scenario "ORB-Can-Help." It shows the one small thing an ORB can do to help you. Finally, the third scenario shows a different technique for doing it the hard way; we'll call it "Yet-Another-Way." We don't want to turn this into a Soapbox, but it appears that the CORBA designers had one too many espressos when they were designing the Dynamic Invocation Interface.

Dynamic Invocation: The Do-It-Yourself Scenario

As we said earlier, creating a request is the hardest part of a dynamic invocation. In this scenario, we assemble the request without any help from the ORB. Here's a step-by-step description of the object interactions shown in Figure 5-3:

1. ***Ask the object for its interface definition****.* You can invoke *get_interface* on any CORBA object to obtain an **InterfaceDef** object that fully describes this interface in the Interface Repository.

2. ***Look up the method you're interested in.*** You invoke *lookup_name* on the **InterfaceDef** object to obtain an **OperationDef** object that fully describes the method you want to dynamically invoke.

3. ***Obtain the method's description.*** You invoke *describe* on the **OperationDef** object to obtain a full description of the method.

4. ***Create an empty NVList****.* You invoke *create_list* on the ORB object to create an empty **NVList**. You must specify the number of items to allocate for this list.

5. ***Populate the NVList.*** You invoke *add_item* and *add_value* for each argument in the method.

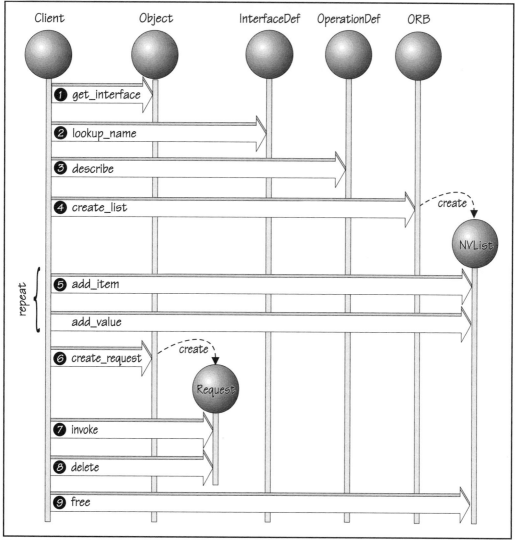

Figure 5-3. Dynamic Invocation: The Do-It-Yourself Scenario.

6. ***Create the request object***. You invoke *create_request* on the object reference to create a **Request** object. You must pass it: 1) the name of the method, 2) the **NVList**, and 3) a **NamedValue** to receive the result.

7. ***Invoke the remote operation.*** You issue *invoke* to call the method on the remote object. This is a synchronous invocation. The results will appear in the **Request** object.

8. ***Free the request object***. You issue *delete* to destroy the **Request** object. Yes, it breaks our heart to do this after all the effort it took to assemble it, but that's life.

9. *Free the NVList*. You invoke *free* to release the space associated with the **NVList**.

As you can see, it takes quite a bit of work to dynamically create a request. In the next scenario, we let the ORB do some of this work for us.

Dynamic Invocation: The ORB-Can-Help Scenario

This scenario is slightly easier because we will let the ORB assemble the parameter descriptions for us. Here's a step-by-step description of the object interactions shown in Figure 5-4:

1. *Ask the object for its interface definition*. You can invoke *get_interface* on any CORBA object to obtain an **InterfaceDef** object that fully describes this interface in the Interface Repository.

2. *Look up the method you're interested in*. You invoke *lookup_name* on the **InterfaceDef** object to obtain an **OperationDef** object that fully describes the method you want to dynamically invoke.

3. *Tell the ORB to create and populate an NVList*. You invoke *create_operation_list* to let the ORB create an **NVList** that it populates with the name and data types of the arguments; you must pass it the **OperationDef**.

4. *Set the values for your arguments*. You invoke *add_value* to set the value of each argument in the **NVList**.

5. *Create the request object*. You invoke *create_request* on the object reference to create a **Request** object. You must pass it: 1) the name of the method, 2) the **NVList**, and 3) a **NamedValue** to receive the result.

6. *Invoke the remote operation*. You issue *invoke* to call the method on the remote object. This is a synchronous invocation. The results will appear in the **Request** object.

7. *Free the request object*. You issue *delete* to destroy the **Request** object.

8. *Free the NVList*. You invoke *free* to release the space associated with the **NVList**.

Even with help from the ORB, it still takes a lot of work to do this dynamic invocation. But it's a step in the right direction.

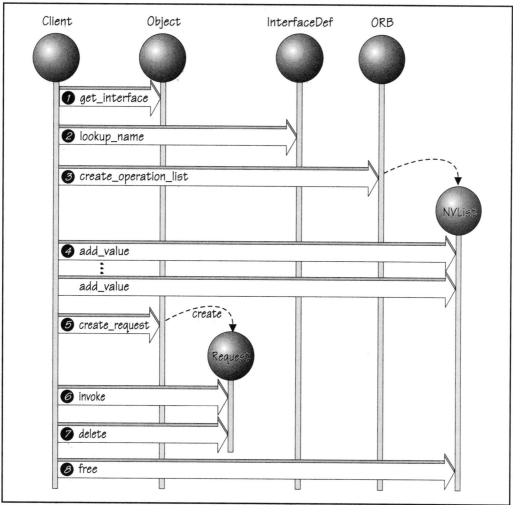

Figure 5-4. Dynamic Invocation: The ORB-Can-Help Scenario.

Dynamic Invocation: The Yet-Another-Way Scenario

This scenario is a variation of the Do-It-Yourself method. Instead of adding your arguments to an **NVList**, you add them to the **Request** object. So you create an empty **Request** for an operation. You then incrementally populate it with arguments. Here's a step-by-step description of the object interactions shown in Figure 5-5:

1. ***Ask the object for its interface definition***. You can invoke *get_interface* on any CORBA object to obtain an **InterfaceDef** object that fully describes this interface in the Interface Repository.

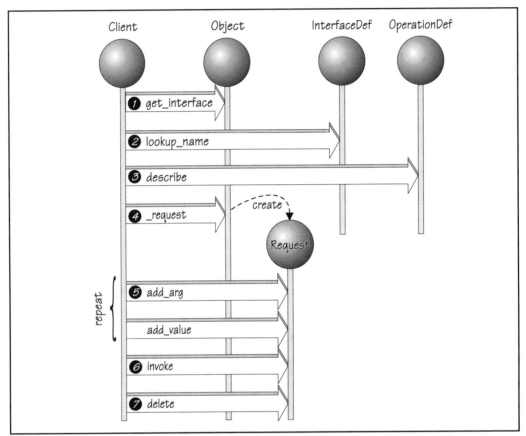

Figure 5-5. Dynamic Invocation: The Yet-Another-Way Scenario.

2. ***Look up the method you're interested in.*** You invoke *lookup_name* on the **InterfaceDef** object to obtain an **OperationDef** object that fully describes the method you want to dynamically invoke.

3. ***Obtain the method's description.*** You invoke *describe* on the **OperationDef** object to obtain a full description of the method.

4. ***Create an empty request object.*** You invoke *_request* on the object reference to create an empty **Request** object; you must pass it the name of the method you want to invoke.

5. ***Populate the request object.*** You invoke *add_arg* and *add_value* for each parameter the method expects.

6. ***Invoke the remote operation.*** You issue *invoke* to call the method on the remote object. This is a synchronous invocation. The results will appear in the **Request** object.

7. *Free the request object*. You issue *delete* to destroy the **Request** object.

As you can see, we took a step backwards. This was just another form of do-it-yourself construction. However, it can be useful in some situations—for example, when the method you invoke takes no parameters. Then you simply create a request and invoke it.

The Price of Freedom

In our programming book, we ran some benchmarks that compare the average response times of static versus dynamic Ping invocations. We used the *VisiBroker for Java* ORB over an Ethernet LAN. The average response time (in milliseconds) is based on running 1000 remote method invocations.[2]

We ran the dynamic benchmark with and without the overhead associated with constructing the requests. Table 5-1 shows the results. The numbers show that a dynamic invocation is about 40 times slower than its static counterpart. The surprise here is the huge overhead associated with preparing a request. It's definitely not cheap. Of course, we're doing several lookups against an Interface Repository every time we construct a request. So it does chew up quite a few machine cycles and disk accesses. But now we can put a price tag on freedom. Are you still willing to trade-off performance for flexibility? We're sure it's worth it in certain situations. But we're not planning to throw away our stubs soon (see the next section).

Table 5-1. Dynamic Versus Static Pings.

	Dynamic Pings		Static Pings
	With Prepare	**Without Prepare**	
Remote Ping Performance	131.4 msecs	3.3 msecs	3.2 msecs

When To Use Dynamic

With traditional CORBA, you only have two choices for your invocations: static precompiled stubs or dynamic invocations using DII. Java gives us a third choice: downloadable stubs. Remember, stub bytecodes are Java classes. You download them along with an applet. So, you get both the client code and the stubs—it's really

---

[2] For more details see our book, **Client/Server Programming with Java and CORBA** (Wiley, 1997).

a downloadable client technique. Now, which of these three techniques should you use? It depends on your usage patterns (see Table 5-2).

Table 5-2. DII Versus the Alternatives.

Usage Pattern	Recommended Invocation Technique
Client invokes server object frequently; server object does not change.	Use static precompiled stubs.
Client invokes server object infrequently.	Use dynamic invocations (DII).
Client discovers server object at run time.	Use dynamic invocations (DII).
Client runs within browser; it discovers new object.	Use downloadable applet and static stubs. Applet becomes the client for this object.

CONCLUSION

The CORBA DII lets you construct a remote invocation "on-the-fly." It introduces a dynamic programming style that encourages the run-time discovery of objects and just-in-time binding. In addition, you don't have the burden of managing stubs and distributing them to the clients. There are no versions to manage; you always bind to the most current interface an object provides. However, this freedom comes with a steep price tag. First, it requires more programming effort. Second, dynamic invocations are about 40 times slower than their static counterparts. So, you're trading off performance and ease of use for maximum flexibility.

Chapter 6

The Existential CORBA

In this chapter, we first look at the CORBA 2.0 initialization protocol. We answer the following question: How does a newly activated object discover its ORB and the universe of CORBA objects? The CORBA 2.0 initialization protocol ensures that an object can find its ORB, BOA, Interface Repository, Trader, Naming Service, and whatever else it needs to bootstrap itself into the intergalactic distributed object universe. Before CORBA 2.0, this bootstrapping was left as an exercise for the ORB vendors. The results were non-portable solutions. Next, we look at how the ORB activates server-side objects. Yes, you can manually activate all your objects, but what happens if a server supports millions of objects? We shouldn't have to prestart all of them before clients can connect to them. If we did, even the largest supercomputer could be brought to its knees. The CORBA philosophy is to keep the client side simple. In this case, simple means that the clients must view all objects on the server as being up and running all the time. These server objects must appear to be always actively waiting on the client to invoke their operations (or methods).

THE CORBA 2.0 INITIALIZATION INTERFACE

CORBA 2.0 defines a set of initialization methods that all ORBs must provide to help an object bootstrap itself into the distributed environment. These methods are implemented by the **CORBA::ORB** pseudo-object. You may recall from the previous chapter that **CORBA::ORB** is one of the ORB's core interfaces. The light methods in Figure 6-1 deal with object initialization.

As we explained in the last chapter, **CORBA::ORB** is a pseudo-object interface that defines general-purpose ORB methods. A *pseudo-object* is an object that the ORB directly creates, but you can invoke it like any other object. The ORB itself is a pseudo-object. You can invoke methods on an **ORB** pseudo-object from either a client or server implementation. Three of these methods are specific to object initialization: *BOA_init*, *list_initial_services*, and *resolve_initial_references* (see light methods in Figure 6-1).

You invoke *BOA_init* to obtain a reference to your **BOA** pseudo-object. You'll need this reference to register your objects with the ORB. You invoke *list_initial_services* to obtain a list of names to well-known services. Think of it as the ORB's mini-naming service. It's your welcome package to the CORBA intergalactic universe. You invoke *resolve_intial_references* to convert the string names of services to object references.

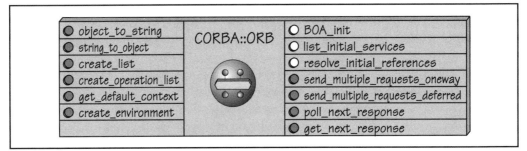

Figure 6-1. The CORBA::ORB Initialization Methods.

An Initialization Scenario

In essence, the initialization service provides a barebones naming service that allows objects to find the services they need to function on an ORB. Figure 6-2 shows the typical calls an object must invoke to bootstrap itself. Let's walk through this initialization scenario:

1. ***Obtain an object reference for your ORB.*** You issue the CORBA API call *ORB_init* to inform the ORB of your presence and to obtain a reference to an ORB *pseudo-object*. Note that we issued an API call and not a method invocation. To invoke a method, you must first bootstrap yourself into the CORBA world.

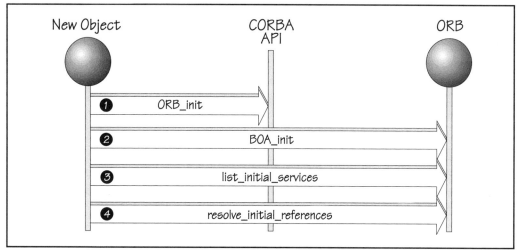

Figure 6-2. CORBA 2.0 Initialization Service—Or, How Does a Component Find Its ORB?

2. ***Obtain a pointer to your Object Adapter***. You invoke the method *BOA_init* on the ORB pseudo-object to tell the BOA you're there and to obtain its object reference (BOA is also a pseudo-object).

3. ***Discover what initial services are available***. You invoke the method *list_initial_services* on the ORB pseudo-object to obtain a list of well-known objects—for example, the Interface Repository, Trader, and the Naming Service. These well-known objects are returned in a list of string names.

4. ***Obtain object references for the services you want***. You invoke the method *resolve_initial_references* to obtain object references for the services you want. You're now a well-connected, first-class citizen on the CORBA ORB.

You should note that an object can initialize itself in more than one ORB.

How You Find Your Other Objects

The initialization service is just a bootstrap Naming Service. It gives you a list of well-known services—for example, the Trader and Naming Services. You can then use these services to find any object in the intergalactic ORB universe. The *Naming Service* is like a telephone White Pages for objects; it lets you look up other objects by name. You can also discover new objects via CORBA's Yellow Pages—the *Trader Service*. The Traders can dynamically keep track of these new objects and their latest and greatest services. We cover the CORBA Trader and Naming Services in Part 3.

WHO ACTIVATES MY OBJECTS?

This section looks at the ORB activation (and deactivation) policies. We explain how your server objects conspire with the *Basic Object Adapter (BOA)* to give clients the illusion that every object they know of is always available. CORBA does not even provide an explicit command for a client to start up a server object.[1] Consequently, it falls upon the server side of the ORB to provide the illusion that all its objects—and there can be millions of them—are up and running and active all the time, even though they are not. This illusion keeps the client code simple, but it shifts the implementation burden to the server side. You must write code that cooperates with the ORB when you start and stop your objects or when the ORB starts up or shuts down. In other words, you must help the ORB provide an automatic startup function. The ORB should be able to either prestart an object or start it on demand when clients invoke it.

Your implementation must also cooperate with a *Persistence Service* to save and restore the state of your server objects; you must do it in a way that is totally transparent to the client. For example, the client must be able to pass around an object reference, store it in a string format in a database or naming service, and then be able—perhaps many years later—to use the reference to retrieve the same object. Your server object must be able to resurrect itself in the same state the client left it in. Of course, if the object is shared, its state can be modified by another client in the interim. But you get the idea.

The Server Side of CORBA

You should be warned that the server side of CORBA is going through a second round of OMG standardization. We will tell you all about it in Part 4. If you use standard language bindings, most of the code you write should be portable. We anticipate the changes will be mostly in the area of object activation. This is where you'll find most of the system-level dependencies. For example, how does an ORB handle multithreading issues across OSs? Can an ORB depend on having DLLs or their equivalent on every OS? This is an area where Java complements CORBA very well; it provides a uniform layer of OS services that lets you write very portable server objects.

The CORBA::BOA Interface

The BOA is also a *pseudo-object*. It provides operations that your server-object implementations can access. In addition, it interfaces with the ORB core and with

---

[1] The one exception is when the client creates a new object via a CORBA factory. The new object is then implicitly started by the factory. We cover CORBA factories in Part 3.

the implementation skeletons through private interfaces, which means they're ORB-specific. This is an area that OMG is also addressing in its second round of server standardization.

Figure 6-3 shows the methods (or operations) that OMG defines for the **CORBA::BOA** interface. You use this interface to create or destroy object references and to query or update the information the BOA maintains for an object reference. The BOA maintains a registry of the active objects and implementations that it controls. You use the **BOA** interface to communicate with this registry and tell the ORB about your objects. You can think of this protocol as a conspiracy between your server objects and the ORB to create the illusion that all server objects are active all the time.

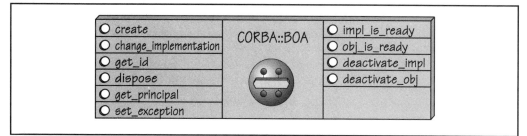

Figure 6-3. The CORBA::BOA Interface.

Let's quickly go over the operations the BOA supports. You invoke *create* to describe the implementation of a new object instance to the BOA and obtain a reference to it. You create the actual object via a language constructor or a factory. You must pass to the ORB three pieces of information it needs to bind the object with a new object reference: 1) an *interface name* that is described in the Interface Repository, 2) an *implementation name* that is described in the Implementation Repository, and 3) some unique *reference data* (or ID) that you define. The reference data is implementation-specific; it is totally opaque to the ORB. You typically use the ID to distinguish between objects or to specify a *Persistent ID (PID)* that points to where the object stores its state. The ORB doesn't care what you do with this ID.

You can update the implementation information associated with an existing object by invoking *change_implementation*. You invoke *get_id* to obtain the reference data associated with this object. You invoke *dispose* to destroy the object reference. You must separately delete the object's resources using the CORBA *Life Cycle Service* or a destructor—or, you can let the Java garbage collector do it for you.

The *get_principal* operation has been superseded by the CORBA Security Service; it should return a null. You invoke *set_exception* to tell the ORB that something went wrong. Servers and ORBs use the last four operations—*impl_is_ready, obj_is_ready, deactivate_impl,* and *deacivate_obj*—to activate and deactivate implementations and the objects that run within them. We describe these activation methods in the next section.

BOA and Other Object Adapters

An *Object Adapter* defines how an object is activated. You can do this by creating a new process, creating a new thread within an existing process, or by reusing an existing thread or process. A server could support a variety of object adapters to satisfy different types of requests. For example, an Object Database (ODBMS) may want to implicitly register all the fine-grained objects it contains without issuing individual calls to the Object Adapter. In such a case, it doesn't make sense for an Object Adapter to maintain a per-object state. The ODBMS may want to provide a special-purpose Object Adapter that not only interfaces with the ORB core but also meets its special requirements. However, OMG prefers not to see a proliferation of Object Adapter types. To avoid this proliferation, CORBA specifies a *Basic Object Adapter (BOA)* that "can be used for most ORB objects with conventional implementations."

CORBA requires that a BOA adapter be available in every ORB. Object implementations that use it should be able to run on any ORB that supports the required language bindings. CORBA requires that the following functions be provided in a BOA implementation:

- An Implementation Repository that lets you install and register an object implementation. It also lets you provide information describing the object.

- Mechanisms for generating and interpreting object references, activating and deactivating object implementations, and invoking methods and passing them their parameters.

- Activation and deactivation of implementation objects.

- Method invocations through skeletons.

BOA supports traditional and object-oriented applications. It does not specify how methods are packaged or located—this could be done through DLLs or a system call at startup that identifies the location of the methods.

CORBA makes a clear distinction between a server and its objects. A *server* is an execution unit; it's a process. An *object* implements an interface. A server can contain one or more objects. It can even contain objects of different classes. In the other extreme, a server can contain code that only implements a single method, instead of an entire interface. In all cases, objects get activated within their servers.

To get the widest application coverage, CORBA defines four activation policies—
shared server, unshared server, server-per-method, and *persistent server*—that
specify the rules a given implementation follows for activating objects. Think of
them as scheduling policies.

BOA Shared Server

In a *shared server* activation policy, multiple objects may reside in the same
program (or process). The BOA activates the server the first time a request is
invoked on any object implemented by that server (see Figure 6-4). After the server
has initialized itself, it notifies the BOA that it is prepared to handle requests by
calling *impl_is_ready.* All subsequent requests are then delivered to this server
process; BOA will not activate another server process for that implementation.

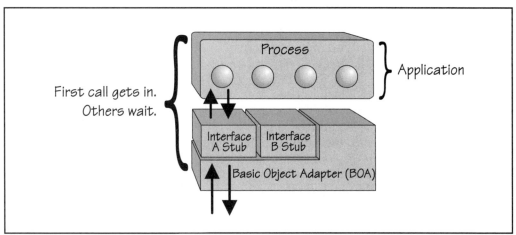

Figure 6-4. The BOA Shared Server Activation Policy.

When the process is ready to terminate, it notifies BOA by issuing a
deactivate_impl call. At this point, all the objects that are running within the
process are automatically deactivated. You can also deactivate an individual object
at any time by issuing *deactivate_obj.* You may want to do this when there are no
active client references to your object. You should note that CORBA does not
require that shared server objects invoke *obj_is_ready* when they first come up.
However, most ORB implementations require it. CORBA also mentions that objects
can be instantiated on demand when an invocation is received. But it leaves the
implementation of this concept as an exercise for the ORB vendors. Consequently,
it is very non-standard.

Most CORBA servers are of the shared server variety. So how do you run multiple objects concurrently within the same process? You do this using threads. You should be warned that this whole area is very implementation dependent. Because Java supports threads (and its libraries are thread-safe), we recommend that you use a thread to represent each active object instance. You can even use multiple threads to represent the same object to multiple clients. If you do this, you must serialize the access to the state information—for example, you can maintain the state in a multiuser database or treat it as a Java critical section. Make sure your ORB is thread-safe.

BOA Unshared Server

In an *unshared server* activation policy, each object resides in a different server process (see Figure 6-5). A new server is activated the first time a request is invoked on the object. When the object has initialized itself, it notifies BOA that it is prepared to handle requests by calling *obj_is_ready*. A new server is started whenever you request an object that is not yet active, even if a server for another object with the same implementation is active. A server object remains active and will receive requests until it calls *deactivate_obj*.

So where would you use an unshared server? You typically use this kind of activation in situations that require a dedicated object. For example, you could have a dedicated object represent a printer or a robot on a manufacturing line. Instead of managing multiple objects, the implementation only handles a single object.

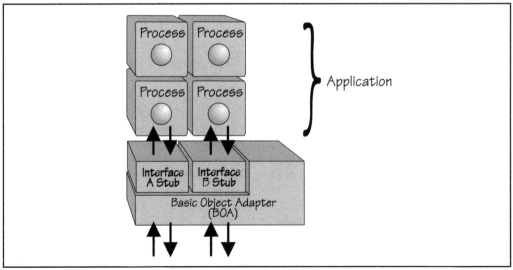

Figure 6-5. The BOA Unshared Server Activation Policy.

BOA Server-per-Method

In a *server-per-method* activation policy, a new server is always started each time a request is made. The server runs only for the duration of the particular method (see Figure 6-6). Several server processes for the same object—or even the same method of the same object—may be concurrently active. A new server is started for each request, so it's not necessary for the implementation to notify BOA when an object is ready or deactivated. BOA activates a new process for each request, whether or not another request for that operation or object is active at the same time.

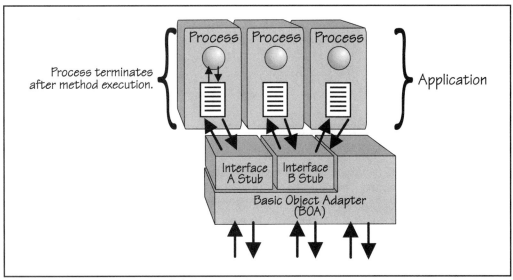

Figure 6-6. The BOA Server-per-Method Activation Policy.

So where would you use a server-per-method? This is probably the most infrequently used activation policy. The best use of this activation policy is for running scripts or utility programs that execute once and then terminate.

BOA Persistent Server

In a *persistent server* activation policy, servers are activated by means outside BOA (see Figure 6-7). Typically you start the server application, which then notifies BOA that it's ready to accept work by means of an *impl_is_ready* call. BOA treats all subsequent requests as shared server calls; it sends activations for individual objects and method calls to a single process. If no implementation is ready when a request arrives, an error is returned for that request.

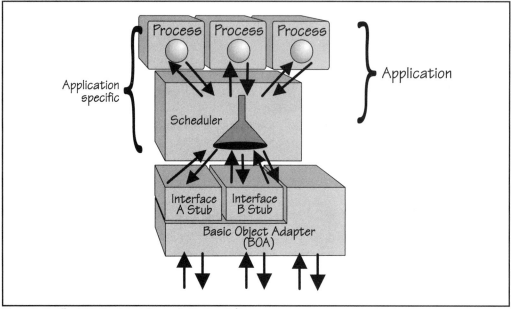

Figure 6-7. The BOA Persistent Server Activation Policy.

So where would you use a persistent server? The persistent server is really just a special case of the shared server. The difference is that the server activation is not handled by the ORB. Generally, you would expect a DBMS, ODBMS, TP Monitor, or Web Server to be up all the time. So these would be good candidate applications for the persistent server policy. Any CORBA program that you start from the command line is a persistent server. You may also want to create your own scripts to start a server.

An Object Activation Scenario

We will now walk you through a shared server scenario to show you how to activate a new object as well as an existing object (see Figure 6-8). Here are the steps a shared server follows:

1. ***The server creates two object instances***. The server either invokes a CORBA factory or a language constructor to create new instances of the objects.

2. ***The new object registers with the BOA***. Your new server object must invoke *BOA::create*. The object must pass the BOA its *interface name, implementation name*, and some unique *reference data* (or ID) that you define. The *create* call returns an object reference for this new object that you can then pass to *obj_is_ready* to let the ORB know that your object is ready for business.

3. **The existing object registers with the BOA.** Your existing server object already has an object reference. You can use this object reference to obtain the Persistent ID (PID) that is associated with this object. You can then use this PID to load the object's state from a persistent store—for example, an ODBMS or RDBMS. Your object then invokes *obj_is_ready* to let the ORB know that it is ready for business.

4. **The server says it's ready for business.** The server has started all its objects. So it invokes *impl_is_ready* to tell the ORB that it's ready to accept client invocations. This starts a do-forever loop for this server.

5. **The objects deactivate.** In our scenario, each object deactivates itself by invoking *deactivate_obj*. There are a variety of strategies for when an object should invoke this method. You may want to issue a *deactivate_obj* when the Object Transaction Service issues a *commit*. The object can then store its

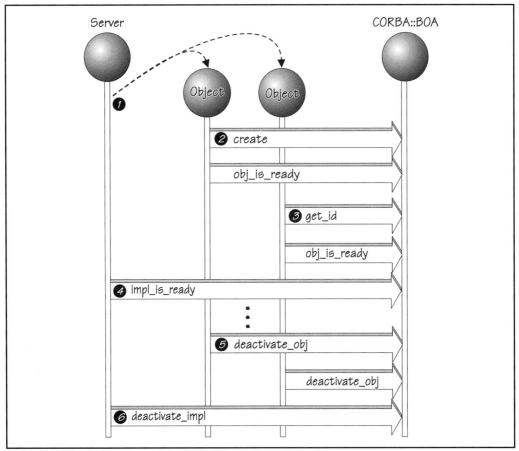

Figure 6-8. A Shared Server Activation Scenario.

state—or, you can issue *deactivate_obj* when the object's thread terminates. Finally, you can issue *deactivate_obj* when there are no clients referencing this particular object.

6. ***The server shuts down***. The server invokes *deactivate_impl* to tell the ORB that it will not accept subsequent requests.

CONCLUSION

This chapter demonstrates how server objects cooperate with their ORB to create an illusion that all objects are always active. A new breed of Object TP Monitors can also participate in this conspiracy to provide load-balancing, fault-tolerance, and scalability. We will need these TP Monitors to transparently manage millions of server objects. The TP Monitor will activate and deactivate the objects that it controls; it will also manage their state. We will have more to say about object activation, the BOA, and TP Monitors in Part 4.

Chapter 7

Metadata: Who Am I?

Metadata is the ingredient that lets us create agile client/server systems. An agile system is self-describing, dynamic, and reconfigurable. The system helps components discover each other at run time; it provides information that lets them interoperate. An agile system lets you write client software without hardcoding all calls to particular servers. Finally, it provides metadata information that application tools can use to create and manage components.

An agile system differentiates itself from a traditional client/server system by its pervasive use of metadata to consistently describe all available services, components, and data. Metadata allows independently developed components to dynamically discover each other's existence and to collaborate. The pervasive dissemination of metadata is a key ingredient in a distributed component infrastructure. Without it, you have a hard-coded client/server system with no flexibility.

CORBA is such an agile system. To be CORBA-compliant, any component you write must be self-describing. Every system-level object or service that lives on a CORBA bus must also be self-describing. Even the CORBA bus itself is self-describing. As a result, CORBA is a totally self-describing system. The CORBA metadata language is the *Interface Definition Language (IDL)*. The CORBA metadata repository is the *Interface Repository.* It's nothing more than a run-time database that contains the interface specifications of each object an ORB recognizes. Think of the

Interface Repository as a queryable and updatable run-time database that contains IDL-generated information.

The IDL precompiler and the Interface Repository are basic ORB services that are shipped with every CORBA-compliant ORB. The pervasive use of IDL and the Interface Repository makes CORBA more self-describing than any other form of client/server middleware. This chapter covers the CORBA IDL and the Interface Repository. We also cover in detail the new services CORBA 2.0 defines to make the Interface Repository metadata available across multivendor ORBs.

THE CORBA IDL: A CLOSER LOOK

As we said in Chapter 1, IDL is a contractual language that lets you specify a component's boundaries and its interfaces with potential clients. The CORBA IDL is language neutral and totally declarative. This means it does not define the implementation details. The IDL provides operating system and programming language independent interfaces to all services and components that reside on a CORBA bus.

What Does an IDL Contract Cover?

An IDL contract includes a description of any resource or service a server component wants to expose to its clients. Server components must support two kinds of clients: 1) run-time clients that invoke their services, and 2) developers who use IDL to extend an existing component's functions by subclassing. In both cases, IDL is required to specify the component's interfaces so that the implementation can be treated as a black box (or binary code).

You can use CORBA IDL to specify a component's attributes (or public variables), the parent classes it inherits from, the exceptions it raises, typed events, pragmas for generating globally unique identifiers for the interfaces, and the methods an interface supports—including the input and output parameters and their data types. The IDL grammar is a subset of C++ with additional keywords to support distributed concepts; it also fully supports standard C++ preprocessing features.

The IDL is a descriptive language; it supports C++ syntax for constant, type, and operation declarations. However, IDL does not include any procedural structures or variables. Note that because it separates implementation from specification, IDL is a good notational tool for software architects. Most notational languages only provide descriptions of interfaces. In contrast, CORBA IDL provides a direct path between a software architecture—defined by its interfaces—and the compiled code that implements it. From IDL descriptions, a precompiler can directly generate client stubs and server implementation skeletons. IDL also provides a great way to encapsulate low-level APIs and legacy software. Client/server architects will find CORBA IDL to be a very useful and versatile tool.

The Structure of the CORBA IDL

The Interface Repository stores metadata that is identical to the components you describe in IDL. In fact, the Interface Repository is simply an active database that contains compiled versions of the metadata information captured via IDL. So, before we jump into the structure of the Interface Repository, let's take a quick look at what's inside a CORBA IDL file.

Figure 7-1 shows the main elements that constitute the CORBA IDL. Let's go over the pieces:

■ **Modules** provide a namespace to group a set of class descriptions (or *interfaces* in OMG terminology). A module is identified by the keyword *module*. A module has a *scoped* name that consists of one or more *identifiers*. This means simple name strings. The identifiers are separated by the characters "::". So the main

Part 2. ORB Fundamentals

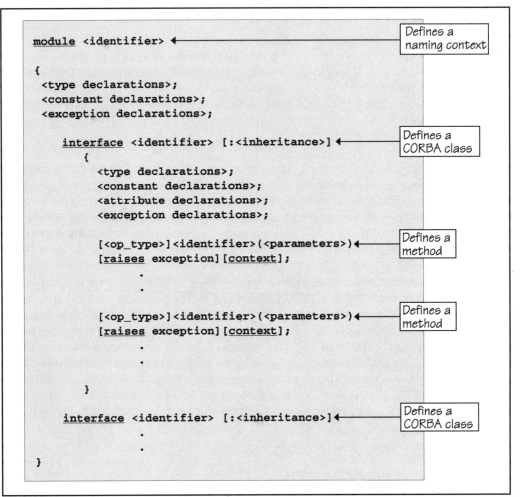

Figure 7-1. The Structure of a CORBA IDL File.

purpose of a module is to introduce an additional level of hierarchy in the IDL namespace.

■ *Interfaces* define a set of methods (or *operations* in OMG terminology) that a client can invoke on an object. Think of it as a class definition, but without the implementation section. An interface can declare one or more *exceptions* that indicate an operation did not perform successfully. An interface may have *attributes*. These are values for which the implementation automatically creates *get* and *set* operations. You can declare an attribute read-only, in which case the implementation only provides the *get* function. An interface can be derived from one or more interfaces, which means IDL supports multiple interface inheritance. You define inheritance relationships using a C++-like syntax.

■ **Operation** is the CORBA-equivalent of a method. It denotes a service that clients can invoke. The IDL defines the operation's *signature*, which means the method's parameters and the results it returns. A parameter has a *mode* that indicates whether the value is passed from client to server (*in*), from server to client (*out*), or both (*inout*). The parameter also has a *type* that constrains its possible values. The *op_type* is the type of the return value. The method signature optionally defines the exceptions that a method *raises* when it detects an error. An optional *context* expression contains a set of attribute values that describe a client's context. It lets a client pass information to a server that describes its local environment.

■ **Data types** are used to describe the accepted values of CORBA parameters, attributes, exceptions, and return values. These data types are named CORBA objects that are used across multiple languages, operating systems, and ORBs. CORBA supports two categories of types: *basic* or *constructed* (see Figure 7-2). CORBA's basic types include short, long, unsigned long, unsigned short, float, double, char, boolean, and octet. CORBA's constructed types include enum, string, struct, array, union, sequence, and any. The *struct* type is similar to a C++ structure; it lets you create any complex data type using *typedefs* (meaning type definitions). The *sequence* type lets you pass a variable-size array of objects, but you must still specify a maximum number of items that can be placed in a sequence. The *any* type is very useful in dynamic situations because it can represent any possible IDL data type—basic, constructed, or object reference. This means you can use *any* to pass any type of information. Each CORBA IDL data type is mapped to a native data type via the appropriate language bindings.

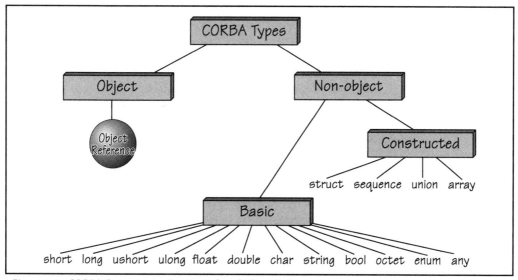

Figure 7-2. CORBA Types: Basic, Constructed, and Object References.

The CORBA IDL is very comprehensive and concise. The entire language is described in 36 pages.[1] This includes the definition of the IDL grammar and all the CORBA data types.

An IDL Example

Was that too much material to digest in one reading? The answer is probably yes. So let's see if we can help make it "perfectly clear" with a quick example. Let's create some IDL to describe the interfaces in Figure 7-3. In the figure, we define two new CORBA interfaces—**Dog** and **Cat**—in a module called *MyAnimals*. Figure 7-4 shows the IDL file that creates these two interfaces (or classes).

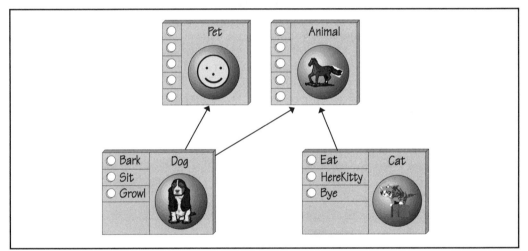

Figure 7-3. MyAnimals With Two Interfaces: Dog and Cat.

The MyAnimals IDL module listed in Figure 7-4 defines two interfaces: **Dog** and **Cat**. **Dog** is derived from the parent classes **Pet** and **Animal**. **Dog** has an attribute called *age* for which the implementation automatically provides *get* and *set* methods. **Dog** supports three methods (or operations): *Bark*, *Sit*, and *Growl*. It *raises* an exception when the dog is not in the mood to obey the master. **Cat** is derived from **Animal** and supports the methods: *Eat*, *HereKitty*, and *Bye* (of course, cats are also pets, but we don't show it in the class hierarchy).

---

[1] See **CORBA: Architecture and Specification** (OMG, 1996). The CORBA references are listed in the back of this book.

```
module MyAnimals
{
    /* Class Definition of Dog */
    interface Dog:Pet, Animal
    {
        attribute integer age;
        exception NotInterested {string explanation};

        void Bark(in short how_long)
            raises (NotInterested);

        void Sit(in string  where)
            raises (NotInterested);

        void Growl(in string  at_whom)
            raises (NotInterested);
    }

    /* Class Definition of Cat */
    interface Cat: Animal
    {
        void Eat();
        void HereKitty();
        void Bye();
    }
} /* End MyAnimals */
```

Figure 7-4. IDL Module MyAnimals With Two Interfaces: Dog and Cat.

Type Codes: CORBA's Self-Describing Data

CORBA defines *type codes* that represent each of the IDL-defined data types. You use these type codes to create self-describing data that can be passed across operating systems, ORBs, and Interface Repositories. Each type code has a globally unique Repository ID. Type codes are used in any CORBA situation that requires self-describing data. For example, they are used:

■ *By Dynamic Invocation Interfaces* to indicate the data types of the various arguments.

■ *By Inter-ORB Protocols*—including IIOP and DCE/ESIOP—to specify the data types of arguments within messages that get passed across ORBs and operating systems. So it serves as the IIOP canonical data representation.

■ *By Interface Repositories* to create ORB-neutral IDL descriptions.

■ *By the any data type* to provide a self-describing generic parameter.

The CORBA **TypeCode** interface defines a set of methods that let you operate on type codes, compare them, and obtain their descriptions (see Figure 7-5). For example, you can invoke a *content_type* operation on an array or sequence to obtain the element type they contain. Note that many of the operations are data-type specific. For example, you can only invoke the member operations on structures, unions, and enumerated data types.

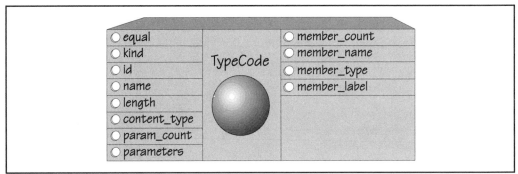

Figure 7-5. The CORBA TypeCode Interface.

THE CORBA 2.0 INTERFACE REPOSITORY

CORBA 2.0 not only greatly enhances the functions of the CORBA 1.1 Interface Repository, it also broadens their inter-ORB scope. So, you can now create federations of Interface Repositories that operate across ORBs while maintaining the autonomy of local administrators. CORBA 2.0 introduces two new features that make this possible: 1) a set of new methods for *incrementally* updating the contents of an Interface Repository at run time, and 2) globally unique *Repository IDs* that can be used in a distributed namespace. This section covers the Interface Repository in some detail. If it gets too detailed, just fast-forward to the next section.

What's an Interface Repository?

A CORBA 2.0 *Interface Repository* is an on-line database of object definitions. You can capture these definitions directly from an IDL-compiler or through the CORBA Interface Repository write functions—CORBA doesn't care how the information gets there. The CORBA specification, however, does detail how the information is organized and retrieved from the repository. It does this creatively by specifying a set of classes whose instances represent the information that's in the repository.

The class hierarchy mirrors the IDL specification. The result is a highly flexible object database that keeps track of collections of objects organized along the same lines as the IDL. Of course, all the objects in the repository are compiled versions of the information that's in an IDL source file.

Why Is an Interface Repository Needed Anyway?

An ORB needs to understand the definition of the objects it is working with. One way to get these definitions is by incorporating the information into the stubs. The other way to get this information is through a dynamically accessible Interface Repository. What does an ORB do with the information in the repository? It can use the object definitions to do the following:

■ *Provide type-checking of method signatures*. The parameter types are checked regardless of whether the request is issued using dynamic APIs or through a stub. Signatures define the parameters of a method and their type.

■ *Help connect ORBs together*. A multi-ORB "federation" of Interface Repositories is used to translate objects that go across heterogeneous ORBs. Note that you must use the same Repository ID to describe these objects. You must define the interfaces of these intergalactic objects in all ORB repositories.

■ *Provide metadata information to clients and tools*. Clients use the Interface Repository to create "on-the-fly" method invocations. Tools—such as class browsers, application generators, and compilers—can use the information to obtain inheritance structures and class definitions at run time.

■ *Provide self-describing objects*. You can invoke the *get_interface* method on any CORBA object to obtain its interface information (after that information is installed in the Interface Repository).

Interface Repositories can be maintained locally or managed as departmental or enterprise resources. They serve as valuable sources of metadata information on class structures and component interfaces. An ORB may have access to multiple Interface Repositories.

Interface Repository Classes: The Containment Hierarchy

The Interface Repository is implemented as a set of objects that represent the information in it. These objects must be persistent, which means they must be stored on a non-volatile medium. CORBA groups the metadata into modules that

---

represent naming spaces. The repository object names are unique within a module. CORBA defines an interface for each of its eight IDL structures:

- *ModuleDef* defines a logical grouping of interfaces. Like an IDL file, the Interface Repository uses modules to group interfaces and to navigate through groups by name. So you can think of a module as providing a namespace.

- *InterfaceDef* defines the object's interface; it contains lists of constants, type-defs, exceptions, and interface definitions.

- *OperationDef* defines a method on an object's interface; it contains lists of parameters and exceptions raised by this operation.

- *ParameterDef* defines an argument of a method.

- *AttributeDef* defines the attributes of an interface.

- *ConstantDef* defines a named constant.

- *ExceptionDef* defines the exceptions that can be raised by an operation.

- *TypeDef* defines the named types that are part of an IDL definition.

In addition to these eight interfaces that represent IDL structures, CORBA specifies a **Repository** interface that serves as the root for all the modules contained in a repository namespace. Each Interface Repository is represented by a global root repository object. Figure 7-6 shows the containment hierarchy for objects that belong to these interfaces (or classes). You'll notice that some of the objects—for example, instances of the **Repository** class—contain other objects. Some objects—for example, instances of the **ModuleDef** class—are both contained and containers. Finally, some objects—for example, instances of the **ExceptionDef** class—are always contained in other objects, but they don't contain objects of their own.

The Interface Repository Class Hierarchy

The CORBA Interface Repository architects noticed these containment hierarchies, and then defined three abstract superclasses—or classes that cannot be instantiated—called **IRObject**, **Contained**, and **Container** (see Figure 7-7). Notice that this figure shows an inheritance hierarchy as opposed to a containment hierarchy. All Interface Repository objects inherit from the **IRObject** interface, which is new to CORBA 2.0. This interface provides an attribute operation for identifying the actual type of an object as well as a *destroy* method. Objects that are containers

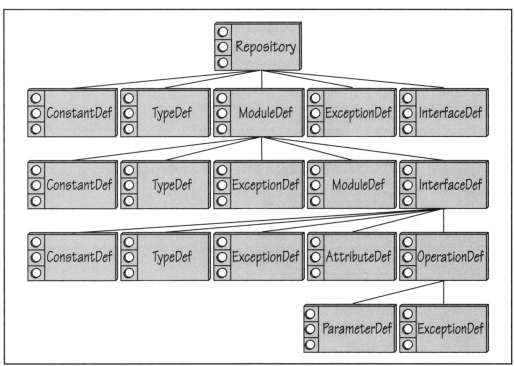

Figure 7-6. The Containment Hierarchy for the Interface Repository Classes.

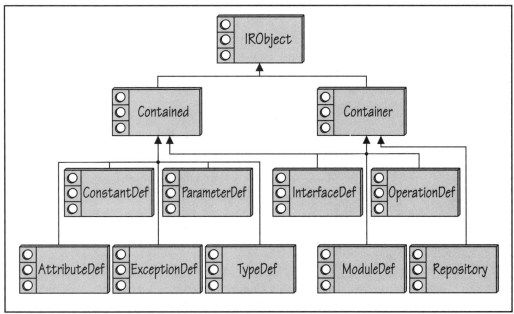

Figure 7-7. The Inheritance Hierarchy of the Interface Repository Classes.

inherit navigation operations from the **Container** interface. The **Contained** interface defines the behavior of objects contained in other objects. All the repository classes are derived from **Container**, from **Contained**, or from both through multiple inheritance. This clever scheme allows the repository objects to behave according to their containment relationships (also see the next Details box).

The Interface Repository: A Closer Look

Details

Figure 7-8 shows a class hierarchy of the more important Interface Repository classes (and their interfaces). The rest of the classes simply inherit from these interfaces; they are not shown here. The Interface Repository classes provide operations that let you read, write, and destroy metadata that's stored in a repository. The *destroy* operation deletes an object from the repository; if you apply this operation on a container object, it will destroy all its contents. The **Contained** interface provides a *move* operation to remove an object from its current container and add it to a target container. The write, destroy, and move operations are new to CORBA 2.0.

You access Interface Repository metadata by invoking methods polymorphically on different object types. Because of this clever design, you can navigate and extract information from repository objects with only nine methods (see Figure 7-8). Five of these methods are derived from the ancestor classes **Container** and **Contained**. The other four methods are specific to the **InterfaceDef** and **Repository** interfaces. Here's a description of the read and navigation methods:

■ *Describe*—when you invoke this method on a target **Contained** object, it returns a Description structure containing the IDL information that "describes" the object.

■ *Lookup*—when you invoke this method on **Container** objects, it returns a sequence of pointers to the objects it contains.

■ *Lookup_name*—you invoke this method on a **Container** object to locate an object by name.

■ *Contents*—when you invoke this method on **Container** objects, it returns the list of objects directly contained or inherited by this object. You use this method to navigate through a hierarchy of objects. For example, you can start with a **Repository** object and list all the objects it contains, and so on.

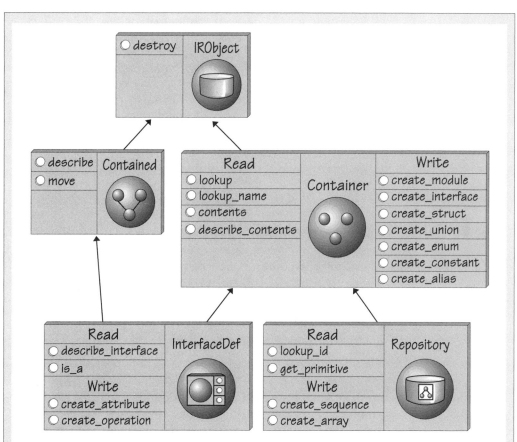

Figure 7-8. Interface Repository: The Top-Level Class Hierarchy and Interfaces.

■ *Describe_contents*—when you invoke this method on a **Container** object, it returns a sequence of pointers to the content descriptions of the objects it contains. This method combines the *contents* and *describe* operations. You can limit the scope of the search by excluding inherited objects or by looking for a specific type of object (for example, of type InterfaceDef).

■ *Describe_interface*—when you invoke this method on an **InterfaceDef** object, it returns a structure that fully describes the interface—including its name, Repository ID, version number, operations, attributes, and all the parent interfaces.

■ *Is_a*—when you invoke this method on an **InterfaceDef** object, it returns TRUE if the interface is identical to or inherits directly from an interface that you specify in an input parameter.

■ *Lookup_id*—you invoke this method on a **Repository** object to look up an object in a repository given its Repository ID.

Part 2. ORB Fundamentals

- *Get_primitive*—you invoke this method on a **Repository** object to obtain a reference on a primitive object. This means an immutable object type that is owned by the repository. Examples of primitive objects include object references, principals, base data types, and type codes.

Together, these method calls allow you to navigate through an Interface Repository. You can search through the namespaces of specific modules to look for objects that meet your search criteria. When you find an object, you use the *describe* method to retrieve the IDL information that defines it. Also, remember that **IRObject**, **Container,** and **Contained** are abstract classes, which means that you never deal with them directly. Instead, you invoke methods on Interface Repository objects that inherit their behavior from these abstract base classes.

How Do You Find an Interface in the First Place?

You can locate an object's interface in one of three ways:

1. ***By directly calling the ORB's Object::get_interface method.*** You can issue this call against any valid object reference. The call will return an **InterfaceDef** object that fully describes the object's interface. This method is useful when you encounter an object whose type you do not know at compile time.

2. ***By navigating through the module namespace using a sequence of names.*** For example, if you know the name of the interface you're after, you can start by looking for it in the root module of the repository. When you find the entry, invoke the method *InterfaceDef::describe_interface* to obtain the metadata that describes that interface.

3. ***By locating the InterfaceDef object that corresponds to a particular Repository ID.*** You do this by invoking the method *Repository::lookup_id*.

Once you obtain an **InterfaceDef** object, you can invoke its interfaces to obtain the metadata you need. You can then use this metadata to dynamically invoke methods on that object. ❑

Federated Interface Repositories

With the new CORBA 2.0 enhancements, we can now create intergalactic federations of Interface Repositories that operate across multiple ORBs. To avoid name collisions, these repositories assign unique IDs—called *Repository IDs*—to global interfaces and operations. You can use these Repository IDs to replicate copies of the metadata across multiple repositories and still maintain a coherent view across them. This means that the unique identity of an interface is preserved across ORB and repository boundaries. For example, with a global Repository ID, you can obtain some metadata on an interface from a local repository. You can then obtain additional metadata on that *same* interface from a remote repository.

To ensure that IDL definitions in various repositories do not contain any duplicates, CORBA 2.0 defines the following naming conventions:

■ **Scoped names** uniquely identify modules, interfaces, constants, typedefs, exceptions, attributes, operations, and parameters within an Interface Repository. A scoped name consists of one or more identifiers separated by the characters "::".

■ **Repository IDs** globally identify modules, interfaces, constants, typedefs, exceptions, attributes, operations, and parameters. They are used to synchronize definitions across ORBs and Repositories.

The next section describes the mechanisms for creating these global Repository IDs.

What Does a Global Repository ID Look Like?

The *Repository ID* itself is a string consisting of a three-level name hierarchy. CORBA 2.0 defines two formats for specifying global Repository IDs:

■ **Using IDL names with unique prefixes**. You create a Repository ID using an IDL name that consists of three components separated by colons ":". The first component is the string "IDL". The second component is a list of identifiers separated by "/" characters. The first identifier is a unique prefix, and the rest are the IDL identifiers that make up a scoped name. The third component consists of major and minor versions in decimal format separated by a period. For example, a valid Repository ID for the interface **Cat** in the module MyAnimals is "*IDL:DogCatInc/MyAnimals/Cat/:1.0*". In this case, *DogCatInc* is a unique prefix that denotes an organization. You can also use an Internet ID for a prefix (or any other unique name).

■ **Using DCE Universal Unique Identifiers (UUIDs)**. DCE provides a UUID generator that calculates a globally unique number using the current date and time, a network card ID, and a high-frequency counter. There's almost no chance for this algorithm to create duplicate UUIDs. The DCE format for the Repository ID also consists of three components separated by colons ":". The first component is the string "DCE". The second component is a printable UUID. The third component is made up of a version number in decimal format. Note that there is no minor version. For example, a DCE Repository ID could look like "*DCE:700dc500-0111-22ce-aa9f:1*".

You can associate Repository IDs with IDL definitions in a variety of ways. For example, an installation tool might generate them for you. Or an IDL precompiler can generate them based on pragma directives that you embed in the IDL (see the next Details box).

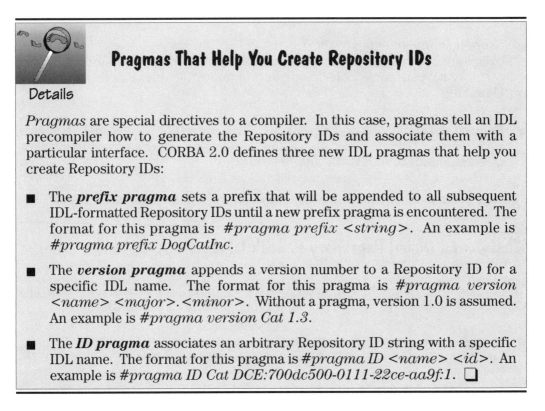

Pragmas That Help You Create Repository IDs

Details

Pragmas are special directives to a compiler. In this case, pragmas tell an IDL precompiler how to generate the Repository IDs and associate them with a particular interface. CORBA 2.0 defines three new IDL pragmas that help you create Repository IDs:

- The ***prefix pragma*** sets a prefix that will be appended to all subsequent IDL-formatted Repository IDs until a new prefix pragma is encountered. The format for this pragma is *#pragma prefix <string>*. An example is *#pragma prefix DogCatInc*.

- The ***version pragma*** appends a version number to a Repository ID for a specific IDL name. The format for this pragma is *#pragma version <name> <major>.<minor>*. Without a pragma, version 1.0 is assumed. An example is *#pragma version Cat 1.3*.

- The ***ID pragma*** associates an arbitrary Repository ID string with a specific IDL name. The format for this pragma is *#pragma ID <name> <id>*. An example is *#pragma ID Cat DCE:700dc500-0111-22ce-aa9f:1*. ❏

CORBA IDL Without Pain

One of the frequent complaints you hear from C++, Java, or Smalltalk programmers is: Why must we go through the extra step of describing our objects in IDL? Why can't the ORB understand our language objects? Some enterprising compiler vendors took up this challenge by directly generating CORBA IDL from language classes—for example, both the MetaWare C++ and VisualAge for C++ compilers can now generate, directly from C++, CORBA IDL for SOM.

More recently, Visigenic/Netscape introduced *Caffeine*; it includes a *Java2IIOP* postprocessor that directly generates CORBA stubs and skeletons from Java byte-codes.[2] Caffeine also lets you generate CORBA IDL from Java using the *Java2IDL*

---

[2] We describe Caffeine in detail, including a programming example, in our book, **Client/Server Programming with Java and CORBA** (see Chapter 13).

postprocessor. Finally, the OMG is also working on a Java-to-CORBA *reverse mapping standard* (see OMG document *orbos/96-12-12*). So if you don't like IDL, help is on the way. Of course, if you're a C programmer, this won't be too helpful. You have no way to define classes from within the language; IDL is your only answer.

THE INTROSPECTIVE CORBA OBJECT

CORBA objects are derived from the root CORBA **Object** interface. As a result, they are supersmart objects that can tell you quite a lot about themselves. An object is *introspective* if it can describe its behavior at run time. These introspective properties make objects very attractive to client/server tool vendors, Trader Services, and dynamic clients. Introspection lets you discover at run time the stuff that only compilers previously recognized. CORBA introspection includes a wealth of information that is contained in Interface Repositories; it provides enough detail to let you dynamically construct and invoke a method at run time.

THE CORBA INTROSPECTION INTERFACE

A CORBA object derives its introspective powers from **CORBA::Object**. In addition, **CORBA::ORB** provides two useful helper functions: *object_to_string* and *string_to_object* (see the light methods in Figure 7-9). Here's a quick description of CORBA introspection:

■ **CORBA::Object** defines operations that are supported by every CORBA object reference. It's the root interface of all CORBA objects. The ORB provides these

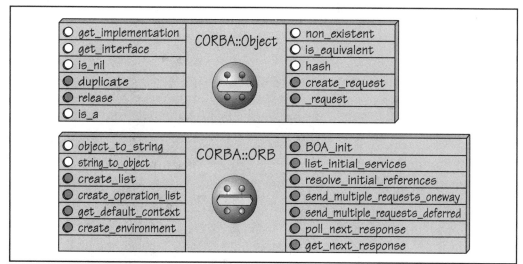

Figure 7-9. The CORBA Object Introspection Methods.

operations for free. You simply inherit them when you create your object. Seven of these methods deal with introspection. You already saw *get_interface* in Chapter 5; it returns a reference to an **InterfaceDef**, which is an object inside an Interface Repository that describes this interface. You invoke *get_implementation* on an object reference to obtain an **ImplementationDef** object. This is an Implementation Repository object that describes the implementation of your object.

You invoke *is_nil* to determine if the object exists. You can also invoke *non_existent* to determine if the object has been destroyed. You invoke *is_equivalent* to determine if two object references are equivalent; the ORB returns TRUE if your object reference is equivalent to the object reference you pass as a parameter. If two object references are identical, they are equivalent. Two different object references that refer to the same object are also equivalent. To improve the performance of object searches, the ORB may maintain an internal hash value for an object reference. If two object references *hash* differently, they are not identical. However, the reverse is not always true. Finally, you invoke *is_a* to determine if an object is really an instance of the Repository Type you specify.

■ **CORBA::ORB** is a pseudo-object interface that defines general-purpose ORB methods. Two of these methods are introspection-related. You invoke *string_to_object* to create a "stringified" version of the object that you can then pass around. You invoke *object_to_string* to convert a string representation to an object reference on which you can invoke methods.

In summary, every CORBA object is introspective. You can invoke ORB-implemented methods on every object reference to obtain information about this object. Note that the actual metadata is stored in the Interface Repository. The introspection methods simply return object references to Interface Repository objects.

CONCLUSION

A CORBA ORB comes with standard mechanisms for generating and managing metadata. You generate metadata that describes your components and their interfaces using IDL. The ORB's IDL precompiler automatically writes your IDL-defined metadata in an Interface Repository. From then on, you can update that metadata using the Interface Repository write and update operations. Clients can query the Interface Repository; they can discover what interfaces are available and how to call them. You can use the same Interface Repository to store the description of components—ranging from very fine-grained system objects to business objects. It's all very regular. With CORBA 2.0, we have a solid foundation for creating federated Interface Repositories that can interoperate across heterogeneous ORBs and operating systems.

Part 3
CORBA Services

An Introduction to Part 3

In Part 3, we cover *all* 15 existing CORBA Services—OMG calls them collectively the *CORBAservices* They include Naming, Events, Life Cycle, Persistence, Relationships, Externalization, Transactions, Concurrency Control, Licensing, Query, Properties, Security, Time, Collections, and Trading Services. Object services are the basic building blocks for a distributed object infrastructure. They provide the next step up in the evolutionary chain toward creating distributed components—or what the OMG calls *business objects*.

As you will discover, the CORBA Services are extremely generic. First, they are totally independent of any application domain. Second, they were designed using the Bauhaus principle. This means that every service does one and only one thing, but it does it well. You should be able to combine these services in different ways in your applications. It's all code that you don't have to reinvent yourself. We anticipate that these services will also be incorporated in higher-level frameworks— for example, one of your authors is incorporating them in a CORBA-based TP Monitor for objects.

We found most CORBA Services to be well-designed and useful. We put some through the ultimate wringer: our graduate students. For example, during one semester we gave the CORBA Trader specification "as is" to our students for their class projects. We then told them to "go build it in Java." Three months later, all the teams demonstrated functional implementations of the Trader. Most teams implemented their Traders using a 3-tier client/server architecture with CORBA and JDBC. One team even combined CORBA server objects with an ODBMS.

So the million dollar question is: Why aren't the ORB vendors delivering commercial implementations of these services at student speeds? We may later answer this question in a Soapbox. But, we first must cover each of these services.

We think Part 3 makes fascinating reading. It captures a tremendous amount of experience in distributed object design—including many useful *design patterns* for distributed objects. This should not be too surprising—after all, the CORBA Object Services were designed by the leading industry experts in their respective fields.

Your authors know first-hand how much know-how went into the design of each of these services. So we are very happy to be able to collect them all in Part 3 for your "instant gratification." You'll find that there's a lot there—it's really a complete course in distributed object design. Of course, we complement the reading with all these inevitable scenarios, tutorials, and Soapboxes. Life would be dull without them.

Chapter 8

CORBA Services: Naming, Life Cycle, and Events

Large lump development hinges on a view of the environment which is static and discontinuous; piecemeal growth hinges on a view of the environment which is dynamic and continuous.

> — Christopher Alexander et al., Authors
> The Oregon Experiment
> (Oxford, 1975)

This chapter introduces the three most basic services you need to simply operate within an ORB environment: Naming, Life Cycle, and Events (the light services in Figure 8-1). Why are these services basic? When objects first get started, they need to find other objects on the ORB. The CORBA *Naming Service* is like the telephone white pages for objects; it lets you find objects by name. The *Trader Service* (see next chapter) is like the telephone Yellow Pages; it advertises object services and helps you find them. The *Life Cycle Service* deals with key existential issues—including life, death, and relocation; it lets you create objects, move them around, and destroy them. The *Event Service* provides asynchronous interactions between anonymous objects; you get notified when significant things happen on the ORB.

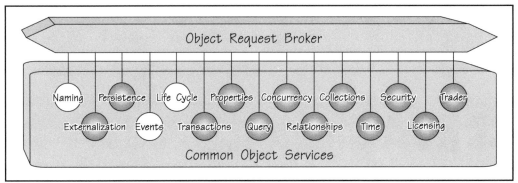

Figure 8-1. CORBA Object Services: Naming, Trader, Life Cycle, and Events.

THE CORBA OBJECT NAMING SERVICE

The *Object Naming Service* is the principal mechanism for objects on an ORB to locate other objects. Names are humanly recognizable values that identify an object. The naming service maps these human names to object references. A name-to-object association is called a *name binding*. A *naming context* is a namespace in which the object's name is unique. Every object has a unique reference ID. You can optionally associate one or more names with an object reference. You always define a name relative to its naming context.

Object Naming in a Nutshell

The Object Naming Service became an OMG standard in September 1993. It was designed to transparently encapsulate existing name and directory services such as the DCE CDS, ISO X.500, Sun NIS+, and the Internet's LDAP. The idea was not to reinvent the wheel. The Naming Service lets you create naming hierarchies. Clients can navigate through different naming context trees in search of the object they want. Name contexts from different domains can be used together to create federated naming services for objects. A CORBA naming hierarchy does not require a "universal" root.

The Naming Service has no dependencies on other CORBA object services. But if your clients need to perform complex searches, you can register naming characteristics for your object with the *Properties Service*. Clients can then use the *Query Service* to look for object names with certain externally visible characteristics—for example, objects whose *time_last_modified* date is greater than 1/1/96 (also see the next Briefing box).

What's in a CORBA Object Name?

You can reference a CORBA object using a sequence of names that form a hierarchical naming tree (see Figure 8-2). In the figure, each dark node is a *naming context*. An object's name consists of a sequence of names (or components) that form a *compound name*. Each component—except for the last one—is used to name a context. The last component is the object's *simple* name.

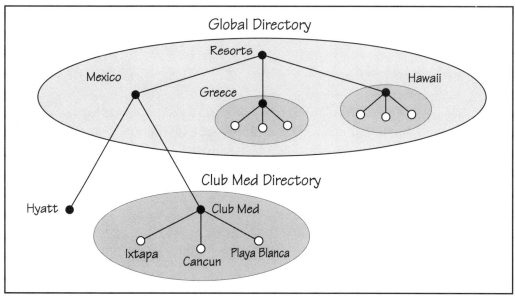

Figure 8-2. CORBA Objects Support Hierarchical Naming.

In Figure 8-3 we show a compound name that consists of a simple name—*Playa Blanca*—and three context names: *Club Med, Mexico*, and *Resorts*. The compound name defines a path for resolving context names until you get to the simple name. You can start from any context and use a sequence of names to resolve an object. To *resolve* a name means to find the object associated with the name in a given context. To *bind* a name is to create a name-to-object association for a particular context.

Each named component is a structure with two attributes: 1) *identifier* is the object's name string; 2) *kind* is a string in which you can put a descriptive attribute for your name—for example, a file type. The service designers prefer that you do not encode meanings directly into names. Instead, they want you to use the *kind* attribute to qualify names. The Naming Service does not interpret, assign, or manage these attributes in any way. They are used by higher levels of software.

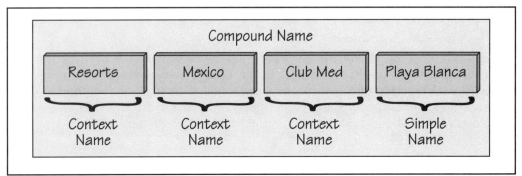

Figure 8-3. A Compound Name.

How Does It Work?

Figure 8-4 shows the two interfaces **NamingContext** and **BindingIterator** that implement the Naming Service. **NamingContext** objects contain a set of name-to-object bindings in which each name is unique. These objects may also be bound to names in other naming context objects to be part of a name hierarchy.

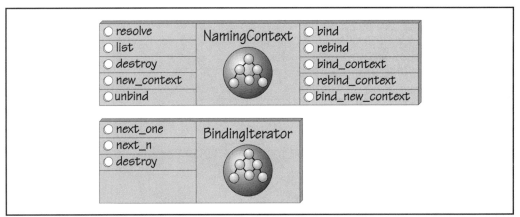

Figure 8-4. The Object Naming Service Interfaces.

You invoke the *bind* method in the **NamingContext** interface to associate an object's name with a binding context. The *rebind* method is the same as *bind* except that it does not return an error if the name has already been bound to another object; it simply rebinds the object to the new name. This is how you create a naming hierarchy. You invoke *unbind* to remove a name from a binding context. The *new_context* method returns the naming context. *Bind_new_context* creates a new context and binds it to a name you supply. The *destroy* method lets you delete a naming context.

The IBM/Sun Interoperable Naming Service

Briefing

In August 1996, IBM and Sun announced an *Interoperable Naming Service* for their respective CORBA ORBs—DSOM 4.0 and NEO/Joe. We briefly cover this Naming Service extension because it demonstrates how you can mix-and-match CORBA services. It also demonstrates how you can extend and specialize a CORBA service. Note that this is a preliminary specification; Sun and IBM have not submitted it to the OMG. They may submit it at a later date—after they work out the kinks in the implementation.

The IBM/Sun Naming Service adds three extensions to the official CORBA Naming Service: 1) a well-known bootstrap port (port 900) that lets you obtain an initial naming context via IIOP, 2) a common namespace definition, and 3) extended naming interfaces. These last two items are especially interesting. We will briefly tell you what they do.

The "Common" Namespace

The Sun/IBM Extended Naming Service divides the CORBA system namespace into three naming trees (see Figure 8-5): *hosts*, *workgroups*, and *cells*. A host contains a local namespace in which you can mount a distributed namespace.

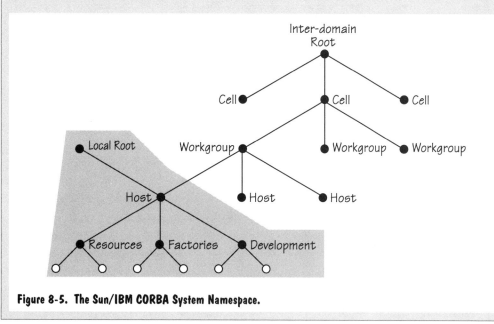

Figure 8-5. The Sun/IBM CORBA System Namespace.

It's very similar to the Unix file system. The workgroup and cells contain namespaces that are shared and distributed. A workgroup typically contains between 10 and 200 hosts; each host belongs to one default workgroup. A cell contains one or more workgroups.

The Extended Naming Interfaces

Figure 8-6 shows the Sun/IBM extended naming interfaces (see dotted area). They extend and combine functions from three CORBA Services: Naming, Properties, and Query. Using these interfaces, you can assign properties to a naming context, and then issue queries against these properties to locate objects. To speed up the search, Sun/IBM provide extensions that let you create indexes on properties. You should be able to specify an index on a property, name, or type.

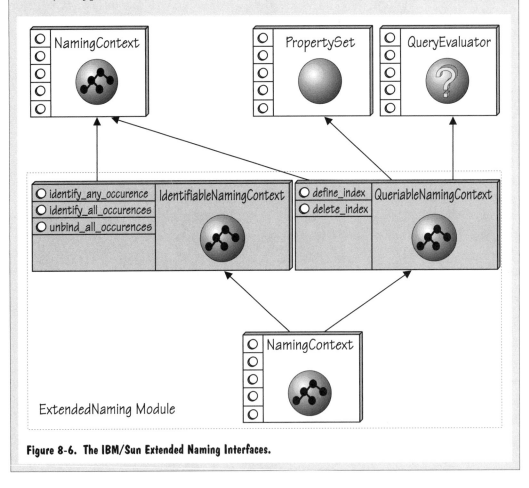

Figure 8-6. The IBM/Sun Extended Naming Interfaces.

> The **ExtendedNaming::NamingContext** interface does not introduce any new methods. It simply aggregates the rest of the interfaces. You use it to create propertied-namespaces that you can then query via SQL or Object SQL. We cover the CORBA Query and Property Services later in Part 3. At this point, we simply wanted to demonstrate that you can combine CORBA services via multiple inheritance. You should be able to create more powerful aggregates that you can further specialize to meet your particular needs. The Sun/IBM scheme can serve as a design pattern. ❑

You can find any named object using the *resolve* method; it retrieves an object bound to a name in a given context. The *list* method lets you iterate through a returned set of names (it returns a **BindingIterator** object). You iterate by invoking *next_one* and *next_n* on the returned **BindingIterator** object. You invoke *destroy* to free the iteration object.

In summary, the Object Naming Service defines interfaces that let you manage namespaces for objects, and then query and navigate through them. The objects that provide these interfaces live on the ORB and can be implemented by encapsulating existing procedural naming services with CORBA wrappers. CORBA simply defines the interfaces to these services, not the implementation.

THE CORBA OBJECT LIFE CYCLE SERVICE

The *Object Life Cycle Service* provides operations for creating, copying, moving, and deleting objects. The Life Cycle Service was recently expanded so that all these operations can now handle associations between groups of related objects. This includes containment and reference relationships, as well as the enforcement of referential integrity constraints between objects. In accordance with CORBA's use of the Bauhaus principle (keep the services simple and single focused), you define these relationships using the *Relationship Service*. To be more precise, the Life Cycle Service provides interfaces that are derived from the Relationship Service.

A Compound Life Cycle Example

Let's walk through an example of how the life cycle operations are implemented on an object that has explicit associations with other objects. Figure 8-7 shows a document object that contains one or more page objects, which in turn contain multimedia and text objects. The document is stored in a folder object and *references* a catalog object that contains an entry for it. The Life Cycle Service maintains a graph of all these associations.

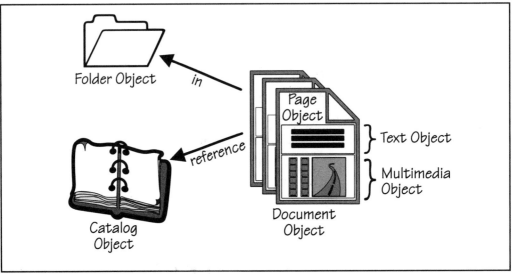

Figure 8-7. Object Life Cycle Services Must Handle Associated Objects.

A "deep move" causes the document to be moved with all its dependent objects (the pages and their contents); the reference in the catalog is updated; and the document gets removed from the source folder and gets inserted into the target folder (see Figure 8-8). Likewise, when the document is externalized to a file, all the objects it contains go with it. When the document is deleted, its page objects and the graphic

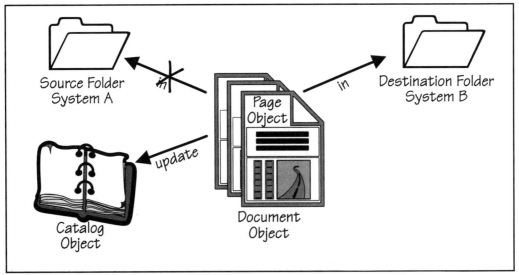

Figure 8-8. A "Deep" Move Handles All the Associations.

objects they contain are also deleted. The references to the document are removed from both the catalog and the folder (see Figure 8-9).

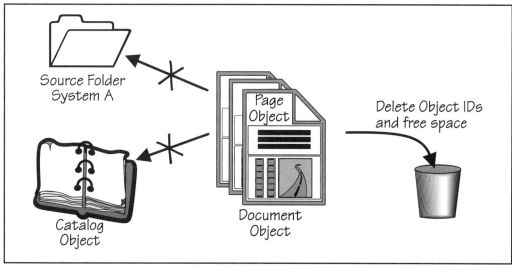

Figure 8-9. Delete Removes Objects and Dependents and Manages References.

The Life Cycle Interfaces

Clients have a simple view of Life Cycle operations. In the previous example, the clients simply invoke methods to *move* and *copy* the document object; all the associated objects are handled transparently. The Life Cycle Service is able to handle both simple containment and referential relationships.

To create a new object, a client must find a *factory* object (meaning an object that knows how to instantiate an object of that class), issue a *create* request, and get back an object reference. A client can also create an object by cloning an existing object with a *copy* operation. The factory objects must allocate resources, obtain object references, and register the new objects with the Object Adapter and Implementation Repository. When an object is copied across machines, the factory object on the target node is involved.

Figure 8-10 shows the three interfaces that provide the basic Life Cycle Service (more interfaces were recently added to support Compound Life Cycle and are described in the next section). The **LifeCycleObject** interface defines the *copy, move,* and *remove* operations; it provides the client's primary view of Life Cycle operations on target objects. The *copy* operation makes a copy of the object and returns an object reference; the *move* operation allows the object to roam to any location within the scope of the factory finder; and the *remove* operation deletes the object. The **FactoryFinder** defines an interface for finding factories. Because every object requires different resource information for its creation, it's impossible to define a single factory interface for all objects. The **GenericFactory** simply defines a general *create_object* operation.

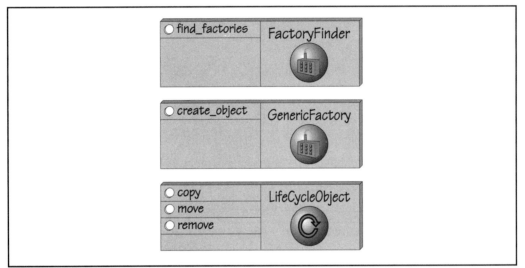

Figure 8-10. The Object Life Cycle Interfaces.

The Compound Life Cycle Interfaces

The Compound Life Cycle interfaces are a recent addendum to the Life Cycle Service. The addendum provides new interfaces that support deep copies, moves, and deletes (see Figure 8-11). The addendum adds a new factory interface called **OperationsFactory**, which creates objects of the class **Operations**. Notice that the **Operations** interface supports the same *copy, move*, and *remove* methods; it also adds a new method called *destroy*.

The three classes **Node**, **Role**, and **Relationship** are derived from corresponding classes in the CORBA Relationship Service. They let you define relationships between objects that know nothing of each other. To define a relationship, you must associate a role with an object and then create relationships between these roles. Complex relationships can be expressed using graphs that keep track of nodes that form the relationship's web. What this all means is that when you invoke an operation—such as *copy, move, remove*, or *destroy*—you're performing it on group of related objects instead of a single object. You define the group using the Relationship classes. We explain these classes in more detail in Chapter 14, "CORBA Services: Object Relationships and Time."

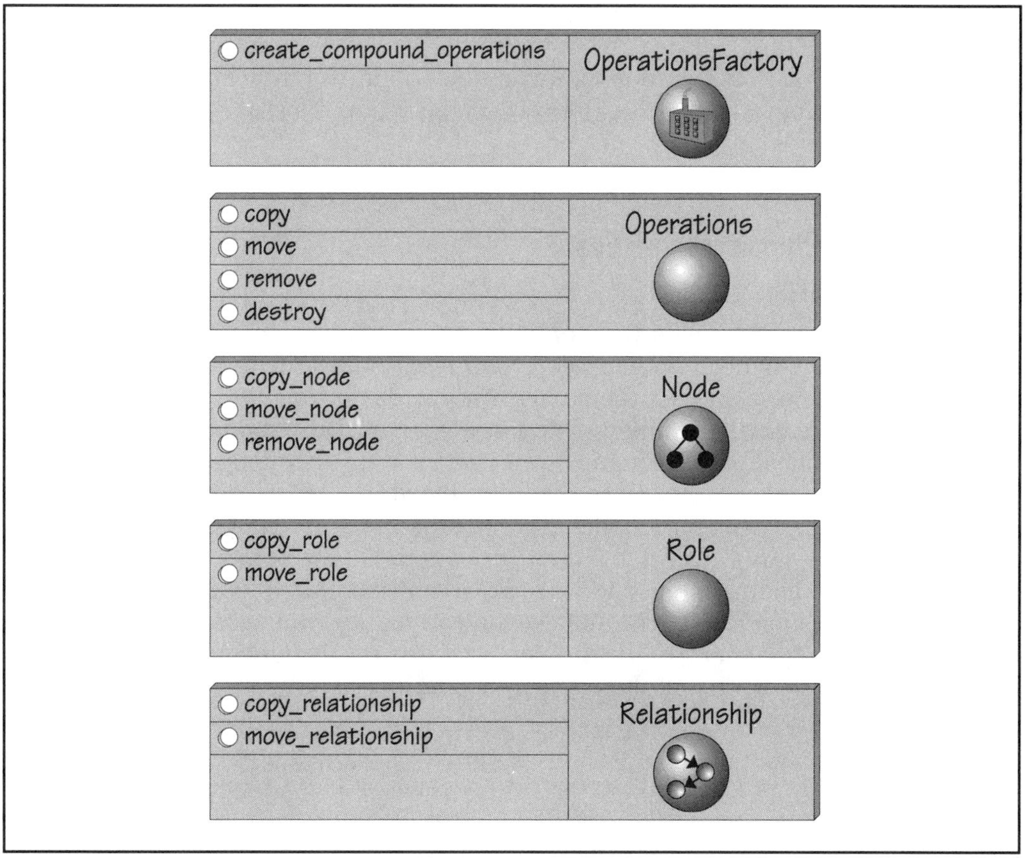

create_compound_operations — OperationsFactory

copy
move
remove
destroy — Operations

copy_node
move_node
remove_node — Node

copy_role
move_role — Role

copy_relationship
move_relationship — Relationship

Figure 8-11. The Compound Life Cycle Interfaces.

You should note that clients of the Life Cycle Service typically interact with the **LifeCycle** object we described in the previous section. If the object participates as a node in a graph of related objects, it will delegate the call to a service that implements the **Operations** interface. The caller must also pass an object reference for a **Node** object to indicate the starting node in a graph of related objects. The delegation mechanism hides most of the compound node complexities from clients. As far as the clients are concerned, they just say copy or move; then the magic occurs "under-the-covers."

THE CORBA EVENT SERVICE

The *Event Service* allows objects to dynamically register or unregister their interest in specific events. An *event* is an occurrence within an object specified to be of interest to one or more objects. A *notification* is a message an object sends to interested parties informing them that a specific event occurred. Normally, the object generating the event doesn't have to know the interested parties. This is all handled by the Event Service, which creates a loosely-coupled communication channel between objects that don't know much about each other. Events are more loosely coupled than RPC but less loosely coupled than Message-Oriented Middleware (MOM).

Suppliers and Consumers of Events

The Event Service decouples the communication between objects. The service defines two roles for objects: *suppliers* and *consumers*. The suppliers produce events; the consumers process them via event handlers. Events are communicated between suppliers and consumers using standard CORBA requests. In addition, there are two models for communicating event data: push and pull. In the *push model*, the supplier of events takes the initiative and initiates the transfer of event data to consumers. In the *pull* model, the consumer takes the initiative and requests event data from a supplier. An *event channel* is an intervening object that is both a supplier and consumer of events. It allows multiple suppliers to communicate with multiple consumers asynchronously and without knowing about each other. An event channel is a standard CORBA object that sits on the ORB and decouples the communications between suppliers and consumers.

The event channel supports both the push and pull event notification models (see Figure 8-12):

- With the **push model**, the supplier issues a *push* method invocation on the event channel object; the event channel, in turn, pushes the event data to the consumer objects. A consumer can stop receiving events by invoking the method *disconnect_push_consumer* on the event channel. The consumer invokes a *connect_push_consumer* method on the event channel to register its interest in some event type.

- With the **pull model**, the consumer issues a *pull* method invocation on the event channel object; the event channel, in turn, pulls the event data from the supplier. Using the *try_pull* method, the consumer can periodically poll for events. A supplier can stop accepting requests for supplying events by invoking a *disconnect_pull_supplier* method on the event channel. The supplier issues an *add_pull_supplier* method on the event channel to register its object reference and offer its services.

An event channel can communicate with a supplier using one style of communication, and it can communicate with a consumer using a different style of communication.

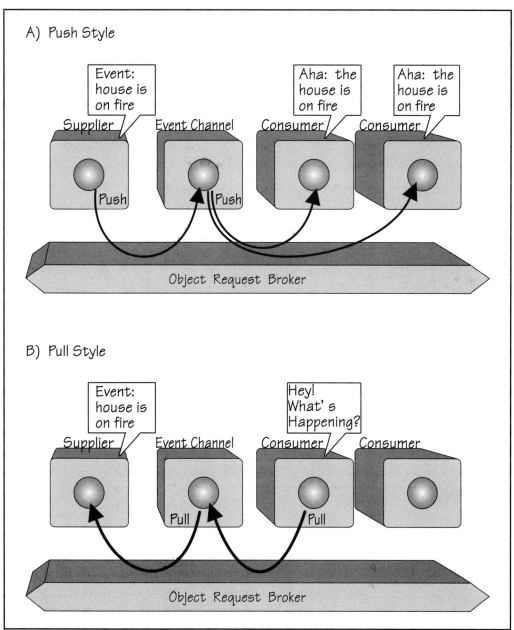

Figure 8-12. The Event Service: Push and Pull Styles.

Figure 8-13 shows an event channel with multiple suppliers and consumers. The channel enables a variety of suppliers to send data asynchronously to a variety of consumers. Notice that a channel can provide a mix of pull and push style communications. The channel insulates suppliers and consumers from having to know which communication model other objects on the channel use—for example, a pull supplier can send events to a push consumer.

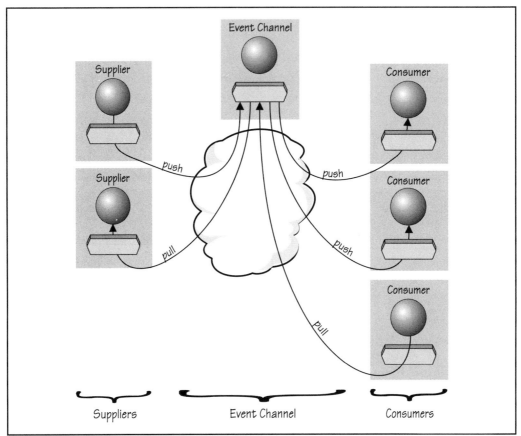

Figure 8-13. An Event Channel With Push-Style and Pull-Style Communications.

The event interface supports multiple levels of service (for example, different levels of reliability). A persistent store of events may be supplied by the event channel object as part of its service (for example, some key events may be stored for up to a week or more). The event channels are *well-known* objects. They can serve as anchor points to help objects discover each other at run time. The consumers and suppliers of events use the standard CORBA IDL interfaces—no extensions are required.

Typed Events

The generic event channel object does not understand the contents of the data it's passing. It just passes a single parameter of type *any*. The producers and consumers must agree on common event semantics. However, the Event Service also supports a *Typed Event* model that allows applications to describe the contents of events using the IDL. The parameters passed must be input only; no information is returned. Typed events support both the pull and push models. Using the IDL, you can define special event types—for example, document or system management events. Consumers can then subscribe to a particular event type; typing becomes a powerful means of filtering event information. You can track the exact events you're interested in (it's a rifle instead of a shotgun).

Point-to-Point Events

The CORBA Event Service also provides interfaces that let suppliers of events directly communicate with consumers. Figure 8-14 shows a direct push-style communication between a consumer and a supplier of events. The two sides must first exchange **PushConsumer** and **PushSupplier** object references. The supplier then invokes the *push* method on the **PushConsumer** interface to deliver an event. To stop receiving events, a consumer invokes *disconnect_push_consumer* on the **PushSupplier** interface.

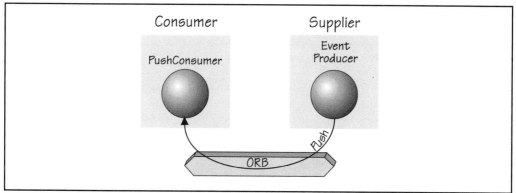

Figure 8-14. A Point-to-Point, Push-Style Event Setup.

The problem with point-to-point event connections is that the supplier must keep track of all its consumers, and vice versa. The supplier must also be able to handle situations where the consumers cannot keep up with it—in some situations, the consumer may not even be connected. Generally, you'll find it more convenient to use an event channel; it decouples the suppliers from their consumers, and it queues events for later delivery.

Event Proxies

An event channel uses proxy objects to decouple consumers and suppliers of events. Instead of directly interacting with each other, suppliers and consumers obtain proxy objects from the event channel to represent them in future exchanges of events. A supplier obtains a consumer proxy, and a consumer obtains a supplier proxy. The event channel brokers the exchange of events via these proxy objects. Figure 8-15 shows a single supplier distributing events to three consumers.

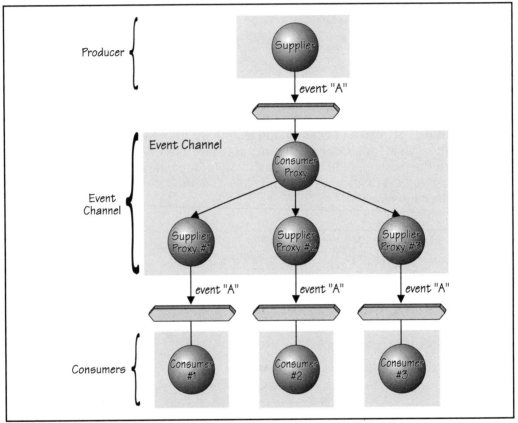

Figure 8-15. Consumer and Supplier Proxy Objects.

The Push Event Interfaces

The push model is the more common way to distribute events. We recommend that you use it—especially on wide area networks. In comparison, the pull model is a drain on communication resources. Figure 8-16 shows the seven interfaces CORBA defines for its push-style generic event communications. Three of these interfaces—**ConsumerAdmin**, **SupplierAdmin**, and **EventChannel**—deal with the administration of event channel proxies. The proxy interfaces simply extend the point-to-point **PushConsumer** and **PushSupplier** interfaces. Here's a quick description of what these interfaces do:

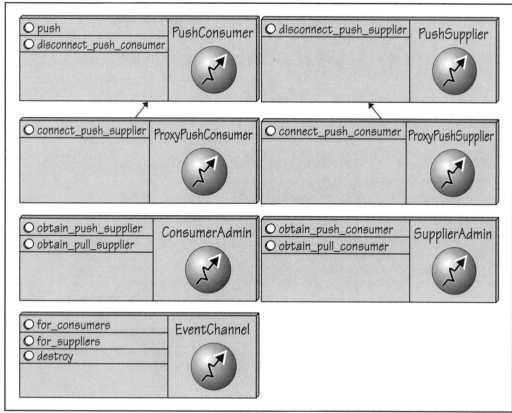

Figure 8-16. CORBA Event Service: The Push Interfaces.

■ **PushConsumer** defines two methods: *push* and *disconnect_push_consumer*. The *push* method receives an event with a single parameter of type *any*. Your implementation must decode the data in the *any* and then service the event. You invoke the *disconnect_push_consumer* method to tell the consumer that it will not be receiving any more events. Note that **PushConsumer** defines a generic way for an object to receive callbacks.

■ **PushSupplier** defines a single method—*disconnect_push_supplier*. You invoke this method to tell the supplier to stop sending events.

■ **ProxyPushConsumer** defines a single method—*connect_push_supplier*. A supplier invokes this method to connect with a proxy consumer object on an event channel. The call registers the supplier's object reference with the event channel.

■ **ProxyPushSupplier** defines a single method—*connect_push_consumer*. A consumer invokes this method to connect with a proxy supplier object on an event channel. The call registers the consumer's object reference with the event channel.

■ **ConsumerAdmin** is a dispenser of proxy supplier objects. To connect to an event channel, a consumer must first obtain a proxy supplier object. The consumer invokes *obtain_push_supplier* to obtain a **ProxyPushSupplier** object; it invokes *obtain_pull_supplier* to obtain a **ProxyPullSupplier** object.

■ **SupplierAdmin** is a dispenser of proxy consumer objects. To connect to an event channel, a supplier must first obtain a proxy consumer object. The supplier invokes *obtain_push_consumer* to obtain a **ProxyPushConsumer** object; it invokes *obtain_pull_consumer* to obtain a **ProxyPullConsumer** object.

■ **EventChannel** defines three administrative methods for event channels. The *for_consumers* method returns a **ConsumerAdmin** object. The *for_suppliers* method returns a **SupplierAdmin** object. Finally, the *destroy* method destroys the event channel and frees its resources.

In the next section, we walk through a scenario that shows how these interfaces play together.

A Push Event Scenario

The scenario in Figure 8-17 shows a push supplier sending an event to a push consumer via an event channel. It's not as complicated as it looks. Let's walk through the steps:

1. *The supplier obtains a SupplierAdmin object.* The supplier invokes *for_suppliers* on the **EventChannel** to obtain a **SupplierAdmin** object.

2. *The supplier obtains an event channel proxy.* The supplier invokes *obtain_push_consumer* on the **SupplierAdmin** to obtain a **ProxyPushConsumer** object.

3. *The supplier registers with the event channel.* The supplier invokes *connect_push_supplier* on the **ProxyPushConsumer** to connect with a proxy consumer object. The supplier must pass its object reference. The event channel uses it to disconnect from this supplier.

4. *The consumer obtains a ConsumerAdmin object.* The consumer invokes the *for_consumers* method on the **EventChannel** to obtain a **ConsumerAdmin** object.

5. *The consumer obtains an event channel proxy.* The consumer invokes *obtain_push_supplier* on the **ConsumerAdmin** to obtain a **ProxyPushSupplier** object.

6. *The consumer registers with the event channel.* The consumer invokes

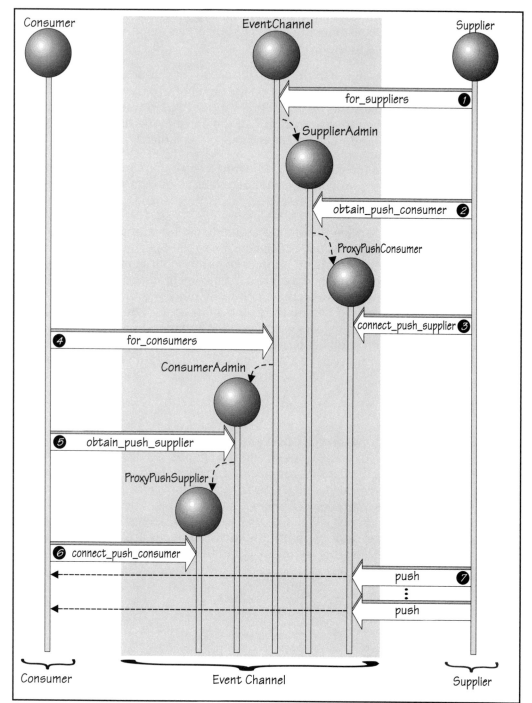

Figure 8-17. A Push Event Scenario.

connect_push_consumer on the **ProxyPushSupplier** to connect with a proxy supplier object. The consumer must pass its object reference. The event channel uses it to *push* events to this consumer.

7. ***The supplier emits one or more events.*** Now that the setup is complete, the supplier can start transmitting events via the channel. To transmit an event, the supplier simply invokes the *push* method on the **ProxyPushConsumer**. The event channel will then invoke *push* on all the consumers that have registered proxies. In our scenario, we only have a single consumer.

This scenario shows that most of the work involves setting up and registering with the event channel. After you connect with an event channel, pushing events is a piece of cake.

In summary, the Event Service introduces a minimalist form of MOM communications into CORBA. It is minimalist because it doesn't support MOM-like message priorities, filters, transaction protection, reception confirmation, time-to-live stamps, or sophisticated queue management.[1] The event channel objects make it easier to develop groupware applications and to help objects discover each other. Event typing allows you to zoom-in on the events of interest. The fan-in and fan-out capabilities of event channel objects can serve as a broadcast or multicast system, which can help create online object bazaars. The Event Service is extremely useful; it provides a foundation for creating a new genre of distributed object applications.

CONCLUSION

We just concluded our first three CORBA object services—the tally is three down and twelve more to go. As you can see from this chapter, each service is carefully designed to do one thing well; it's as complicated as it needs to be. The services are typically divided into several distinct interfaces that provide different views for different kinds of clients of the service. For example, the Life Cycle Service exposes a set of interfaces to its regular clients as well as a set of delegation interfaces that service providers can use. More importantly, all the services are designed from the ground up to work together; they all use IDL and the CORBA bus.

---

[1] OMG is working on adding MOM capabilities to CORBA; it issued a MOM RFP (the Messaging RFP) in mid-96. The RFP received strong responses from key MOM vendors including Tibco, Digital, IBM, Nortel, Expersoft, and PeerLogic. So you may be seeing some full-blown CORBA MOMs by late 1997. We cover CORBA Messaging in Part 4.

Chapter 9

CORBA Services: Object Trader

The *Object Trader Service* became a CORBA standard in mid-1996. The Trader Service is like a Yellow Pages for objects; it lets you discover objects based on the services they provide. In contrast, the *Naming Service* is like a telephone White Pages for objects; it lets you look up other objects by name. Using these two services, you should be able to locate any object in the intergalactic ORB universe.

In an Object Web environment, objects will be dynamically discovered by spiders, crawlers, bots, search engines, publish-and-subscribe services, and agents of all types. The traders will dynamically keep track of these new objects and their latest and greatest services. In this chapter, we cover the CORBA Trader Service (see Figure 9-1).

So what's a trader? A *trader* is an object that provides "matchmaking" services for other objects. *Exporters*—or service providers—advertise their services with the trader. *Importers*—or service consumers—use the trader to discover services that match their needs. The trader matches the needs of clients with the advertised capabilities of servers. In CORBA terminology, it matches exporters of services with importers (see Figure 9-2). Traders let you dynamically discover services and facilitate the late binding to these services.

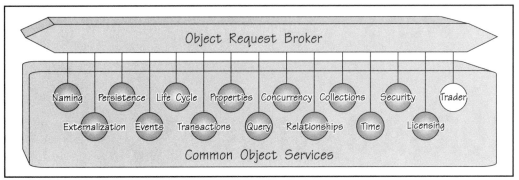

Figure 9-1. CORBA Object Services: Trader.

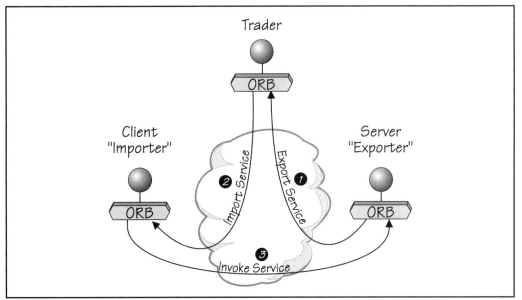

Figure 9-2. The Trader Service: Importers Meet Exporters.

TRADING: THE BIG PICTURE

A new service provider will first register its service with the trader. Then it will give it all the relevant information, including:

- **An object reference**. This is the reference clients use to connect to the advertised service and invoke its operations. It's the object reference to the interface that provides the service.

■ ***The service type name***. A service type includes information on the names of the operations (or methods) to which the service will respond along with their parameters and result types. It also includes distinguishing properties of the service and its trading context.

■ ***The properties of the service***. These are name-value pairs that define the offer. This is how you advertise application-level information. *Properties* describe the capabilities of a service. An exporter specifies (or asserts) values for properties of the service it is advertising. A property can be mandatory or optional. The exporter must specify values for all mandatory properties.

The trader maintains a repository of *service types*. For example, you can have a service type called *restaurant*. The restaurant type would include the interfaces to the service and a set of properties that describe individual restaurants. For example, a restaurant has a menu, specials, a street address, business hours, reviews, and so on. In true CORBA fashion, types can extend other types via multiple inheritance.

A service offer can also contain *dynamic properties*. The value for a dynamic property is not held within the trader. The trader obtains it on-demand using a registered dynamic property evaluator. This is an interface to a service that can provide the value at run time. For example, in response to a query, a trader could obtain the "specials of the day" by directly contacting a restaurant object. You should note that these dynamic evaluations can be slow. You can always tell the trader not to consider offers with dynamic properties when it matches your import request.

The trader stores service type descriptions—for example, restaurant—in its **ServiceTypeRepository**. It also maintains a database of service objects that are instances of these types. These are the objects exporters advertise via the trader. In our example, these are the actual restaurants. Clients—or importers—can get in touch with the trader to find out what services are listed or to ask for a service by type. It's like the telephone Yellow Pages. The trader will find the best match for the client based on the context of the requested service and the offers of the providers. A matching service will have a type that matches the client's request. It also has properties that match a client's criteria for a service.

Federated Traders

Traders from different domains can create *federations* and pool their offers. This lets traders in different domains advertise their services in a pool while maintaining control of their own policies and services. These loose federation of traders

resemble an electronic bazaar. When a trader links to other traders, it makes the offer spaces of those other traders implicitly available to its own clients.

Each trader's horizon is limited to traders to which it is explicitly linked. But the target traders may in turn be linked to yet more traders. This means that you can reach a large number of traders from your starting trader. These linked traders form a *trading graph*.

Typically, the client talks to one trader that can then fulfill the import request by propagating it to all the traders to which it is linked. Obviously, this can create problems like cyclical searches. To avoid these endless loops, the Trader Service lets you control the number of trader hops a request traverses. You can also specify a *Link_follow_rule-policy* that keeps the request from being forwarded to other traders. Or you can specify that a request only be forwarded if the original trader cannot fulfill it. In general, a trader federation is a good thing. It allows traders to provide larger and more diverse offer spaces to their clients.

Policies, Constraints, and Preferences

The total offer space of a set of linked traders can potentially be very large. The Trader Service lets you prune a search via *policies*, *constraints*, and *preferences*. Here's a quick explanation of what they each do:

■ **Policies** let you define the scope of the search. You specify a policy using a name-value pair. A policy identifies the set of service offers to examine. You specify how the search is to be performed instead of what services to pursue. Each policy partly determines the behavior of the trader. For example, you can set a *hop_count* policy to limit the number of trader links traversed during a search. *Scoping policies* allow you to specify the upper bounds of offers to be searched or returned. You can also use policies to limit a search to a single trader or to specify a starting trader. We previously explained how you can use a policy to exclude dynamic offers. You set default policy values using the trader's **Admin** interface. You can then always override these defaults when you submit an import request.

■ **Constraints** let you specify the search criteria. An importer selects a service type and then specifies a constraint. So what exactly is a constraint? It is a well-formed expression conforming to a constraint language. The Trader Service defines a standard constraint language for interworking between traders. You can specify a different constraint language by including its name between << >> at the start of a constraint expression. For example, you can specify SQL to be your constraint language; you then pass an SQL statement in the constraint string.

■ **Preferences** let you specify the order in which the matching offers are returned. If you do not specify a preference string, the default is *first*—meaning the trader will return the offers in the order it discovers them. Valid preferences are *max*, *min*, *random* and *with constraint*. You can specify a preference language by preceding the string with the name of that language—for example, <<SQL>>.

The bottom line is that you use policies to identify the set of service offers to examine. You then specify the search criteria using the service type and constraint. The search is applied against the set of service offers. The trader will then order the results using your preferences.

The Core Trader Interfaces

Figure 9-3 shows the core trader interfaces. These are the interfaces that provide the trader functions. Here's a brief description of these interfaces:

■ The **Lookup** interface is used by clients and traders to discover and import services. This interface defines a single operation called *query*. You can pass six parameters when you invoke *query*: 1) the *service type* you request, 2) a *constraint* string, 3) a *preference* string, 4) a *policies* string, 5) *how_many* objects to return without an iterator, and 6) the set of *property* name-value pairs you want returned. This last parameter gives you three options: all properties should be returned without naming them, no properties should be returned, or you can explicitly name each property you want returned. The results are returned in an array of offers. Each offer contains an object reference and the name-value pairs for the properties you requested. The method returns an **OfferIterator** object, if the number of offers exceeds the number you specified in the *how_many* parameter.

■ The **OfferIterator** interface lets you navigate a set of service offers returned by the **Lookup** object. You invoke *next_n* to return the next n offers; you specify n to return an array of offers. The *max_left* method returns the number of offers remaining in the iterator. You invoke *destroy* to free the iterator.

■ The **Register** interface is used by service providers to advertise their objects. You invoke *export* to advertise your object via this trader. You must pass an object reference, the service type, and a list of property-value pairs that describe the service you offer. The trader will return an *OfferId* that uniquely references your offer. You invoke *withdraw* to remove a specific service offer. You invoke *withdraw_using_constraint* to remove all offers that meet a certain constraint. You invoke *modify* to change the terms of the contract. You invoke *describe* to obtain the offer description held by the trader. You invoke *resolve* to obtain a **Register** object for a named trader. This operation only works if your trader is linked to this named trader.

■ The **Link** interface allows a trader to use the services of another trader. You invoke *add_link* to add the name as well as the **Lookup** object reference of the target trader. You can also specify a policy for doing remote lookups on this link name. You invoke *remove_link* to break your link with the target trader. You invoke *modify_link* to change the information associated with the link name you provide. You invoke *describe_link* to obtain information on a link. You invoke *list_links* to obtain a list of all the trader name links held by this trader.

■ The **Proxy** interface allows a trader to determine at offer time the object reference that can service an offer. The trader knows about this offer and its type via an OfferId. However, it does not possess the actual object reference. So how does the trader find the object that provides the service? It finds it by invoking a *query* operation on a **Lookup** object held in the OfferId. You create this OfferId by invoking the *export_proxy* method; you must give it the object reference of the target **Lookup**. Yes, this is confusing. This is typically what happens when an object chooses to hide behind other objects. However, proxies can also be very useful. For example, a server pool can publicize its service via the trader and then dynamically assign the offer to a particular server object based on load, availability, and other such factors.

■ The **DynamicPropEval** interface is used to resolve the value of dynamic properties at offer time. Instead of providing a value for a dynamic property, the provider passes a reference to a **DynamicPropEval**. The trader invokes the *evalDP* method to obtain the value for that property before returning an offer. Dynamic properties allow producers to provide very timely information about their services. For example, you can obtain a stock price at the time an offer is made. Of course, you must balance the value of this just-in-time information against the performance impact—each dynamic property resolution costs a remote method invocation.

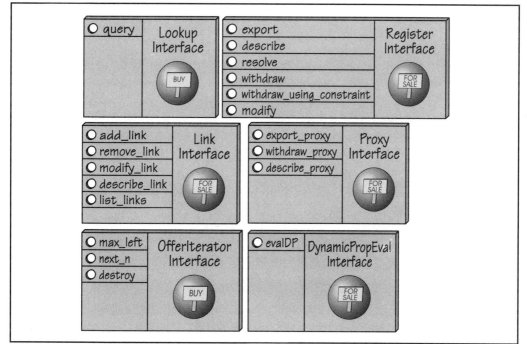

Figure 9-3. The Trader Service: The Core Interfaces.

The Trader Administration Interfaces

A *service type* is really a dynamically composed class. Even an end-user should be able to create one. For example, you can create a *restaurant type* by dynamically associating a set of properties with an object class. You can do this without writing a single line of code. The trader does all the work on your behalf via its **ServiceTypeRepository** interface. This interface is part of the system management services a trader provides; it's a type repository for traders. The other management aid is an **Admin** interface that lets you define your trader's policies. Here's a brief description of the functions these two interfaces provide (see Figure 9-4):

■ The **ServiceTypeRepository** interface allows you to create and manage service types. It manages a service type repository. You invoke the *add_type* method to create a new service type. You must supply the name of the type, its object interface, and its properties. You delete a service from the type repository by invoking *remove_type*. You invoke *list_types* to obtain the names of all the service types in a repository. You invoke *describe_type* to obtain the description of a particular type. Or you can invoke *fully_describe_type* to obtain the description of a type and all its parent interfaces. You invoke *mask_type* to stop advertising a particular type; the type will continue to exist in the repository because other types could be derived from it. You invoke *unmask_type* to bring a masked type back to life.

■ The **Admin** interface lets you configure the system and set its various parameters. Administrators use these parameters to constrain the search.

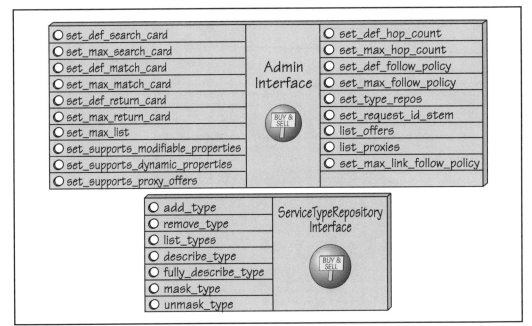

Figure 9-4. The Trader Administration Interfaces.

A Trader Scenario

It's time for a scenario that shows how all these interfaces play together. Figure 9-5 shows a complete trading cycle. Let's walk through the steps:

1. *The server creates a new service type*. In this scenario, the server directly

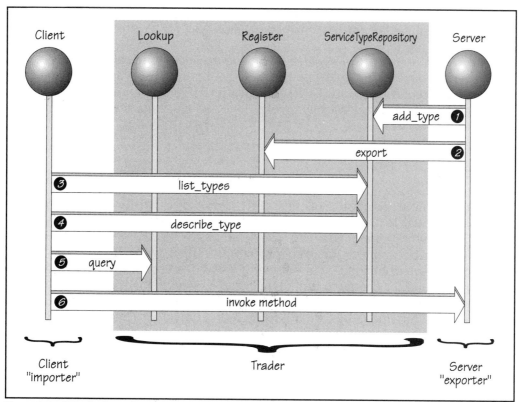

Figure 9-5. A Trader Scenario.

creates a new service type by invoking *add_type* on a trader's **ServiceType-Repository** interface. You should also be able to create a service type with a visual administrative tool.

2. ***The server advertises its service***. The server advertises its service by invoking the *export* method on the trader's **Register** interface. It passes the name of the service type, the object reference that will service the request, and values for the parameters.

3. ***The client obtains a list of service types***. The client invokes *list_types* on the trader's **ServiceTypeRepository** interface to obtain the list of service types.

4. ***The client obtains a type description***. The client invokes *describe_type* on the trader's **ServiceTypeRepository** interface to obtain a particular type's description. This includes the type's parameters and its object interface.

5. ***The client requests a service type***. The client invokes the *query* method on the trader's **Lookup** interface to obtain a list of objects that can provide this service. The client must pass the service type and the parameters it wants

returned. It can narrow the query by specifying constraints and policies. It can also order the results by specifying its preferences.

6. ***The client invokes the service***. The client picks an object that can provide the service and then invokes its methods to obtain the service. The client can invoke the request via static CORBA invocations if it has a stub for this interface. Otherwise, it must dynamically invoke the interface using the CORBA dynamic invocation service.

CONCLUSION

This concludes our discussion of the Trader Service. CORBA's federated traders have the potential to transform the Object Web into a gigantic online bazaar for objects. At a minimum, you can use traders to create very powerful publish-and-subscribe systems for Web objects. Traders will help us create very dynamic ORB environments. They provide a way for server objects to advertise their services and for clients to find them. Traders complement CORBA's dynamic invocation service; together, they provide the ultimate form of late-binding. Traders can grow in all directions by forming loose federations that can easily scale. You can start with a small trader and expand it to intergalactic proportions.[1]

---

[1] In one of our CORBA/Java graduate classes, we assigned a class project to implement a minimalist CORBA Trader Service. Most students were able to complete their project in one semester working in groups of three. They created 3-tier client/server versions of the Trader Service using CORBA, Java, and JDBC. So, we know it can be done. Now, where are the commercial implementations?

Chapter 10

CORBA Services: Transactions and Concurrency

If we could combine the power of objects with the reliability of transactions, we would catapult commercial computing into a new era.

— *John Tibbetts and Barbara Bernstein*

Transactions are essential for building reliable distributed applications. So it should come as no surprise that transactions and distributed objects are getting married. OMG's *Object Transaction Service (OTS)* defines IDL interfaces that let multiple distributed objects on multiple ORBs participate in atomic transactions—even in the presence of catastrophic failure. OTS optionally supports nested transactions. The support of nesting and inter-ORB transactions provides an object foundation for dealing with the complex world of multistep consumer-to-business and business-to-business transactions.

The *Concurrency Control Service* allows objects to coordinate their access to shared resources using locks. An object must obtain an appropriate lock from the service before accessing a shared resource. Each lock is associated with a single resource and a single client. The service defines several lock modes that correspond to different categories of access and multiple levels of granularity. This

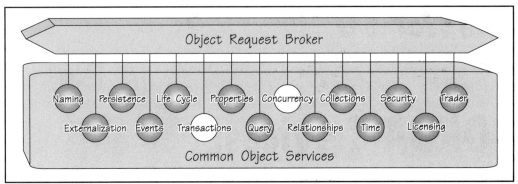

Figure 10-1. CORBA Object Services: Transactions and Concurrency Control.

service complements OTS by letting you obtain and release locks on transactional boundaries. This chapter covers both services (see Figure 10-1).

THE CORBA OBJECT TRANSACTION SERVICE

The *Object Transaction Service (OTS)* is possibly the most important piece of middleware for intergalactic objects. OTS does a superb job of marrying transactions with objects at the ORB level.[1] With OTS, ORBs provide a seamless environment for running mission-critical components. This feature alone gives ORBs a leg up over any competing form of client/server middleware. An ORB becomes the next-generation TP Monitor. In this section, we first go over what makes transactions so important. Then we introduce OTS.

What Is a Transaction?

The idea of distributed systems without transaction management is like a society without contract law. One does not necessarily want the laws, but one does need a way to resolve matters when disputes occur.

— *Jim Gray*

Transactions are more than just business events: They've become an application design philosophy that guarantees robustness in distributed systems. In an ORB

---

[1] OTS is the result of the work of some of the best technologists in the transaction processing business. The key architects were Pete Homan and Ed Cobb, now both with BEA; Tony Storey and Ian Houston from IBM; Graeme Dixon from Transarc; Alan Snyder from SunSoft; Annrai O'Toole from Iona; and Brian Vetter from Tivoli.

environment, a transaction must be managed from its point of origin on the client, across one or more servers, and then back to the originating client. When a transaction ends, all parties involved agree as to whether it succeeded or failed. The transaction is the contract that binds the client to one or more servers. A transaction becomes the fundamental unit of recovery, consistency, and concurrency in a distributed object system. Of course, all participating objects must adhere to the transactional discipline; otherwise, a single faulty object can corrupt an entire system. In an ideal world, all distributed object interactions will be based on transactions.[2]

Transaction models define when a transaction starts, when it ends, and what the appropriate units of recovery are in case of failure. The flat transaction model is the workhorse of the current generation of TP Monitors (and other transactional systems). It is called *flat* because all the work done within a transaction's boundaries is at the same level. The transaction starts with *begin_transaction* and ends with either a *commit_transaction* or *abort_transaction* (see Figure 10-2). It's an all or nothing proposition—there's no way to commit or abort parts of a flat transaction. However, the newer transaction models—for example, *nested transactions*—provide a much finer granularity of control over the different threads that

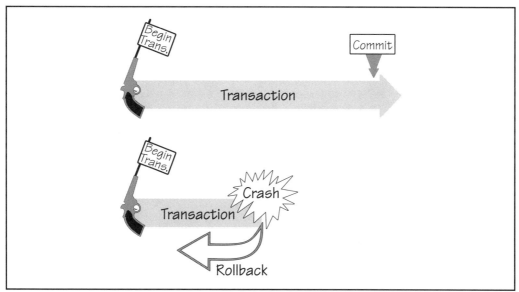

Figure 10-2. The Flat Transaction: An All-Or-Nothing Proposition.

---

[2] If you need more information on transactions, we recommend Jim Gray and Andreas Reuter's **Transaction Processing Concepts and Techniques** (Morgan Kaufmann, 1993). This 1000-page book is the Bible of transaction processing. If you want a lighter introduction, try our book **The Essential Client/Server Survival Guide, Second Edition book** (Wiley, 1996). Our book covers transactions and TP Monitors in less than 100 pages.

constitute a transaction. The newer transaction models are attractive because they have the potential to better mirror their real-world counterparts (see the next Briefing box).

FYI

What's a Nested Transaction?

Briefing

Most of the alternatives to the flat transaction are based on mechanisms that extend the flow of control beyond the linear unit of work. Two of the most obvious ways to extend the flow of control are by chaining units of work in linear sequences of "mini" transactions (the chained transaction or Saga models) or by creating some kind of nested hierarchy of work (the nested transaction).

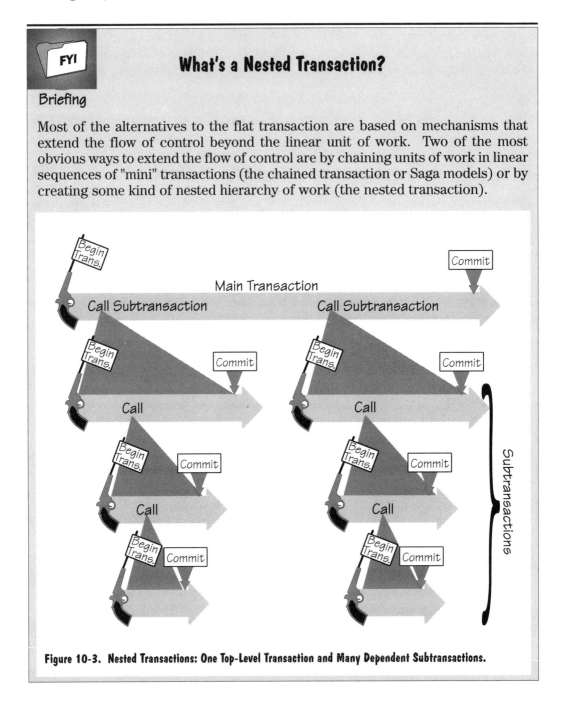

Figure 10-3. Nested Transactions: One Top-Level Transaction and Many Dependent Subtransactions.

Nested transactions provide the ability to define transactions within other transactions. They do this by breaking a transaction into hierarchies of "subtransactions," very much like a program is made up of procedures. The main transaction starts the subtransactions, which behave as dependent transactions. A subtransaction can also start its own subtransactions, making the entire structure very recursive. A subtransaction's effects become permanent after it issues a local commit and all its ancestors commit. If a parent transaction aborts, all its descendent transactions abort—regardless of whether they issued local commits.

Figure 10-3 shows a main transaction that starts nested transactions, which behave as dependent transactions. Each subtransaction can issue a commit or rollback for its designated pieces of work. When a subtransaction commits, its results are only accessible to the parent that spawned it. The main benefit of nesting is that a failure in a subtransaction can be trapped and retried using an alternative method, still allowing the main transaction to succeed. ❏

Object Transaction Service Features

CORBA's OTS provides the following features:

- ***Supports flat and nested transactions.*** All OTS implementations must support flat transactions; nested transaction support is optional. In a nested environment, the flat transaction is the top-level transaction.

- ***Allows both ORB and non-ORB applications to participate in the same transaction.*** OTS lets you interoperate object transactions with procedural transactions that adhere to the X/Open DTP standard.

- ***Supports transactions that span heterogeneous ORBs.*** Objects on multiple ORBs can participate in a single transaction. In addition, a single ORB can support multiple transaction services.

- ***Supports existing IDL interfaces.*** A single interface supports both transactional and non-transactional implementations. To make an object transactional, you use an ordinary interface that inherits from an abstract OTS class. This approach avoids a combination explosion of IDL variants that differ only in their transaction characteristics.

OTS is a well-designed, low-overhead service that should perform at least as well as an X/Open-compliant procedural transaction service.

The Elements of the Object Transaction Service

Figure 10-4 shows the elements of OTS. Objects involved in a transaction can assume one of three roles: *Transactional Clients, Transactional Servers,* or *Recoverable Servers.* Let's go over these roles and see what they each do:

■ *A transactional client* issues a set of method invocations that are bracketed by begin/end transaction demarcations. The calls within the bracket may be for both transactional and non-transactional objects. The ORB intercepts the begin call and directs it to the Transaction Service, which establishes a transaction context associated with the client thread. The client then issues method invocations on remote objects. The ORB implicitly tags the transaction context and propagates it in all subsequent communications among the participants in the transaction. The ORB also gets involved when the client issues a commit or rollback and notifies the Transaction Service. The client is oblivious to all this under-the-covers activity; it simply starts a transaction, issues its method invocations, and commits or rolls back the transaction.

■ *A transactional server* is a collection of one or more objects whose behavior is affected by the transaction but have no recoverable states or resources of their own. The ORB implicitly propagates the transaction's context whenever these objects call a recoverable resource. A transactional server does not participate in the completion of the transaction, but it can force the transaction to be rolled back.

■ *A recoverable server* is a collection of one or more objects whose data (or state) is affected by committing or rolling back a transaction. *Recoverable objects* are transactional objects with resources to protect. Examples of recoverable resources are transactional files, queues, or databases. Recoverable objects use *register_resource* method invocations to tell the Transaction Service that a recoverable resource has just joined the transaction whose context was propagated in the client call. In addition, recoverable objects provide methods that are used by a transaction coordinator (the *coordinator* is the transaction service) to orchestrate an ORB-mediated, two-phase commit protocol.

OTS is seamlessly integrated with the ORB mechanisms. It relies on the ORB to automatically propagate the transaction context. Notice that the scope of a transaction is defined by a *transaction context* that is shared by the participant objects. The transaction context is a pseudo-object that's maintained by the ORB for each ORB-aware thread. The context is null when there is no transaction associated with a thread. The transaction service manages and propagates the transaction context with help from the ORB.

OTS provides "IDL-ized" interfaces for the objects that make up the transaction service. So it is possible for clients and transactional objects to get more intimately involved in the details of the transaction propagation via explicit method invocations. However, most transactions will depend on the ORB to transparently do all the work using its built-in facilities. Fewer interventions means better performance.

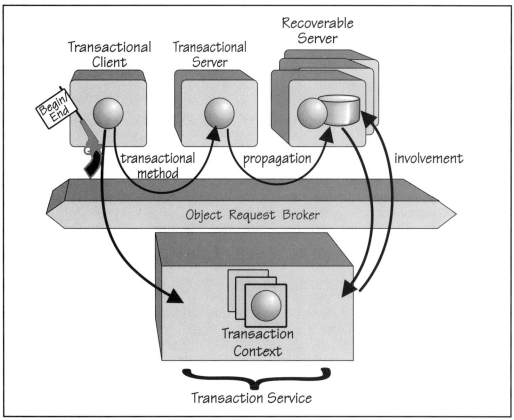

Figure 10-4. Object Transaction Service: Meet the Players.

The OTS Interfaces

Figure 10-5 shows the four key interfaces of OTS; we left out the minor ones. The following is a brief description of what each of these interfaces do:

■ **Current** defines a CORBA pseudo-object that makes it easy for clients to use OTS. Clients invoke *begin* and *commit* to start and end a transaction. The ORB will transparently propagate the context of the pseudo-object to the transaction service and to all participants in the transaction. The context contains an ID that uniquely identifies the transaction; it also contains status information. The client can invoke *rollback* to abort the transaction. It can *suspend* the transaction to stop propagating the context with each message; it can *resume* it when it wants the context to be propagated. *Get_control* returns a **Control** object that you can use to directly interact with the transaction service—a recoverable server typically invokes this method to obtain a reference to its transaction coordinator. A top-level transaction invokes *set_timeout* to define maximum elapsed time (in seconds) for its subtransactions to complete before it aborts them.

■ **Coordinator** is implemented by the transaction service. Recoverable objects use it to coordinate their participation in a transaction with the OTS. A server invokes *register_resource* to participate in a transaction. If it supports nested transactions, it instead invokes *register_subtran_aware*. It invokes *create_subtransaction* to create a nested transaction that's a child of the current transaction. It invokes *rollback_only* to abort the entire transaction. The *get_* and *is_* operations are useful to servers that need to explicitly control their participation in a transaction. The *hash_* operations return a handle to the current transaction. Before invoking *register_resource*, servers use the hashed value to quickly find out if the current resource is already registered.

■ **Resource** is implemented by a recoverable server object to participate in a *two-phase* commit protocol. OTS uses the two-phase commit protocol to coordinate a transaction's commit or abort across multiple server objects so that they either all fail or all succeed. To do this, OTS centralizes the decision to commit but gives each participant the right of veto. It's like a Christian wedding: You're given one last chance to back out of the transaction when you're at the altar. If none of the parties object, the marriage takes place.

In the first phase of a commit, OTS invokes *prepare* on all the participant resource objects. Each resource object returns in a parameter a "vote" value that is either vote_commit, vote_rollback, or vote_readonly. Based on the vote's outcome (everyone has veto power), the transaction service either issues *commit* or *rollback*. It can also issue a *forget* to a resource object that's fuzzy about its outcome. If the coordinator has only a single registered resource, it avoids the two-phase commit altogether and invokes *commit_one_phase* instead.

■ **SubtransactionAwareResource** is implemented by a recoverable server object with nested transaction behavior. Notice that this interface is derived from the **Resource** interface. It adds two new methods *commit_subtransaction* and *rollback_subtransaction*. These methods are invoked when subtransactions complete. Subtransaction aware server objects must first register with the **Coordinator** object by invoking *register_subtran_aware*.

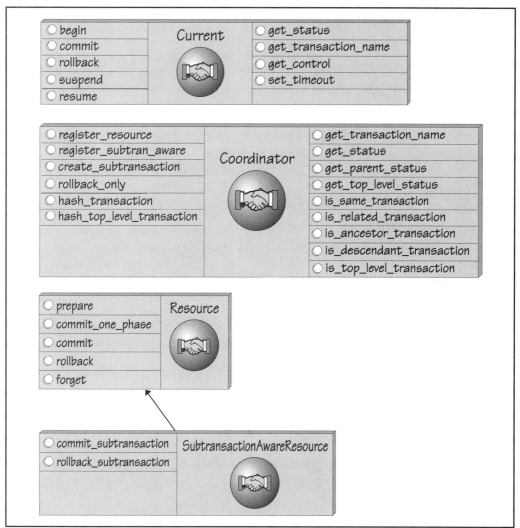

Figure 10-5. Object Transaction Service: The Key Interfaces.

You should also be aware of the existence of a **TransactionalObject** interface. This is an abstract class that defines no operations. What is it good for? It's actually a very important class. It serves as a marker objects use to indicate that they're transactional. To make your object transactional you simply inherit from the **TransactionalObject** class. The ORB will then propagate the transaction context associated with a client's thread whenever the client invokes any method on your object. Note that the ORB passes this context in a special field (the context field) that is totally transparent as far you're concerned. It's something ORBs do implicitly.

An Object Transaction Scenario

Are you getting overwhelmed with all these interfaces? As you know by now, our tradition in this book is to explain how interfaces are really used with an annotated scenario (too bad we can't animate a book). This next scenario will be fun. It's like going to a movie and seeing us squirm through these interface patterns. You get to sit back, relax, and munch on popcorn. Just look at the figure and the annotated text that comes with it. Then follow the numbers and read the explanations. Warning: We only do scenarios after we introduce a particularly heavy dose of interfaces; you don't get them all the time—they're hard work!

Figure 10-6 shows a scenario of a client doing a debit against one server object and a credit against another one. The example is "get a $100,000 dollars out of Jeri's account in Bank A and put it in your account in Bank B." You don't want this to fail, do you? The objects representing Bank A and Bank B are recoverable server objects that multiply inherit from the **Resource** class and the **TransactionalObject** abstract class (remember, this is the indicator that does nothing). We also show two transaction service objects that are instances of the **Current** and **Coordinator** classes. The client initiates this transaction across the two servers and issues a *commit* when it's done. Hopefully the money will get tucked away safely in your account. Here's the explanation that goes along with the numbers in the picture:

1. ***Client begins transaction***. The client invokes *begin* on the **Current** pseudo-object. The ORB passes this information to the transaction service that maintains a **Current** object for each active transaction.

2. ***Client makes a debit on Bank A's object***. The client invokes a *debit* method on an object in Bank A. This object implements the logic of the transaction (something you write) but it also inherits its behavior from the OTS classes **Resource** and **TransactionalObject**. So we're dealing with a recoverable resource object.

3. ***Bank A's recoverable object registers its resource.*** The recoverable server object first invokes the method *get_control* on the **Current** object (the shorthand notation is *Current::get_control*) to obtain a reference to the **Coordinator** object. Then it invokes *Coordinator::register_resource* to register with the coordinator object for this transaction. The coordinator keeps track of all the participants.

4. ***Client makes a credit on Bank B's object***. The client invokes a *credit* method on an object in Bank B. This object implements the logic of the transaction (again, something you write) but also inherits its behavior from the OTS classes **Resource** and **TransactionalObject**. So we're dealing with a recoverable resource object.

5. ***Bank B's recoverable object registers its resource.*** It's a repeat of what Bank A's server just did.

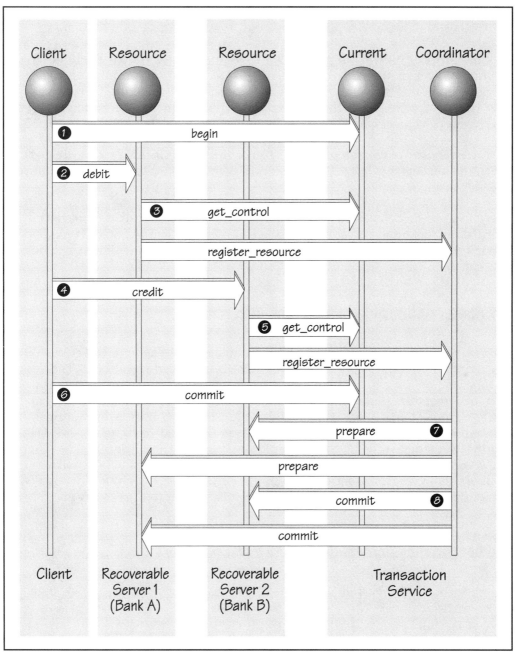

Figure 10-6. Object Transaction Service: A Two-Phase Commit Scenario.

6. **Client issues a commit.** The client invokes the method *Current::commit*. The ORB informs the transaction service that the transaction has ended.

7. **Coordinator performs phase 1 of two-phase commit.** The coordinator invokes each participant's *prepare* method to get a vote from all the participants on whether this transaction should be committed for posterity (i.e., you get your $100,000). Let's give this scenario a happy ending by assuming everyone returns a "vote_commit."

8. **Coordinator performs phase 2 of two-phase commit.** The coordinator tells all the participants to *commit*. You now have $100,000 more to spend in your bank account.

Are you all feeling richer, or just tired? It would have been better for Jeri if the coordinator had issued a rollback instead of a commit. She could have kept her $100,000. Luckily, our scenarios are only fiction. This happy ending concludes our OTS story.

THE CORBA CONCURRENCY CONTROL SERVICE

The *Concurrency Control Service* provides interfaces to acquire and release locks that let multiple clients coordinate their access to shared resources. The service does not define a *resource*. For example, an object could be a resource; it would then implement the Concurrency Control Service to let its clients access it concurrently. The Concurrency Control Service supports both transactional and non-transactional modes of operation. It was designed to be used with OTS to coordinate the activities of concurrent transactions. The design for the Concurrency Control Service originated from Transarc—a company that specializes in TP Monitors for nested transactions. Consequently, the service is tightly coupled to transactional locks and is even designed to work with nested transactions.

The Concurrency Control Service and Transactions

The client of the Concurrency Control Service can choose to acquire locks in one of two ways:

- **On behalf of a transaction**. In this case, the Transaction Service drives the release of locks as the transaction commits or aborts. Typically, a transaction will retain all its locks until it completes.

- **On behalf of a non-transactional client.** In this case, the responsibility for releasing locks lies with the client.

The Concurrency Control Service will ensure that both transactional and non-transactional clients serially access a resource. It doesn't matter to the service whether a lock was acquired by a transactional or non-transactional client. A lock is, after all, a lock.

Locks

A *lock* is a token that lets a client access a particular resource. The role of the Concurrency Service service is to prevent multiple clients from simultaneously owning locks to the same resource if their activities conflict. The service defines several lock modes that correspond to different categories of access—including *read*, *write*, *intention read*, *intention write*, and *upgrade*. An *upgrade* lock is a *read* lock that conflicts with itself. You use it to prevent deadlocks. For example, a deadlock occurs when multiple clients have *read* locks to a resource, and one of these clients requests a *write* lock. If, however, each client requests an *upgrade* lock followed by a *write* lock, the deadlock will not occur.

Locksets

The Concurrency Control Service does not define the granularity of resources that are locked. However, it defines a *lockset*, which is a collection of locks associated with a single resource. You must associate a lockset with each protected resource. For example, if an object is a resource, then it must internally create a lockset and maintain it. Locks are acquired on locksets. You can manage related locksets as a group.

The Concurrency Control Service defines a *lock coordinator* that manages the release of related locksets. For example, the coordinator can free all locks associated with a particular transaction when the transaction commits. In addition, the coordinator may manage the release of locks on behalf of a group of related transactions—for example, nested transactions.

Nested Transactions and Locking

The general rule is that transactions must not be able to observe partial effects of other transactions that might later abort. However, the Concurrency Control Service relaxes this rule for nested transactions. It will tolerate a certain level of *lock conflicts* within a nested transaction family. It can do this because nesting creates abort dependencies among parent/child transactions. If the parent aborts, all its subtransactions also abort. As a result, it doesn't matter if the child observes the partial effects of a parent transaction that may later abort because the child will also abort.

When a nested transaction requests a lock that is held by its parent, it becomes the new owner of the lock. When a nested transaction commits (or aborts), the Concurrency Control Service will automatically transfer ownership of all its locks to the parent transaction. A child transaction can acquire a lock on a resource locked by its parent; it can then drop that lock without causing its parent to lose its lock.

The Concurrency Control Interfaces

Figure 10-7 shows the four key interfaces that make up the Concurrency Control Service. The following is a very brief description of what each of these interfaces do:

- **LocksetFactory** lets you create locksets. You invoke *create* to create a regular lockset or *create_transactional* to create a transactional lockset. To create new locksets that are related to existing locksets, you either invoke *create_related* or *create_transactional_related*. When locksets are "related," they release their locks together.

- **Lockset** lets you acquire or release locks. You invoke *lock* to acquire a lock or block until it's free. If you don't want to block waiting, use *try_lock* instead; it returns control immediately if the lock is not available. You invoke *unlock* to release a lock. You invoke *change_mode* to change the mode on an individual lock. Finally, *get_coordinator* returns a lock coordinator object.

- **TransactionalLockset** supports the same methods as **Lockset**. The difference is that you must now pass a parameter that identifies your transaction ID. This interface is only used by transactional objects that need to pass their transaction ID explicitly. In contrast, the **Lockset** interface implicitly uses the transaction context associated with the caller's thread. As a result, **Lockset** can support implicit transactional clients as well non-transactional clients (their transaction context is null).

- **LockCoordinator** defines a single method called *drop_locks*. OTS invokes this method to release all locks held by a transaction when it commits or aborts.

This concludes the section on the Concurrency Control Service. As you can see, it's a straightforward locking system with built-in transactional support.

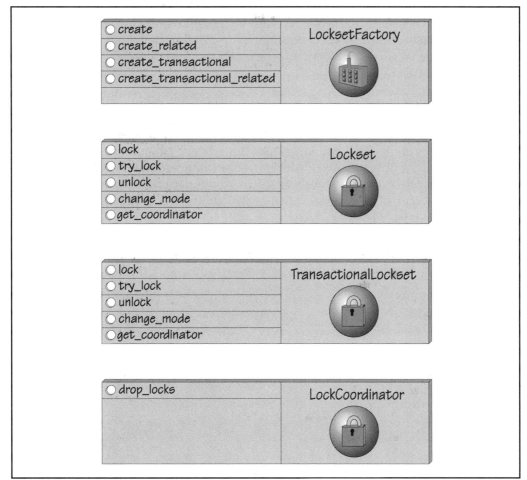

Figure 10-7. Concurrency Control Service: The Interfaces.

CONCLUSION

The marriage of ORB and TP Monitor technologies will create a new infrastructure that exploits the strengths of TP Monitors while providing a robust application development environment based on reusable objects. It's a truly superior client/server alternative.

— *Edward E. Cobb, BEA*

OK, we've covered two more services—the tally is now six down and nine more to go. But OTS was a particularly important service. As Ed Cobb notes, the marriage of objects and transactions can lead to some very potent client/server middleware.

OTS is a service that can integrate other services. For example, the Concurrency Control Service releases locks on transaction boundaries. The Persistent Object Service could also use transaction boundaries to commit data changes in memory to a non-volatile store. So transactions become a generic unit of resource allocation.

In addition to being important at the system level, OTS will redefine the way we build our client/server middleware. For starters it will encourage developers to use transactions pervasively. Transactions are now part of the ORB. As a result, most objects that live on the ORB will be transactional. The ubiquitous use of transactions on the ORB will result in TP Monitors morphing into ORBs (or vice versa). This means that ORBs may very well be the next generation TP Monitor. What else would you expect from a service that was designed from scratch by the best TP Monitor people in the business?

Chapter 11

CORBA Services: Object Security

Security is a pervasive requirement that affects nearly every aspect of distributed object computing. In the middle of 1996, the OMG finally released its long-awaited *Security Service*. After two years in gestation, this service defines a comprehensive security framework. It addresses all aspects of distributed object security—from the security needs of small local systems to those of large intergalactic enterprises. You can use CORBA security within a local enterprise as well as across IIOP Internets.

The security system was designed to be totally unobtrusive to application developers. In theory, your objects should be able to run on a secure ORB without any involvement on your part. The ORB provides security for objects that know nothing of security and have no security interfaces. This makes it easy to port objects across environments that support different security mechanisms. However, System Administrators are not as lucky. They must intimately understand the ORB's security policies to manage it.

In this chapter, we cover the CORBA Security Service (see Figure 11-1). We start with an overview of the security needs of distributed objects. To put it mildly, distributed objects introduce new security "challenges" over and above those of intergalactic client/server systems. It's almost impossible to secure a distributed object environment without a secure ORB. So what is a secure ORB? It's an ORB

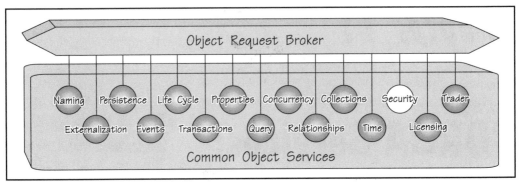

Figure 11-1. CORBA Object Services: Security.

that implements the CORBA Security Service, of course. So we cover the features of the CORBA Security Service. Then we go over its key interfaces. We conclude with object interaction scenarios that show you how the pieces play together.

ARE DISTRIBUTED OBJECTS LESS SECURE?

Distributed objects face all the security problems of traditional client/server systems—and more. The client/server environment introduces new security threats beyond those found in traditional time-shared systems. In a client/server system, you can't trust any of the client operating systems on the network to protect the server's resources from unauthorized access. And even if the client machines were totally secure, the network itself is highly accessible. You can never trust information in transit. Sniffer devices can easily record traffic between machines, and they can introduce forgeries and Trojan horses into the system. This means the servers must find new ways to protect themselves without creating a fortress mentality that upsets users. In addition to these threats, distributed objects must also be concerned with the following added complications:

■ **Distributed objects can play both client and server roles**. In a traditional client/server architecture, it is clear who is a client and who is a server. Typically, you can trust servers, but not clients. For example, a client trusts its database server, but the reverse is not true. In distributed object systems, you cannot clearly distinguish between clients and servers. These are just alternate roles that a single object can play.

■ **Distributed objects evolve continually**. When you interact with an object, you're only seeing the tip of the iceberg. You may be seeing a "facade" object that delegates parts of its implementation to other objects; these delegates may be dynamically composed at run time. Also, because of subclassing, the implementations of an object may change over time. The original programmer neither knows nor cares about the changes.

■ ***Distributed objects interactions are not well understood***. Because of encapsulation, you cannot fully understand all the interactions that take place between the objects you invoke. There is too much "behind the scenes" activity.

■ ***Distributed object interactions are less predictable***. Because distributed objects are more flexible and granular than other forms of client/server systems, they may interact in more ad hoc ways. This is a strength of the distributed object model, but it's also a security risk.

■ ***Distributed objects are polymorphic***. Objects are flexible; it is easy to replace one object on the ORB with another that abides by the same interfaces. This makes it a dream situation for Trojan horses; they can impersonate legitimate objects and thus cause all kinds of havoc.

■ ***Distributed objects can scale without limit***. Because every object can be a server, we may end up with millions of servers on the ORB. How do we manage access rights for millions of servers?

■ ***Distributed objects are very dynamic***. A distributed object environment is inherently anarchistic. Objects come and go. They get created dynamically and self-destruct when they're no longer being used. This dynamism is, of course, a great strength of objects, but it could also be a security nightmare.

To maintain a single system illusion, every trusted user (and object) must be given transparent access to all other objects. How is this done when every PC poses a potential threat to network security? Will system administrators be condemned to spend their working lives granting access level rights to objects—one at a time—for each individual object on each server across the enterprise?

The good news is that many of these problems can be solved by moving the security implementation into the CORBA ORB itself. The ORB must manage security for a range of systems from trusted domains (within a single process or machine) to intergalactic inter-ORB situations. Components that are not responsible for enforcing their own security are easier to develop, administer, and port across environments. In addition, moving security inside the ORB can minimize the performance overhead.

CORBA SECURITY: THE KEY FEATURES

Figure 11-2 shows the model for a secure CORBA ORB. In this model, all object invocations are mediated by the appropriate security functions to enforce policies such as access control. These functions are built into the ORB and cannot be tampered with. Most objects will be unaware of the security policy or how it is enforced by the ORB. A security-aware object can influence the security policy an ORB enforces on its behalf.

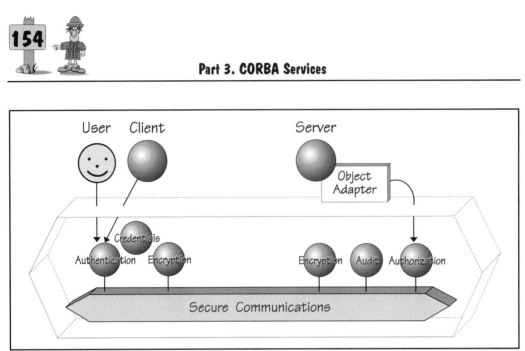

Figure 11-2. CORBA Security Is Built Into the ORB.

The CORBA Security Service allows an ORB to provide up to B2 security for distributed objects. B2 is near the high end of the government security profiles defined in the so-called "Orange Book." To comply with these stringent security requirements on a network, all clients must provide an authenticated user ID, all resources must be protected by access control lists, audit trails must be provided, and access rights must not be passed to other users that reuse the same items.

The CORBA specification also allows ORB vendors to provide systems with lower levels of security, when needed. For example, you may have to downgrade the security of an ORB to comply with the U.S. export laws. Finally, CORBA defines some standard security profiles for out-of-the-box interoperation between secure IIOP ORBs.

In this section, we cover the security mechanisms and issues an ORB must deal with—including authentication, authorization, privilege delegation, non-repudiation, auditing, encryption, and secure federations (or trust domains). We also look at some of the system administration issues.

Authentication: Are You Who You Claim to Be?

An active entity must first establish its identity on a secure ORB. A client needs an identity to access other objects. An active entity is either a *principal* or a client acting on behalf of a principal. So what's a principal? It's a human user or object that is authenticated once by the ORB and given a set of *credentials*—including one or more roles, privileges, and an authenticated ID. A principal only has to log on once to obtain its security clearance, regardless of the number of objects it uses.

Authentication results in a unique authenticated ID that cannot be changed by an object; only the authentication server can change it. The authenticated client can access any server object from anywhere—including hotel rooms, offices, homes, and cellular phones—using a single sign-on. How's that done? With ORB-propagated context security. You simply log on once, get authenticated, and then obtain a set of security tickets (also called *tokens*) for the objects with which you want to communicate. All this activity is conducted "under-the-covers" by the ORB's security mechanisms. No password is stored in the login script on the client, and no telephone callbacks are required.

An authenticated ID is automatically propagated by a secure CORBA ORB; it's part of a caller's context. The authenticated ID serves the following purposes: 1) makes clients (or users) accountable for their actions, 2) lets a server determine which resources a user can access, 3) uniquely identifies the originator of a message, 4) helps service providers determine who to charge for the use of a service, and 5) serves as a *privilege* that can be delegated by a server to its helper objects.

Figure 11-3 shows what goes on under-the-covers in an authenticated client/server interaction. In this scenario, the principal has not yet been authenticated. Here's a step-by-step description:

1. ***Authenticate the principal.*** The *User Sponsor* is a piece of code that interacts with a user to obtain an ID and password. It passes this information to the CORBA Security **PrincipalAuthenticator** object by invoking *authenticate*.

2. ***Create the Credentials object.*** The **PrincipalAuthenticator** returns an authenticated **Credentials** object for this principal. This object serves as the principal's security ticket. It contains attributes such as the principal's authenticated ID and privileges.

3. ***Set the credentials of the execution environment.*** The User Sponsor invokes *set_credentials* to pass its **Credentials** to the **Current** pseudo-object. Note that this is the same **Current** object that is used by the Object Transaction Service. The **Current** object represents the current execution context in a client/server interaction. In this case, **Current** provides access to security information—it holds a reference to the **Credentials** associated with the execution environment.[1]

4. ***The client invokes a secure method on the server.*** On the surface, a secure method invocation is like any other method invocation. However, underneath the surface, the Security Service mediates the client/server interaction based on

---

[1] Credentials for security-unaware applications can be generated when the ORB is initialized. In this case, the user must be authenticated outside the object system. This lets an application propagate its credentials with no involvement on its part.

a security policy. The Security Service obtains its security information from the **Current** object.

5. ***The server executes the secure method.*** A security-aware server can invoke the *get_attributes* method on its local **Current** object to obtain information about the incoming client call. The method returns the identity and privileges of the principal that issued the call on the client side. The server can use the information to make its access decisions.

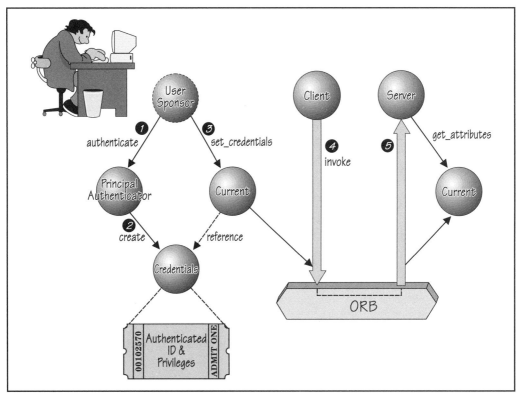

Figure 11-3. Object Security: How CORBA Propagates Authenticated Contexts.

The CORBA Security Service works with different authenticating mechanisms—for example, Kerberos, public keys, and smart cards. The *authenticate* method can work with any system that can help it generate an authenticated **Credentials** object.

Privilege Delegation: Whose Credentials Are These Anyway?

In a distributed object system, the object a client calls to perform an operation may in turn call other objects to perform the operation. This may result in a chain of interobject calls (see Figure 11-4). So how does an ORB enforce an access policy in this world of chained calls? And, which client credentials does the target use to control access? The CORBA Security Service requires that an access decision be made at each point in the chain.

A security-aware object can explicitly control the delegation of its privileges using the security interfaces that we describe later in this chapter. In addition, administrators can specify default delegation policies. The ORBs use these policies to determine which credentials to propagate at each point in an object chain.

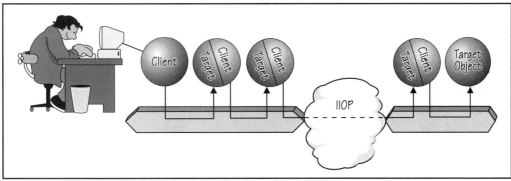

Figure 11-4. Object Call Chaining.

Figure 11-5 shows the *privilege delegation schemes* a client (or intermediary) uses to propagate its privileges:

■ ***No delegation*** means that the intermediary cannot use the client's privileges to invoke the next object in the chain. The intermediary uses the client's credentials to make its own access control decisions. Then, depending on the outcome, it may use its own credentials to invoke the next object in the chain.

■ ***Simple delegation*** means that the intermediary assumes the client's privileges. The intermediary then *impersonates* the client in its dealings with target objects. The intermediary can also delegate the client's credentials to others.

■ ***Composite delegation*** means that the intermediary can subsume the client's privileges as well as its own when dealing with target objects. The intermediate can keep the client's credentials separate or it can combine them with its own. In the latter case, the target won't be able to tell which privileges come from which principal.

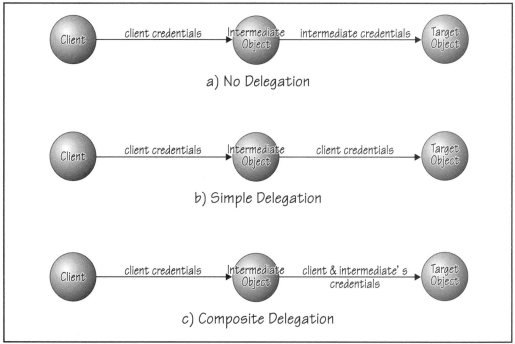

Figure 11-5. Privilege Delegation Schemes.

A client can further control the delegation of its credentials by specifying a time window during which the delegated privileges are valid. The privileges will automatically expire outside this time interval. The client can also specify the maximum number of method invocations for which a delegated credential is valid.

Authorization: Are You Allowed to Use This Resource?

Once clients are authenticated, the server objects are responsible for verifying which operations the clients are permitted to perform on the information they try to access—for example, a payroll server may control access to salary data on a per-individual basis. Servers use *Access Control Lists (ACLs)* and a derivation called *Capability Lists* to control user access. ACLs can be associated with any computer resource. They contain the list of names—as well as group names and roles—of principals and the type of operations they are permitted to perform on each resource. You should be able to have multiple ACL policies in an ORB. The ORB can implement some of the policies; the server object can implement the others.

In a distributed object system, an object is typically the unit of access control. However, you may also want to control access at a lower level of granularity by making each method of an object a controlled resource. To make it easier on the administrator, you may want less granularity, and you may want to provide controls on collections of objects instead of individual objects or methods. In addition, it requires a lot more overhead to run an access control check on every method for every object. So you can cut down the explosion of objects and subjects in your access control lists by specifying coarser levels of security controls. It's a classic trade-off.

The CORBA access model is based on a *trusted ORB* model. You must trust that your ORB will enforce the access policy on a server resource. The access policy determines whether the ORB will invoke a method on the target object. The ORB determines if *this* client—on behalf of *this* principal—can do *this* operation on *this* object. The ORB bases its access decision on the following:

- ■ *The current privileges of the caller.* The caller's privileges are defined by its credentials—including its delegated credentials. These privileges may include: 1) the principal's *access identity*; 2) one or more *roles* that are typically related to the principal's job functions—for example, manager; 3) one or more *group* affiliations—for example, the engineering department; 4) a *security clearance*; and 5) other privileges that an enterprise may use to control access.

- ■ *Any controls that are applied to the privileges.* The ORB must check against controls that limit the life of a privilege. Examples of these controls are the time interval for which a privilege is valid or the number of invocations that are permitted.

- ■ *The operation to be invoked.* The Security Service typically enforces access controls for a set of operations instead of individual operations. For example, it can check whether an operation belongs to an interface or an object *domain*. An object is typically assigned to a security administration domain when it is first created.

- ■ *The access policies of the target object*. These are typically ACLs that identify what category of users can access what category of objects (see Figure 11-6). In the figure, we associate the control attributes with a set of operations on an object (or object domain) instead of with each operation. So a principal with a specified role may have *rights* to invoke a specific set of operations. Of course, you can use ACLs to enforce more granular levels of control. For example, you could create an ACL that controls the access to each method on each object for every principal on your ORB. However, you should be warned that this type of granular control can quickly turn into an administrative nightmare.

The CORBA Security Service defines a standard **AccessDecision** interface that the ORB uses for all its object invocation access decisions. You can manage the ORB's access control policies via the administrative interfaces that we describe later in this chapter.

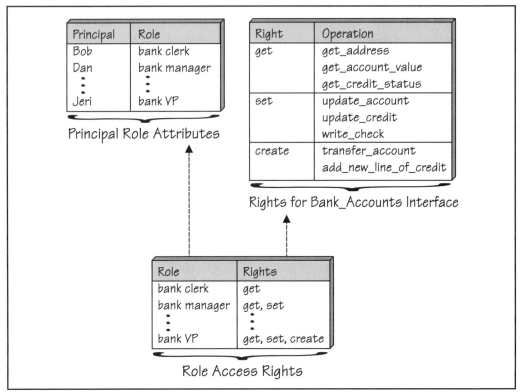

Figure 11-6. Access Control Lists.

Audit Trails: Where Have You Been?

Audit services allow system managers to monitor ORB events. For example, you can monitor attempted logons. Or, you can monitor which objects or services are used. Audit services are a piece of the arsenal needed by system managers to detect intruders in their own organizations. You should be able to monitor all the network activity associated with a suspect client workstation (or principal). Knowing an audit trail exists usually discourages insiders from tampering with servers using their own logon, but they can do it under somebody else's logon.

The CORBA Security Service defines a set of interfaces that allow security-aware objects to log system and application events based on the *audit policies* that you define. *System events* include the authentication of principals, updating privileges, and failed object invocations. *Application events* are specific to the security needs of your application. For example, an application that accepts credit card payments could maintain an audit log of each payment.

The CORBA Security Service lets you select events to be audited by: 1) object or object type, 2) operation, 3) time, 4) principal attributes such as audit-id or role, and 5) success or failure of an operation. For example, you could audit all the after-midnight *update_account* method invocations on **Bank_Account** objects by a bank VP named Jeri.

If you're not careful, your audit logs can quickly explode in size. To help you keep things under control, CORBA defines a set of administrative interfaces that let you restrict the types of events you may want to audit. Events will be audited based on *audit policies* you specify. You can also specify the conditions that will trigger an audit—for example, after midnight. System audit policies are automatically enforced by the ORB for all applications—including the ones that are not security-aware.

Security-aware applications use the **AuditChannel** interface to record their events. They use the **AuditDecision** interface to decide if an audit is needed. And they use the **AuditPolicy** interface to manage audit policies. These interfaces are specified by the CORBA Security Service. We cover them later in this chapter.

Non-Repudiation: Can You Prove It in Court?

An ORB must be able to provide irrefutable evidence that an action took place. For example, the ORB must be able to prove that a method invocation was really originated by you and only you. The ORB must also be able to prove that the recipient got your method invocation (or data). *Non-repudiation* has become a hot topic in electronic commerce circles. It means providing irrefutable evidence that two parties were involved in a client/server interaction. Neither party should be able to deny this evidence in a court of law.

To support non-repudiation, an ORB must provide safeguards that protect all parties from false claims that data was tampered with or not sent or received. In other words, the ORB must provide the electronic equivalent of a sealed envelope. The information must be protected against corruption or replay. To do this, the ORB must provide the sender with proof of delivery and the receiver with proof of a sender's identity. You don't want the data in an electronic fund transfer to be intercepted and rerouted from your account to someone else's.

The CORBA Security Service defines a *non-repudiation framework* and a set of non-repudiation interfaces. The idea is to make principals totally accountable for their actions by providing irrefutable evidence about a claimed event or action. The framework is based on the ISO non-repudiation model (see Figure 11-7). It defines the following non-repudiation services:

■ *Evidence of message creation* proves that the originator created the message. The sender must create a *proof-of-origin* certificate using the non-repudiation service. It then sends the certificate along with the message using the non-repudiation *delivery authority* service. The receiver stores this evidence using the non-repudiation *storage* service. In the case of a dispute, it can later retrieve this evidence.

- ■ ***Evidence of message receipt*** proves that the message was delivered. The recipient must create and send a *proof-of-receipt* certificate using the non-repudiation delivery authority service. The sender receives this evidence and stores it using the non-repudiation storage service; it can later retrieve it if there is a dispute.

- ■ ***An action timestamp*** is generated by the non-repudiation service as part of the evidence. It records the date and time when an event or action took place.

- ■ ***The evidence long-term storage facility*** is used to store the certificates of origin and receipt. If there is a dispute, the adjudicator uses this facility to retrieve the evidence.

- ■ ***The adjudicator*** is used to settle disputes based on the stored evidence.

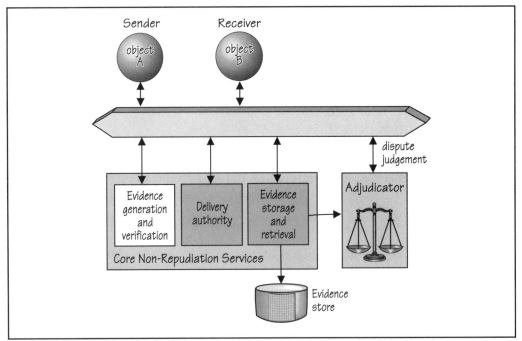

Figure 11-7. The Non-Repudiation Framework.

The CORBA Security Specification defines an interface called **NRCredentials** (see white area in Figure 11-7) that you can use to generate and verify evidence certificates and then relate them to a method invocation. The service also specifies an **NRPolicy** interface that lets you define and manage non-repudiation policies (see Figure 11-8). So what happened to the rest of the non-repudiation functions? For now, they're left as an exercise for the vendors. In our book, this means "buyer beware."

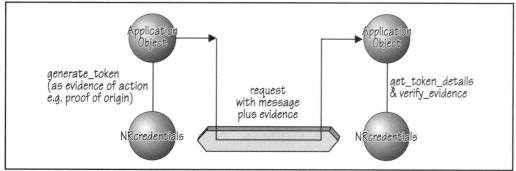

Figure 11-8. Non-Repudiation: What CORBA Defined.

Non-Tampering and Encryption

CORBA ORBs can provide at least two mechanisms for dealing with the non-tampering issue: 1) *Encryption* allows two principals to hold a secure communication, and 2) *Cryptographic checksums*—a less extreme solution—ensures that data is not modified as it passes through the network. Messages are protected according to the *quality of protection* you specify. The request and response may be protected differently. Some systems may provide protection below the ORB message layer—for example, using the *Secure Socket Layer (SSL)* or even more physical means. The ORB does not provide its own message protection when it operates on a secure transport layer.

The CORBA Security Service defines replaceable subsystems that allow ORBs to use standard industry encryption and electronic signature mechanisms such as RSA's public/private keys, OSF's Kerberos, Internet's SSL, NetWare 4.X, and NIS+. Note that the underlying cryptography mechanism is not visible outside the security service. The CORBA Security specification does not define any cryptographic interfaces; it happens transparently under-the-covers.

Security Domains

ORB-based security must also deal with the following issues: inter-ORB security, federated security domains, trusted domains, protection boundaries, and coexistence with existing standards and security mechanisms. An ORB must also be able to interoperate with systems that do not provide security. And, of course, the ORB must deal with the issue of how to manage and administer the security policies.

According to CORBA, "a *security domain* is a set of objects to which a security policy applies for a set of security-related activities administered by a *security authority*." The objects belong to a domain. *Policies* are the rules and criteria that constrain the objects' activity to make the domain secure. The security policies define the rules for access control, authentication, privilege delegation, non-repudiation, and auditability. Security policies are administered at the domain level. So a domain is also a unit of security administration (see Figure 11-9). Security policies let you apply security rules on security-unaware objects without requiring changes to their code.

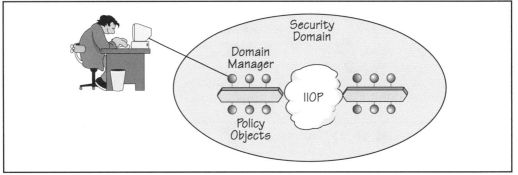

Figure 11-9. A CORBA Security Domain.

A domain can have *subdomains* that reflect organizational subdivisions. For example, a department could specify its own security policies within the umbrella of an enterprise-wide security scheme. In addition to subdomains, you can also have loose *federations of security domains* (see Figure 11-10).

In a federation, each domain retains most of its authority but agrees to give members of other domains limited rights. A federation must also be able to handle policy differences across domains. For example, it must be able to map roles across domains.

A *trusted domain* is formed by objects that trust one another. Objects in a trusted domain can relax their security requirements. This removes the extra overhead that security-checking mechanisms introduce. Consequently, you get better performance.

How do objects interoperate across security domains? The Security Specification defines how security information is passed inside an *Interoperable Object Reference (IOR)*. An IOR specifies both the security an object requires and the mechanisms it supports. The CORBA Security Service also specifies how the *security context* is transmitted inside IIOP messages. It is similar to the way OTS propagates the transaction context. The security context—like the transaction context—is implicitly passed inside an IIOP message. A server can always invoke operations on

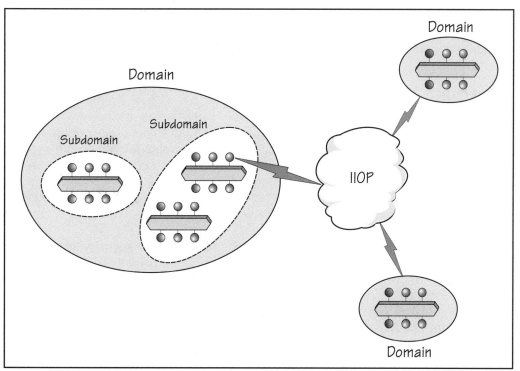

Figure 11-10. CORBA Security: Subdomains and Federated Domains.

its **Current** pseudo-object to obtain the security context associated with a client invocation.

To interoperate across security domains, objects must use the same security technology. For example, if you use a public key to encode a message, then the recipient must possess the corresponding private key. The CORBA Security interfaces were designed to be implemented using a wide variety of security mechanisms. So you must make sure that both the sender and receiver objects belong to the same *security technology domain*.

Managing Security Policies

The CORBA Security Service defines interfaces that let you create, delete, and update policy objects for the different security functions—including access control, auditing, delegation, secure invocation, and non-repudiation. We cover these interfaces in the next section. The Security Service does not define interfaces for creating and managing domains and associating objects with domains. They left this task as an exercise for the CORBA Common Facilities.

In an operational system, administrators are responsible for setting the security policies for the different domains. They are also responsible for creating the domains, assigning objects to them, and moving objects across domains.

THE SECURITY INTERFACES

The Security Service interfaces fall into four categories: 1) new security operations that extend the core CORBA object model, 2) interfaces that let you obtain security services, 3) interfaces that let you create and administer security policies, and 4) interfaces that are only of interest to implementors of security services. In this section, we only cover the first three types of interfaces. We assume that security implementors will need more details than we can provide in this chapter.

Remember that these interfaces should only be of interest to security-aware applications. You can still run your security-unaware applications using the default security an ORB provides. Of course, a security-aware application can use the security interfaces to fine-tune its control of the security environment. It can use the CORBA Security Service to do the following: 1) discover what security features this ORB supports; 2) establish a principal's credentials and, if necessary, authenticate it; 3) control the *Quality of Security (QOS)* for a secure invocation; 4) control delegation; 5) handle security at a target object; 6) use credentials for access control; 7) define what needs to be audited; 8) handle audit events; 9) use non-repudiation to generate and verify evidence; and 10) find the security policies that apply to this object.

The Security Extensions to the CORBA Object Model

Figure 11-11 shows the new functions that ORB pseudo-objects must provide to support security. As you can see, security goes right to the heart of a CORBA ORB. Nothing is left untouched. Here's a quick summary of how the ORB's pseudo-objects must be extended to support security:

■ **CORBA::ORB** supports a new operation called *get_service_information* that returns detailed information on the services an ORB supports. You must specify the service type as an *in* parameter—for example, Security, Transactions, Events, and Persistence. If you specify security, the call will return all the security features this ORB supports—for example, non-repudiation, secure IIOP interoperability, and secure DCE interoperability.

■ **CORBA::BOA** must extend the *create* operation to associate a new object with one or more security policy domains. The object may later be moved to other domains using domain management facilities.

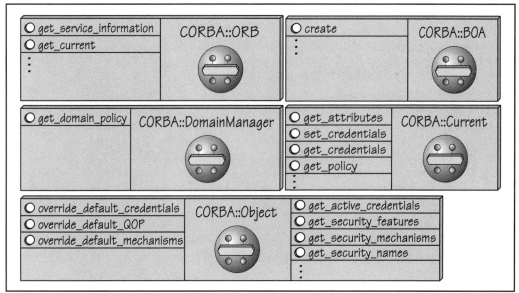

Figure 11-11. CORBA Extensions for Security.

- **CORBA::DomainManager** is a new interface that specifies a single operation—*get_domain_policy*. You invoke this method to obtain the policy types that this domain manager supports. Every domain is represented by its **Domain-Manager** object.

- **CORBA::Current** was first introduced by the Object Transaction Service to represent an object's transaction context. The Security Specification generalizes **Current** to represent the execution context of a client or server object. The execution context includes the object's transaction state and its security credentials. You obtain your **Current** object by invoking *ORB::get_current*.

  Current now includes four new operations that let you manipulate your object's security context. You invoke *get_attributes* to obtain your object's privileges and roles. The User Sponsor invokes *set_credentials* to associate credentials with **Current** at authentication time. A client may subsequently invoke *set_credentials* to downgrade its privileges or to delegate received credentials. You invoke *get_credentials* to obtain your object's credentials. You can use the *received_credentials* attribute to obtain the security credentials of the calling object. You invoke *get_policy* to discover the security policies that are enforced on your object.

- **CORBA::Object** represents a target object reference and also returns information about the object. This interface defines seven new methods that you can invoke to discover and override the security features of a remote object. A security-aware client invokes *get_security_features* to discover the security features a server object supports. The client invokes *get_security_mechanisms* to obtain the list of security mechanisms that both the client and server objects support. The client invokes *get_active_credentials* to obtain a reference to the active credentials object. The client invokes *get_security_names* to obtain from the target a named security mechanism.

The client invokes *override_default_credentials* to change the credentials object it uses with this target. For example, the client may want to downgrade its privileges for subsequent method invocations on this target object. The client invokes *override_default_QOP* to change the "Quality of Protection." For example, the client can change the QOP to enable encryption because the target requests it. The client invokes *override_default_mechanisms* to change the default security mechanisms.

Scenario: How You Manipulate Secure Objects

Let's walk through a brief scenario that shows how a client uses these interfaces to control its security attributes (see Figure 11-12):

1. *What security does this ORB provide?* The client invokes *get_service_information* to obtain a description of the ORB's security features.

2. *What is my current object?* The client invokes *get_current* on the ORB to obtain a reference to its **Current** pseudo-object.

3. *What are my current credentials?* The client invokes *get_credentials* on its **Current** object to obtain a reference to its active **Credentials** object.

4. *Change the credentials privileges*. The client invokes *set_security_features* on its **Credentials** object to change both the QOP of messages and its credentials. A client can downgrade its credentials without requiring a reauthentication. The client may also add some delegated credentials to its own. Any changes the client applies to the **Credentials** object are reflected in all subsequent calls this client makes to any target object. We explain the **Credentials** interface in the next section.

5. *Change my QOP when dealing with this target object*. The client can change its QOP when dealing with specific target objects. It does this by invoking *override_default_QOP* on the target object. For example, the client could enable encryption in its communications with this particular target object. This very fine form of security control is available to security-aware applications.

6. *Invoke methods on the target object*. The client invokes one or more methods on the target object within the security context that it established.

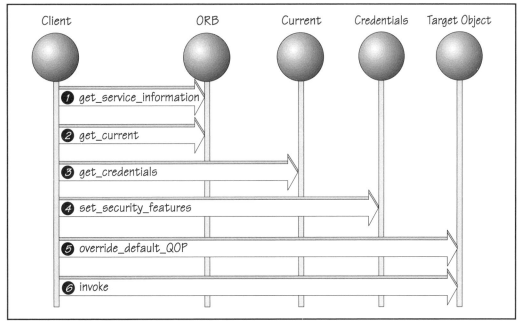

Figure 11-12. Scenario: How a Client Controls Its Security Environment.

Interfaces for Security-Aware Applications

Figure 11-13 shows the key security interfaces that a security-aware application can use. Here's what these interfaces can do for you:

■ **Credentials** represents a principal's current credential information for the session. You invoke *set_security_features* to turn on or turn off security features. You invoke *get_security_features* to find out what security features are active. You invoke *get_attributes* to obtain privileges and other attributes from the **Credentials** object. You invoke *set_privileges* to change a privilege attribute. For example, you could request a new role. You invoke *is_valid* to check if a **Credentials** object is still valid—credentials may have limited lifetimes. You invoke *refresh* to update an expired **Credentials** object. You invoke *copy* to create a duplicate of the **Credentials** object.

■ **PrincipalAuthenticator** encapsulates the ORB's underlying authentication systems. You invoke *authenticate* to authenticate the principal and to obtain its authenticated **Credentials** object. You pass as input parameters the authentication mechanism, the principal's identification, and the requested privilege attributes. The method can ask for more information. You pass any additional information using the *continue_authentication* method.

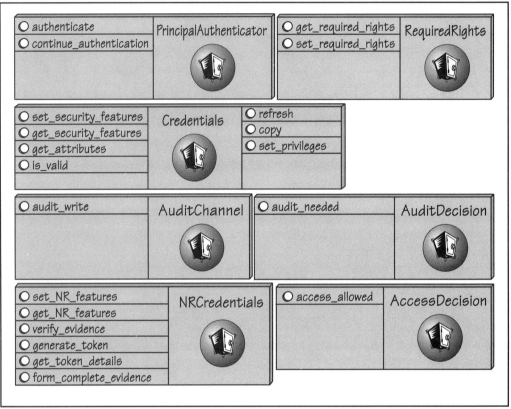

Figure 11-13. Interfaces for Security-Aware Applications.

- **RequiredRights** encapsulates a database of policy information. You invoke *get_required_rights* to retrieve the rights required to execute a method. You must specify as input parameters the target object, the operation, and the interface. You invoke *set_required_rights* to associate lists of rights with an object.

- **AccessDecision** supports a single operation called *access_allowed*. You invoke this operation to check if the specified credentials allow this operation to be performed on this target object.

- **NRCredentials** defines operations that let you generate and verify non-repudiation evidence. You invoke *set_NR_features* to specify the features to apply in the generation and verification operations. You invoke *get_NR_features* to obtain the current features. You invoke *generate_token* to create a non-forge-able evidence called a token. You invoke *form_complete_evidence* to provide added evidence in addition to a token—for example, a timestamp. You invoke *verify_evidence* to verify the evidence. You invoke *get_token_details* to obtain evidence-related information.

■ **AuditChannel** supports a single operation called *audit_write*. You invoke this method to record an audit record. You must pass it the event type, the principal responsible for the action, the time when the event occurs, and event-specific data. Note that the ORB automatically audits events according to its audit invocation policies. You typically use the **AuditChannel** to audit activities that are not ORB-related.

■ **AuditDecision** supports a single operation called *audit_needed*. You invoke this operation to decide if you should write an audit record to the **AuditChannel**.

We will now go through four scenarios that demonstrate how security-aware applications can use these interfaces to control access to server resources, delegate credentials, enforce non-repudiation, and audit events.

Scenario: Do-It-Yourself Access Control

Figure 11-14 shows what happens when a security-aware object receives a call. Let's walk through the steps:

1. *Client invokes server.* In a secure CORBA invocation, the ORB transparently passes the client's security credentials using the *Secure IIOP* facilities.

2. *Server gets the security context from Current.* The **Current** pseudo-object on the server—as on the client—contains the security context associated with this server object; it also contains the incoming client call's **Credentials**. But, how do these credentials get there? It's part of the Secure IIOP magic. The ORB transparently passes the security context of the client to the server. On the receiving end, the server can obtain the client's credentials using the **Current** *received_credentials* attribute. The server invokes *get_attributes* to obtain the privilege attributes it needs to make its own access decisions.

3. *Is this client allowed to invoke this method?* The server invokes the *access_allowed* method on the **AccessDecision** object to check if this client can access this method. In this case, the application is enforcing its own access policies on the parameters of a request. For example, a funds transfer application may want to take into account the amount of money requested.

Remember that the ORB can do most of this work for you. You only write this type of code if you need to provide application-level access controls. Your application's access controls supplement the ORB's standard invocation access policies.

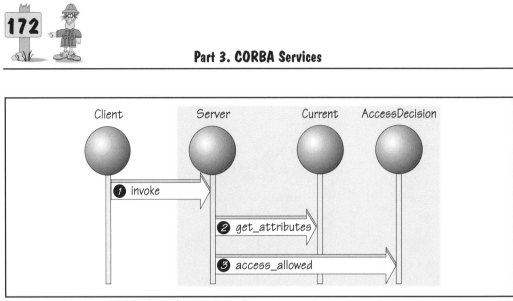

Figure 11-14. Scenario: Do-It-Yourself Access Control.

Scenario: Do-It-Yourself Delegation

Figure 11-15 shows how a security-aware intermediate object influences the delegation of its credentials. Let's walk through the steps:

1. *Client invokes an intermediate object.* In this case, the receiving object needs to call another object to fulfill the client's request.

2. *The intermediary reads in the client's credentials.* The intermediary invokes *get_credentials* on the **Current** pseudo-object to obtain its current **Credentials**. It obtains the client's credentials via the *received_credentials* attribute on the **Current** object.

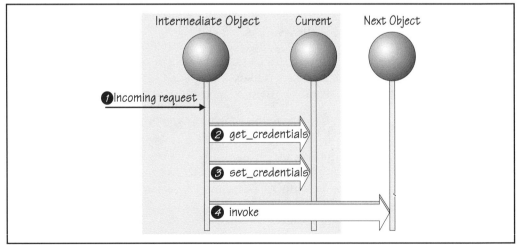

Figure 11-15. Scenario: Do-It-Yourself Delegation.

3. ***The intermediary acquires the client's credentials.*** The intermediary decides to add the client's credentials to its own before invoking the next object in the chain. So it invokes *set_credentials* to add the received credentials to its own. The composite credentials become the default in future invocations.

4. ***The intermediary invokes the next object.*** A Secure IIOP ORB automatically copies the composite credentials to the next object's **Current**.

Typically, you only write this type of code if you need to control the passing of credentials at a very fine-grained level. Normally, you would just set a delegation policy and let the ORB automatically enforce it.

Scenario: Do-It-Yourself Audits

Figure 11-16 shows how a security-aware application can enforce its own audit policies. Let's walk through the steps:

1. ***An object receives an event.*** An event could be a method invocation, server callback, or CORBA event. It's something your application may want to audit.

2. ***Obtain an AuditDecision object.*** The receiver invokes *get_policy* on the **Current** pseudo-object to obtain a reference to an **AuditDecision** object.

3. ***Does this event need to be audited?*** The object invokes *audit_needed* on the **AuditDecision** object to find out if this event needs to be audited.

4. ***Record the event.*** The object invokes *audit_write* on an **AuditChannel** to record the event in an audit trail.

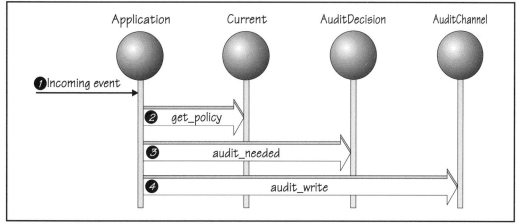

Figure 11-16. Scenario: Do-It-Yourself Audits.

Typically, you only write this type of code if you need to audit application-specific events. The ORB will automatically audit system-level events based on the audit policy you define.

A Non-Repudiation Scenario

Figure 11-17 shows how two security-aware applications use the ORB's security services to generate and validate tokens of non-repudiated evidence. Let's walk through the steps:

1. ***What is the non-repudiation policy?*** The client invokes *get_NR_policy_info* on the **NRPolicy** object to obtain the NR policy.

2. ***The client generates a token of evidence.*** The client invokes *generate_token* to create a piece of non-refutable evidence called a token. A token is like a security certificate signed by the **NRCredentials** object. Hopefully, it cannot be forged.

3. ***The client completes the evidence.*** The client invokes *form_complete_evidence* to provide added evidence in addition to a token. For example, it could add a timestamp.

4. ***The client invokes the remote service.*** The client invokes the remote service and also passes it the non-repudiation evidence. For example, this invocation could be placing an order for a Rolls Royce. The evidence serves as non-refutable proof that the client placed the order. Ideally, the non-repudiation service should deliver the evidence.

5. ***The server verifies the evidence.*** The server invokes *verify_evidence* to verify the evidence. If everything is in order, it should store the evidence in an evidence store.

6. ***The server generates evidence.*** The server invokes *generate_token* to generate evidence that it received the order for the Rolls Royce.

7. ***The server completes the evidence.*** The server invokes *form_complete_evidence* to provide additional information—for example, an order number for the Rolls Royce.

8. ***The server sends the evidence.*** Ideally, the non-repudiation service should deliver the evidence. Unfortunately, this function is not defined by the CORBA service. Consequently, you must deliver the evidence using normal CORBA invocations.

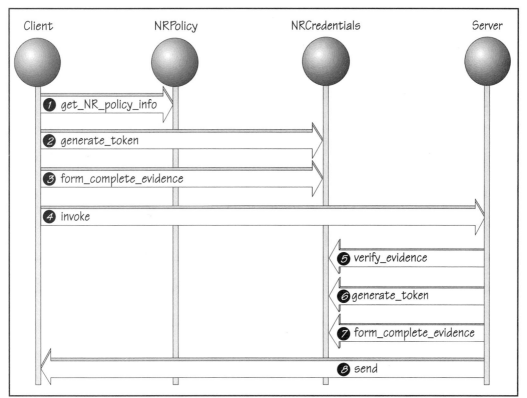

Figure 11-17. A Non-Repudiation Scenario.

Interfaces for Security Administration

Most of security administration consists of defining policies that are then automatically enforced by the ORB. These policies are defined by security administrators
using visual tools. Security-aware applications can modify theses policies within
the boundaries defined by the administrator. Figure 11-18 shows the key policy
interfaces. There should be no surprises at this point. Here's what these interfaces
provide:

■ **AccessPolicy** is the root interface for various kinds of invocation access control
   policies. It provides a single operation called *get_effective_rights*. You invoke
   this method to obtain a list of rights that are granted to a client with privileges
   you specify.

■ **DomainAccessPolicy** lets you define and manage access policies. You use this
   interface to *grant_rights*, *revoke_rights*, *replace_rights*, and *get_rights*.

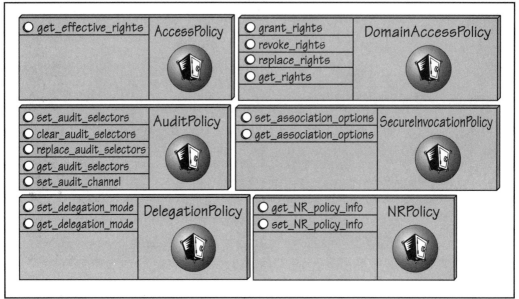

Figure 11-18. Interfaces for Security Administration.

- **AuditPolicy** lets you define and manage audit policies. You use this interface to specify the audit selection criteria that you want to apply to a set of events types. You invoke *set_audit_selectors* to specify the type of objects that you want to audit, the event types, and the audit selection criteria. You invoke *get_audit_selectors* to obtain the current value of the audit selectors for the event types you specify. You invoke *clear_audit_selectors* to delete all the selectors for the event types you specify. You invoke *replace_audit_selectors* to replace the selectors you specify. You invoke *set_audit_channel* to specify the **AuditChannel** object to be used with this audit policy.

- **SecureInvocationPolicy** lets you define the security options that an ORB will apply on secured invocations. It defines how the ORB will protect its messages and how clients and servers establish a trusted association. You invoke *set_association_options* to associate a set of security options you specify with an object type. You can specify the direction as request, reply, or both. You can invoke *get_association_options* to obtain the security features for this object type.

- **DelegationPolicy** lets you define which credentials are used when an intermediate object in a chain invokes another object. You invoke *set_delegation_mode* to apply a delegation policy to the object type you specify (i.e., object interface). The policy choices are no-delegation, simple-delegation, and composite-delegation. You invoke *get_delegation_mode* to obtain the delegation mode for this object type.

- **NRPolicy** lets you define the non-repudiation rules of engagement. These rules specify the third-party authorities that can generate an evidence type. They also specify the time duration for which the generated evidence is valid. If your system supports it, the rules can specify the authorities that adjudicate disputes for this type of evidence. You invoke *set_NR_policy_info* to specify the non-repudiation rules that this policy object supports. You invoke *get_NR_policy_info* to obtain the non-repudiation information associated with this policy object.

Out-of-the-Box Security: Common Secure IIOP

One of IIOP's great strengths is that it provides "out-of-the-box" interoperability across mulivendor ORBs. So how is Secure IIOP interoperabilty achieved? It's achieved via a set of profiles that mandate the underlying security mechanisms— including message encryption, public or private keys, and the level of privilege delegation. CORBA currently defines three *Common Secure IIOP (CSI)* profiles:

- *CSI level 2* supports all the security features described in this chapter— including authentication, message protection, full delegation of privileges, audits, and so on. CSI level 2 can optionally support SESAME (or ECMA 235) for secret and public key encryption.

- *CSI level 1* supports authentication and access protection, but only the initiating principal's credentials can be delegated. This means that the access policy can only rely on the principal's identity—no other attributes can be passed or delegated. CSI level 1 must support MIT's Kerberos V5 (RFC 1510) for secret key encryption. It can optionally support SESAME for public key encryption.

- *CSI level 0* is the same as level 1, but with no delegation. Security is based on the identity of the immediate invoker. CSI level 0 must support Kerberos V5 for secret key encryption. It can optionally support Secure Sockets Layer, SESAME, or SPKM for public key encryption.

Out-of-the-box security is a balancing act. Before they could mandate a security technology, the CORBA architects had to weigh factors such as royalties (and patents), government regulations, technology features, market acceptance, and the Internet. The public key market is growing, but volatile. The private (or secret) key market is more stable—it is dominated by Kerberos—but the technology is less versatile.

CONCLUSION

This long chapter described the state-of-the-art in distributed object security. The CORBA Security Service weighs over 250 pages; it was developed by some of the industry's top security specialists over a period of two years. Is it overkill? Not really. The rule-of-thumb in distributed systems is that there's no such thing as too much security.

Chapter 12

CORBA Services: Persistence and Externalization

Unlike C++ objects, most distributed objects are persistent. This means they must maintain their state long after the program that creates them terminates. To be persistent, the object's state must be stored in a non-volatile datastore—for example, a database or file system. So, who controls the object's persistence? At one end, the *Object Database Management System (ODBMS)* vendors believe that object persistence is totally transparent. An ODBMS magically moves your object between memory and disk to meet your usage needs. All you see is a single-level store of objects. At the other end of the spectrum are those of us with terabytes of existing data. We need a way to get data from our existing stores into objects (and vice versa). As a result, we may need to be more intimately involved with how to access this data and associate it with an object's state. In the middle are those of

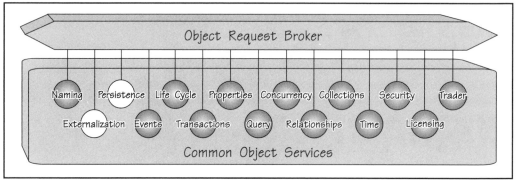

Figure 12-1. CORBA Object Services: Persistence and Externalization.

us that save our data in flat files. All we may need is a streaming service that moves object data into and out of a file. This chapter covers *POS*, which stands for the CORBA *Persistent Object Service* (see Figure 12-1). We also cover ODBMSs because they are so intimately related to object persistence. However, POS works with both relational and object databases. Finally, we cover the CORBA *Externalization Service*. It lets you write an object's contents into a stream so that you can exchange it or move it around. It complements the Persistence and Life Cycle Services.

THE CORBA PERSISTENT OBJECT SERVICE (POS)

The *Persistent Object Service (POS)* allows objects to "persist" beyond the application that creates the object or the clients that use it. The lifetime of an object could be relatively short or indefinite. POS allows the state of an object to be saved in a persistent store and restored when it's needed (see Figure 12-2). When the object is in local memory, you can access its data at native programming language speeds.

What Is POS?

POS is the result of the merging of the IBM and SunSoft/ODBMS-vendor submissions to the OMG. The merger resulted in a specification that can accommodate a variety of storage services—including SQL databases, ODBMSs, document filing systems (like Bento), and others (see Figure 12-3). POS defines the interface to data and persistent objects using IDL-defined interfaces. The implementations of the interface can be lightweight file systems or heavyweight full-featured SQL or Object Database systems. The idea was to create an open implementation that meets the different persistent storage requirements of objects—it encompasses the needs of large-grained objects (such as documents) as well as fined-grained objects (such as SQL table rows). So the main idea behind POS is a single object interface to multiple datastores.

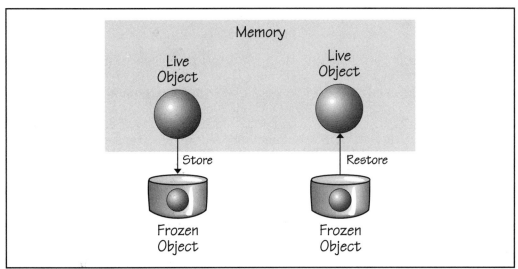

Figure 12-2. A Persistent Object Is Either Live or Frozen.

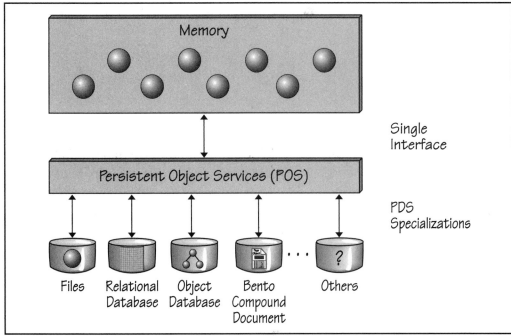

Figure 12-3. Persistent Objects: One Interface, Multiple Datastores.

Single-Level Stores Versus Two-Level Stores

POS provides a single client interface for storing objects regardless of their persistent storage mechanism. POS can handle both *single-level stores* (for example, ODBMSs) and *two-level stores* (for example, SQL databases and simple file systems). In a single-level store, the client is not aware of whether the object is in memory or disk. It's one big virtual store—memory and persistent storage are the same thing. Although ODBMSs sometimes let you use transaction boundaries to flush a cache, they provide most of object storage management transparently. In contrast, two-level stores separate memory from persistent storage. The object must be explicitly staged from a database (or file) into memory, and vice versa.

Almost all the world's existing data is stored in two-level stores. In an ideal world, all objects would be stored in ODBMSs, which are single-level stores for objects. The beauty of ODBMSs is that they do not introduce an impedance mismatch between an object and its storage. ODBMSs provide the most direct path for storing objects. They also provide the best performance and most versatility. We cover ODBMSs in this chapter to give you an idea of where things are going. Remember, however, that POS is not limited to supporting ODBMSs. The whole point of POS is to provide datastore-independent persistence for objects. POS is database secular; it supports them all and lets you make the choice.

POS: The Client's View

Sometimes clients of an object need to control or assist in managing persistence. POS can accommodate different levels of client involvement. At one extreme, the service can be made transparent to client applications. This means the client is completely ignorant of the persistence mechanism; objects appear magically on demand from whatever state they're in. At the other extreme, client applications can use storage-specific protocols that surface all the details of the underlying persistence storage mechanism. Again, the idea is to accommodate different client needs. Some clients need a fine-grain level of control over their persistent store, and for others, ignorance is pure bliss.

The client makes the choice of how much persistent data management it wants. Note that this is a two-way street: Persistent objects can choose not to expose their persistence to clients. POS provides nine operations on three interfaces that clients use to control persistence. These interfaces do not abandon the principle of data encapsulation, but they give clients some of the visibility they may need. More specifically, they let the client decide when the persistent object is stored and restored.

POS: The Persistent Object's View

The *Persistent Object (PO)* is ultimately in charge of its persistence; it decides what datastore protocol to use and how much visibility to give its clients. The PO can also delegate the management of its persistent data to the underlying persistent services. Or, it can maintain fine-grained control over all its interactions with the storage system. The PO can also inherit most of the function it needs to be persistent. At a minimum, a PO must collaborate with its datastores to translate its state into something the underlying service can handle.

The Elements of POS

Figure 12-4 shows the elements of the Persistent Object Service. Let's quickly review what they each do, starting from the top down:

- *Persistent Objects (POs)* are objects whose state is persistently stored. An object can be made persistent by inheriting (via IDL) the **PO** class behavior. It must also inherit (or provide) a mechanism for externalizing its state when asked to do so by the underlying storage mechanism (via a "protocol"). Every persistent object has a *Persistent Identifier (PID)* that describes the location within a datastore of that object using a string identifier. Clients typically interact with the **PO** interface to control the object's persistence.

- *Persistent Object Manager (POM)* is an implementation-independent interface for persistence operations. It insulates the POs from a particular Persistent Data Service. The POM can route PO calls to the appropriate Persistent Data Service by looking at information that's encoded in the PID. A Persistent Object Service has a single POM that typically sits between the objects and the Persistent Data Services. The POM is a router for datastores. It provides a uniform view of persistence in the system across multiple data services.

- *Persistent Data Services (PDSs)* are interfaces to the particular datastore implementations. The PDSs perform the actual work of moving data between an object and a datastore. The PDSs must all implement the IDL-specified **PDS** interface. In addition, some PDSs may support an implementation-dependent *protocol*. This protocol provides a mechanism for getting data in and out of an object. Rick Cattell of SunSoft calls it a "conspiracy" between the object and a PDS. The conspiracy is straightforward between objects and ODBMSs. But it can be quite convoluted when it maps between objects and two-level stores— for example, SQL databases. POS currently specifies three protocols for creating these conspiracies: *Direct Attribute (DA), Object Database Management Group (ODMG-93),* and *Dynamic Data Object (DDO).*

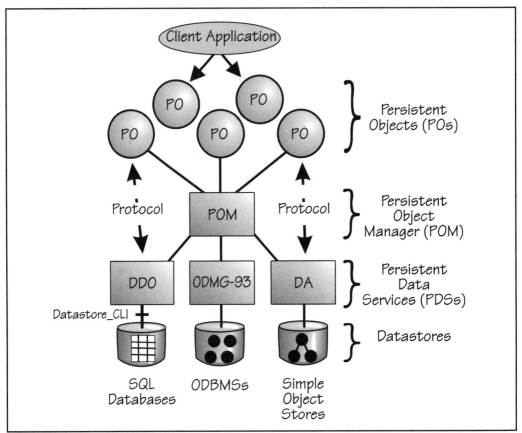

Figure 12-4. The Components of the OMG Persistent Object Service.

■ ***Datastores*** are the implementations that store an object's persistent data independently of the address space containing the object. Examples of datastores are ODBMSs, Posix files, Bento, and SQL databases. POS also provides a set of IDL-defined interfaces that encapsulate the *X/Open Callable Level Interface (CLI)*; it's called the *Datastore_CLI*. This CLI provides an API-like interface to SQL databases; it combines Microsoft's ODBC and Borland's IDAPI.[1]

In a nutshell, POS defines three levels of abstraction that hide different storage implementations. For most client applications, the persistence mechanism will be totally transparent. If you need to control your object's persistence, use the **PO** interface. Of course, the object is responsible for storing and restoring its state. You simply tell it when to do so using the **PO** interface.

---

[1] If these terms are unfamiliar to you, please refer to our book **The Essential Client/Server Survival Guide, Second Edition** (Wiley, 1996). We cover SQL and the CLI in some detail.

POS Protocols: The Object-PDS Conspiracy

The **POM** router provides a generic interface that allows different PDSs to plug-and-play transparently. Datastores provide a single interface to **POM** called the **PDS** interface. In addition, they provide datastore-specific protocols. These are the conspiracies that let an object expose its data to a datastore. Think of it as an agreement between object providers and the PDS implementors on how to get data in and out of an object.

Roger Sessions suggests that if all objects use the stream protocol (it is part of the CORBA *Externalization Service*), then two-level store PDSs only need to support one conspiracy. This conspiracy is between the PDS and the streams to which an object externalizes (and internalizes) its persistent state. We are not aware of the performance implications of streaming. You typically use streams to externalize data to a file or to another process. But is it the most efficient mechanism for an object to exchange data with an SQL database? Perhaps Roger can answer this question (we cover the streaming protocol later in this chapter).

Excluding streams, POS defines three implementation-specific protocols for moving data between an object and different PDSs:

- *The Direct Access (DA)* protocol provides direct access to persistent data using an IDL-like Data Definition Language (DDL) that's a subset of ODMG-93.

- *The ODMG-93* protocol provides direct access from C++, Smalltalk, and Java using an ODMG-specific Data Definition Language. We cover ODMG in the Object Database section of this chapter.

- *The Dynamic Data Object (DDO)* protocol is a datastore-neutral representation of an object's persistent data; it defines a structure that contains all the data for an object. You can use this protocol to dynamically describe an object's data without going through IDL. Clients can use DDOs (with the Datastore_CLI) to formulate dynamic SQL queries. DDO is the basis for the original IBM proposal (from Dan Chang of IBM). Several commercial implementations use DDO to access data from relational databases via the Datastore_CLI. For example, the IBM VisualAge C++ visual builder uses DDO and the Datastore_CLI to access SQL databases. DDO is no panacea. But there's no panacea for mapping between objects and SQL databases; every approach requires some messy mapping constructs. Visual tools make it easier. We cover the Datastore_CLI later in this chapter.

To summarize, protocols simply map between object and datastore views of data (for example, between an object and SQL tables). ODBMSs use a superset of the OMG IDL to describe their objects; they represent objects in a very straightforward way (there is no impedance mismatch). Consequently, ODBMSs and objects have minimal conspiracies. This is not the case for SQL databases and other non-object

Part 3. CORBA Services

stores—their impedance mismatch with objects is large. As a result, it takes quite a bit of "conspiring" to smooth the exchange path between the two. But this is a small price to pay to bring the bulk of the world's data into the object domain.

The POS Interfaces

Figure 12-5 shows the six required interfaces that provide the Persistent Object Service. Clients only need to be aware of the factories and the **PO** and **PID** interfaces. Also notice that **PO**, **POM**, and **PDS** provide the same set of functions, but at different levels of abstraction. Let's go over these interfaces:

- **PIDFactory** lets you create a *Persistent Object ID (PID)* three different ways. Every object must have a PID to store its data persistently. The PID describes where the underlying data for an object lives.

- **POFactory** provides a single operation *create_PO* that lets you create an instance of a persistent object.

- **PID** provides a single operation *get_PIDString* that returns a string version of the PID.

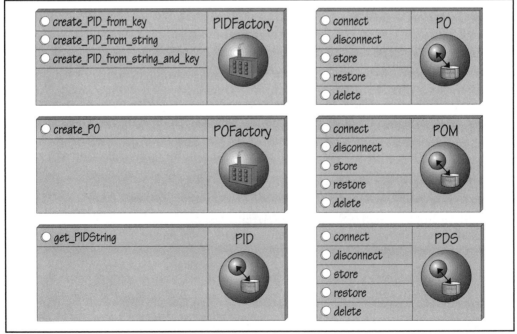

Figure 12-5. The Persistent Object Service Interfaces.

- **PO** provides five operations that let a client externally control the persistent object's relationship with its persistent data. You invoke *store* to get the state data out of the object into the datastore location designated by a PID. *Restore* does the reverse. All persistent objects are derived from the **PO** interface.

- **POM** provides five operations that a persistent object uses to communicate with its underlying datastore; these are the same operations a persistent object exposes to its clients.

- **PDS** provides five operations that a **POM** uses to communicate with its underlying datastore; these are the same operations a persistent object exposes to its clients. The **PDS** is ultimately the interface that moves data between the object and the datastore. To plug a new datastore into the Persistent Object Service, all you need to do is specialize the **PDS** and **PID** interfaces (and work out the protocols).

Most of these operations are self-explanatory. The main idea here is that POMs mediate between multiple datastores.

The POS CLI Interfaces

The POS CLI interfaces encapsulate the X/Open CLI, IDAPI, and ODBC functions. These three database interface standards let you access relational databases, XBase file systems, and even hierarchical databases. The POS CLI allows objects to access these databases via ORBs using IDL-defined interfaces. POS prefers that you avoid going directly to the CLI even if it's via an ORB. Instead, it wants you to use the higher-level persistent object interface. The CLI is meant to be used by PDSs to get to the data. However, if you're an ODBC fan, you should know this interface is available on ORBs using CORBA's POS.

CLI (it used to be called SAG) is an X/Open standard that is being merged with the SQL3 specification. Microsoft promised to make ODBC conform to CLI at some future date. The POS CLI is a superset that covers both ODBC and CLI. You can use the select/cursor CLI operations alone when there is no Query Service. These interfaces hook into the Query Service when it exists. Actually, the Query Service uses the POS CLI to query persistent objects. As a result, the Query Service does not have to repeat what the Persistence Service provides—for example, schema mapping, datastore access, and so on.

Figure 12-6 shows the four key interfaces that constitute the POS CLI (we do not show three minor interfaces). The **Datastore_CLI** interface is the workhorse that provides most of the operations. Typically, you first create a **Connection** object and set the appropriate options. Then you open a connection to the datastore by invoking *connect*. To store an object, you invoke *add_object* or *update_object*.

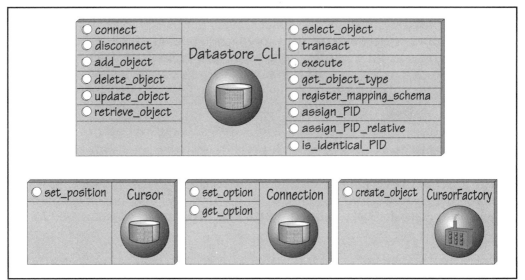

Figure 12-6. POS: The Four Key POS CLI Interfaces.

You invoke *retrieve_object* to restore an object. *Select_object* lets you retrieve sets of objects that match certain keys from the datastore. You can navigate a select's result set using a **Cursor** object (if necessary, get the mapping information first). The CLI is a recoverable object; it participates in an OTS transaction via *transact*. You can invoke a command or stored procedure in the database using *execute*. Finally, you invoke *delete_object* to delete an object.

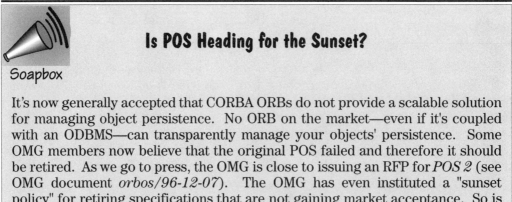

Is POS Heading for the Sunset?

Soapbox

It's now generally accepted that CORBA ORBs do not provide a scalable solution for managing object persistence. No ORB on the market—even if it's coupled with an ODBMS—can transparently manage your objects' persistence. Some OMG members now believe that the original POS failed and therefore it should be retired. As we go to press, the OMG is close to issuing an RFP for *POS 2* (see OMG document *orbos/96-12-07*). The OMG has even instituted a "sunset policy" for retiring specifications that are not gaining market acceptance. So is POS heading for the sunset? We don't think so. The new RFP mandates that "coexistence with POS 1.0 interfaces is a requirement."

According to the POS 2 RFP, the new Persistence Service must provide interfaces for managing: 1) multiple persistent object services at the same time, 2) protocol-independent persistent data—i.e., no conspiracies allowed, 3) schema specification on a per-datastore basis, and 4) the life cycle of persistent objects. The new POS must totally decouple the persistent data from the protocols that access it. In contrast, the current POS only manages the location of persistent information in a protocol-specific manner.

So, will POS 2 solve all your persistence problems? Will ORBs be able to transparently manage the state of millions objects? Will they be able to manage state on transaction boundaries? And, will they be able to work with any database—object or relational? In our opinion—and this is a Soapbox—the problems of distributed object persistence cannot be solved alone by either ORBs, ODBMSs, RDBMSs, OSs, or persistent languages. They can only be solved by a run-time framework that orchestrates all these disparate pieces using transactions; it's a cooperative effort. This framework must provide load-balancing and manage the life cycle of objects. In the procedural world, these frameworks are called *TP Monitors*. They were built to manage and run the application logic on servers. TP Monitors also know how to orchestrate and synchronize multiple applications across multiple DBMSs using transactions.

We need the object version of a TP Monitor. We call it an *Object TP Monitor* (or a *Component Coordinator*). These critters must provide mission-critical run times that transparently manage the life cycle of objects in a scalable manner. So who's going to provide these Object TP Monitors? As we go to press, it appears that the TP Monitor vendors have taken on this challenge. We know of two major projects that are creating ORB-based TP Monitors for CORBA: IBM's *Business Object Server Solution (BOSS)* and BEA Systems' Tuxedo-based *ObjectWare*. The DCOM camp also has its Component Coordinator—it is called *Viper*. So help is on the way. ❑

THE CORBA EXTERNALIZATION SERVICE

Streams are quite fascinating because they can be used for so many purposes. It will be virtually impossible to develop a serious object which does not support the streamable interface.

— Roger Sessions, Author
Object Persistence
(Prentice Hall, 1996)

The *Externalization Service*—originally from Taligent—defines interfaces for externalizing an object to a stream and internalizing an object from a stream. Most programmers are already familiar with the power and simplicity of streams. A *stream* is a data holding area with an associated cursor. A *cursor* is a mobile pointer that moves forward and backward as you write and read data to and from a stream. The data holding area can be in memory, on a disk file, or across a network. You can't tell the difference. You *externalize* an object to a stream to transport it to a different process, machine, or ORB. You *internalize* the object when you need to bring it back to life at its new destination.

Stream Power

In a sense, externalizing and then internalizing an object is similar to copying it using the Life Cycle Service. The difference is that both externalization and internalization break the copy into two steps: You first copy the object to a stream; then you copy from the stream into the final destination object. This two-step process lets you export the object outside of its ORB environment. You do not create a new object until the stream is internalized somewhere else. Streams become an import/export medium for objects. As opposed to a Life Cycle copy, the Externalization Service stops along the way—by breaking a move or copy operation into two steps. It gives you a chance to do something with the intermediate results

Streams let you copy and move objects. They also let you pass objects by value in a parameter (today, CORBA only lets you pass objects by reference in a method call). Roger Sessions predicts that every object will be streamable. If this happens, streams will become the universal protocol for getting data into and out of objects. Every Persistent Data Service will only need to translate from streams to their own persistent store mechanism.

Externalization Service: The Base Interfaces

Figure 12-7 shows the six interfaces that provide the core Externalization Service. The client's view of externalization is very simple. A client creates (or locates) a **Stream** object and passes it one or more objects to be externalized. You create a **Stream** by invoking a **StreamFactory**. You can also create a file-based stream by invoking **FileStreamFactory**. You then invoke *externalize* to request that the object write itself to a stream. You can also write several objects to the same stream as follows: 1) invoke *begin_context*; 2) invoke *externalize* for each object you want to store in the stream; and 3) invoke *end_context*. You invoke the same *externalize* call to store a simple object or a graph of related objects.

When the **Stream** object receives an *externalize* invocation, it turns around and invokes the *externalize_to_stream* method on the target object's **Streamable** interface. All streamable objects must implement this interface (typically as a mixin using multiple inheritance). The streamable object calls the **StreamIO** operations to read or write its state to or from that stream. This interface is implemented by the Stream Service; it provides operations to write and read—to and from a

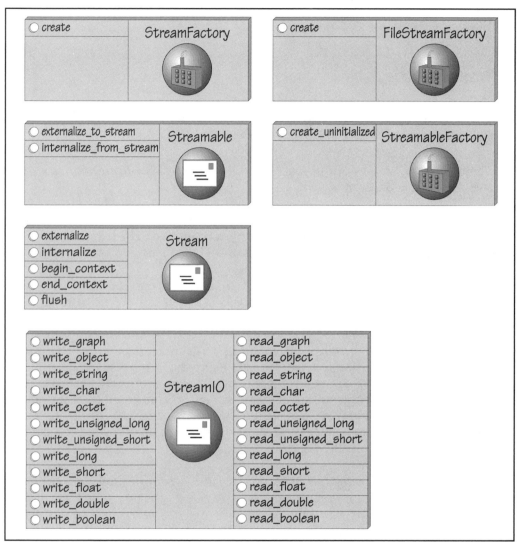

Figure 12-7. Externalization Service: The Base Interfaces.

stream—all the IDL data types. It also lets you read and write related objects using the *write_graph* and *read_graph* operations. The **Stream** object either directly implements the **StreamIO** interface or passes an object reference to it when it calls the streamable object.

To internalize an object from a stream, the client invokes *internalize* on a **Stream** object. The **Stream** object must locate (or create) a **Streamable** object that can internalize its state from a stream; it uses the **StreamableFactory** interface to create the object. The stream then invokes the streamable object's *internalize_from_stream* method. Of course, the streamable object uses the **StreamIO** interface to read the stream contents. Does it sound complicated? It really isn't. We'll back our claim with a little scenario.

A Stream Scenario

The scenario in Figure 12-8 demonstrates how objects are externalized and internalized using streams. Let's walk through the steps:

1. ***Client obtains a Stream object***. The client invokes *StreamFactory::create* to obtain a new **Stream** object.

2. ***Client tells stream to externalize an object***. The client invokes *Stream::externalize* and passes it the object reference to be externalized (note that this object must support the **Streamable** interface).

3. ***Stream tells the streamable object to externalize itself***. The stream invokes *Streamable::externalize_to_stream* to tell the object to externalize itself to stream.

4. ***Object writes its contents to stream***. The object uses the **StreamIO** *write_<type>* operations to write its data contents. It invokes *write_object* to stream embedded objects. A streamable object may also participate as a node in a graph of related objects. This means it may be connected to other objects via the Relationship Service. Connected objects invoke *write_graph* to let the stream service coordinate the externalization of the graph of related objects with the help of the Relationship Service.

5. ***Later, the client needs to internalize the stream***. You can store the externalized form of an object inside a stream for arbitrary amounts of time. You can even transport it to an outside ORB. When you're ready to internalize the object, you invoke *Stream::internalize*. The **Stream** object looks inside the stream for a key that helps it locate a factory that can create an object with an implementation that matches the object in the stream.

6. ***Stream tells the streamable object to internalize itself***. The stream invokes *Streamable::internalize_from_stream* to tell the object to internalize itself to stream.

7. ***Object reads its contents from the stream***. The object uses the **StreamIO** *read_<type>* operations to read its data contents. It invokes *read_object* to read embedded objects. If the streamable object is a node within a graph of related objects, it invokes *read_graph* to let the stream service coordinate the internalization of the related objects with the help of the Relationship Service.

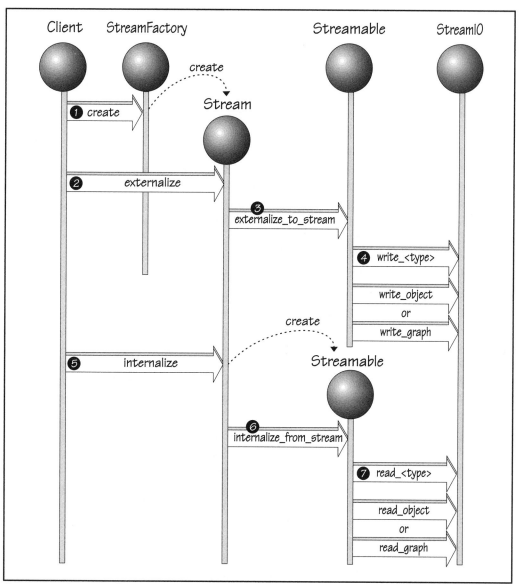

Figure 12-8. Scenario: Object Externalization and Internalization via Streams.

The Externalization Service also defines a *Standard Stream Data Format* that lets you exchange streams across dissimilar networks, operating system platforms, and storage implementations. This standard stream representation uses self-describing IDL data type formats as well as headers that describe the types of objects that are contained within the stream. The **StreamIO** object is responsible for encoding the data within a stream using this canonical representation and for recreating a stream's contents.

OBJECT DATABASES

We define an ODBMS to be a DBMS that integrates database capabilities with object-oriented programming language capabilities. An ODBMS makes database objects appear as programming language objects in one or more existing programming languages.

— **Rick Cattell, Chairman**
ODMG-93 Committee

An ODBMS provides a persistent store for objects in a multiuser client/server environment. The ODBMS handles concurrent access to objects, provides locks and transaction protection, protects the object store from all types of threats, and takes care of traditional tasks such as backup and restore. What makes ODBMSs different from their relational counterparts is that they store objects rather than tables. Objects are referenced through *Persistent Identifiers (PIDs)*, which uniquely identify objects, and are used to create referential and containment relationships between them. ODBMSs also enforce encapsulation and support inheritance. The ODBMS combines object properties with traditional DBMS functions such as locking, protection, transactions, querying, versioning, concurrency, and persistence.

Instead of using a separate language like SQL to define, retrieve, and manipulate data, ODBMSs use class definitions and traditional OO language (usually C++, Smalltalk, and Java) constructs to define and access data. The ODBMS is simply a multiuser, persistent extension of in-memory language data structures (see Figure 12-9). In other words, the client is the C++ or Java program; the server is the

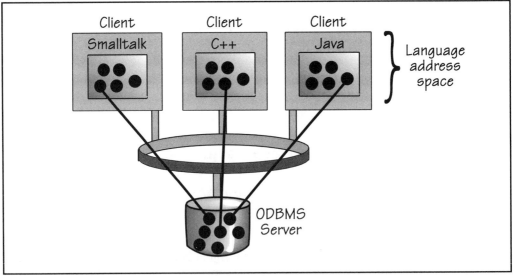

Figure 12-9. ODBMS: An Extension to OO Language Data Structures.

ODBMS—there are no visible intermediaries like RPCs or SQL. The ODBMS integrates database capabilities directly into the language.

Of course, not everything is transparent to the language. By necessity, the ODBMS introduces extensions to the OO language such as container classes and operations that help you navigate through the containers. The ODMG specification includes a full-blown *Object Manipulation Language (OML)* that supports queries and transactions. In an attempt to make the data definition language neutral, ODMG specifies a generic *Object Definition Language (ODL)*. As a result, the ODBMS, like SQL, requires a precompiler to process the object definitions, language extensions, and queries. The output of the compiler, like SQL plans, must also be linked to the ODBMS runtime. So we've come full circle.

What's an ODBMS Good For?

Rather than trying to mangle the data or tear it apart and put it into relational tables, obviously it was best to store those objects in their natural form.

— *Jonathan Cassell, IS Manager*
Granite Construction

ODBMSs are perfect fits for users whose data isn't simple enough to line up in relational tables. For a long time, ODBMSs were an area of great interest to academicians and OO researchers. The earliest commercial ODBMSs made their appearance in 1986 with the introduction of Servio (now GemStone) and Ontos. These two pioneers were joined (in the 90s) by Object Design (ODI), Versant, Objectivity, O2 Technology, Poet, Ibex, UniSQL, and ADB MATISSE. The ODBMS vendors first targeted applications that dealt with complex data structures and long-lived transactions—including computer-aided design, CASE, and intelligent offices. With the emergence of multimedia, groupware, distributed objects, and the Web, the esoteric features of ODBMSs are now becoming mainstream client/server requirements. ODBMS technology fills the gap in the areas where relational databases are at their weakest—complex data, versioning, long-lived transactions, nested transactions, persistent object stores, inheritance, and user-defined data types.

Here's a list of the features that were pioneered by the ODBMS vendors (see Figure 12-10):

■ *Freedom to create new types of information*. ODBMSs give you the freedom to create and store any data type using standard object descriptions. The data type is part of the object class definition. You can easily store arbitrarily complex data structures in an ODBMS (like container hierarchies). In contrast, traditional databases offer a limited number of hard-wired data types; complex structures must be converted into artificially "flattened" table representations.

- ***Fast access.*** ODBMSs keep track of objects through their unique IDs. A search can move directly from object to object without the need for tedious search-and-compare operations using foreign keys and other associative techniques.

- ***Flexible views of composite structures.*** ODBMSs allow individual objects to participate in a multiplicity of containment relationships, creating multiple views of the same objects. Objects can maintain pointers to other objects in a very recursive manner; there's no limit to the different container relationships that you can create. A container typically maintains references to object IDs as opposed to the objects themselves—it's a form of *linking* as opposed to *embedding*.

- ***Tight integration with object-oriented languages.*** ODBMSs present themselves as persistent extensions of the OO languages' in-memory data structures. This allows them to minimize the impedance mismatch between programs and data while maintaining the strong encapsulation features that are inherent in OO languages. OO programmers should find an ODBMS to be a natural extension of their paradigm. ODBMSs provide the fastest and most direct access to objects they store; they also do a good job of preserving the characteristics of these objects. In contrast, RDBMSs require multiple transformations to represent the complex in-memory data structures of an OO language in tabular form. Relational systems can store objects, but they must first break them down into chunks and flatten them into structures that can fit in tables. SQL people, of course, may think that chasing corporate data via in-memory C++ pointers is a travesty. (We'll resume this discussion in the next Soapbox.)

- ***Support for customizable information structures using multiple inheritance.*** The ODBMS data types are defined using object classes. This means that any class can be subclassed to create custom structures that meet exceptional data needs. In addition, the ODBMS lets you mix desirable characteristics from different classes and combine them using multiple inheritance. So the ODBMS extends the concept of object reuse through inheritance to the database.

- ***Support for versioning, nesting, and long-lived transactions.*** Many commercial ODBMSs (including ObjectStore, Ontos, and Objectivity) support nested transactions and versioning for long-duration transactions. Objects can be grouped in configurations and managed as one transaction. ODBMSs are most popular in engineering design applications that require the management of complex documents. A typical Computer Aided Design (CAD) system also depends on version control to track the progressively more enhanced versions of an engineering design. Because of their long involvement with CAD, ODBMSs have perfected the art of versioning and long-lived transactions. ODBMSs have

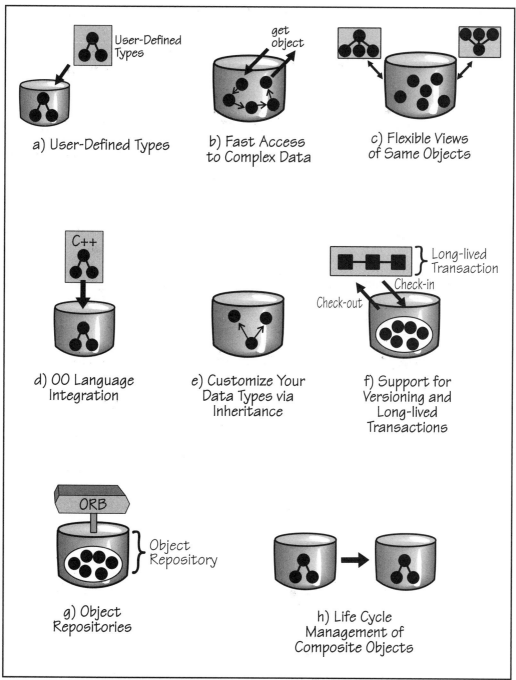

Figure 12-10. The Eight Wonders of ODBMS.

introduced the concept of *configurations*—meaning a collection of objects that are managed as a locking and versioning unit. CAD users typically *check out* a configuration of objects from the ODBMS, work on it, and *check in* their configuration as a new version.

■ *Repositories for distributed objects.* ODBMSs provide natural multiuser repositories for run-time objects. We believe the ODBMS vendors have a huge lead in providing solutions for concurrent access to large numbers (in the millions) of fine-grained objects with ACID protection. ODBMSs also provide true stores for *mobile components* such as Java applets and Beans; they serve as object servers for roaming objects—think of them as object Hiltons.

■ *Support for life cycle management of composite objects.* ODBMSs have also perfected the art of managing composite objects as a unit. For example, you can assemble, disassemble, copy, store, restore, move, and destroy composite objects. The ODBMS automatically maintains the relationships between the parts and treats the aggregate as a single component. This is also a result of their long involvement with CAD. This technology is now used to create very scalable Web servers. The ODBMS becomes a replacement for the file system; it provides a very efficient database for the rich multimedia data types that are starting to proliferate on the World Wide Web.

In summary, ODBMS vendors have had the luxury of being able to create pure object databases without being encumbered by a debt to history. As a result, they were able to provide some missing pieces of technology needed to create the new generation of multimedia-intensive databases with flexible data types. An ODBMS has the advantage over a relational database of knowing the overall structure of a complex object (like a document) and sometimes its behavior (or methods) as well; it can refer to any constituent object by its ID. In contrast, RDBMS vendors are attempting to provide object technology (with SQL3) by using a hybrid approach that decomposes the data from the object and then stores it in tables. This is an area where relational databases are at a disadvantage, but we'll defer that discussion to the Soapbox, too.

ODMG-93 and CORBA

There is no object database life left outside the ODMG-93 standard.

> — *Francois Bancilhon*
> *O2 Technology*

The ODMG-93 standard is the ODBMS answer to SQL. The standard is the result of work done by the *Object Database Management Group (ODMG)*—a consortium that includes all the major ODBMS vendors. The ODMG is a working subgroup of the OMG, and it intends to submit its standard to both ISO and ANSI. In theory, the adoption of ODMG-93 should allow applications to work with ODBMSs from any of the major vendors. Version 1.0 of the standard was published in 1993 (hence the name ODMG-93). Revision 1.1 was published in 1994. Revision 1.2 was published in December 1995. Finally, the ODMG Java bindings were published in December 1996. Each revision strengthened the standard both in scope and depth.

ODMG-93 is an extension of the CORBA Persistent Object Service that defines how to implement a protocol that provides an efficient *Persistent Data Service (PDS)* for fine-grained objects. The standard uses the OMG object model as its basis. The ODBMS's role in an ORB environment is to provide concurrent access to persistent stores capable of handling millions of fine-grained objects. To do this, the OMG refers to a special PDS protocol called ODMG-93. This protocol supplements the IDL-defined RPC invocations with direct API calls to the objectstore for faster access to data.

The ODBMS vendors are also actively promoting within the CORBA ORB task force a *Library Object Adapter (LOA)* that provides direct access via the ORB to specialized high-speed APIs. ODMG-93 states that the ODBMS vendors would like CORBA to standardize on a specialized version of LOA called the *Object Database Adapter (ODA)*. Figure 12-11, adapted from ODMG-93, shows the differences

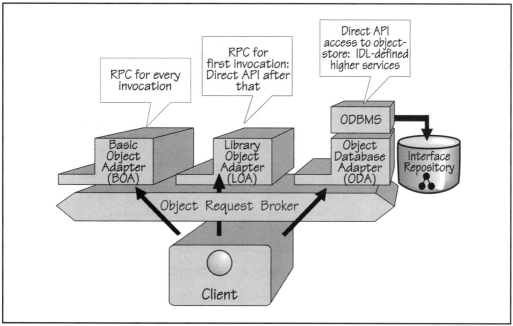

Figure 12-11. ODMG-93 ODBMS as Object Manager on an OMG ORB.

among BOA, LOA, and ODA—yes, more TLAs (three-letter acronyms) you can use to impress the folks back home.

The ODA should provide the ability to register subspaces of object identifiers with the ORB instead of all the millions of objects that are stored in the ODBMS. From the client's point of view, the objects in the registered subspace appear just as any other ORB-accessible objects. The ODA should allow for the use of direct access—as in the LOA—to improve the performance of ORB/ODBMS applications. To summarize, the ODBMS vendors are pushing CORBA to be more flexible when it comes to dealing with applications that manage millions of fine-grained objects. The POS2 RFP indicates that OMG got the message. But it remains to be seen if OMG will extend this new permissiveness to the ORB itself.

The Elements of ODMG-93

The ODMG-93 standard consists of three major components (see Figure 12-12):

■ *Object Definition Language (ODL)*—ODMG-93 uses the OMG IDL as its data definition language. ODL is a "clean" superset of IDL in the sense that it defines elements that are not in IDL, such as collection classes and referential relationships. The ODL lets you describe metadata independently of the programming language. The ODL is processed through a precompiler, which generates stubs that get linked to the ODBMS and the client language (C++ or Smalltalk). ODL

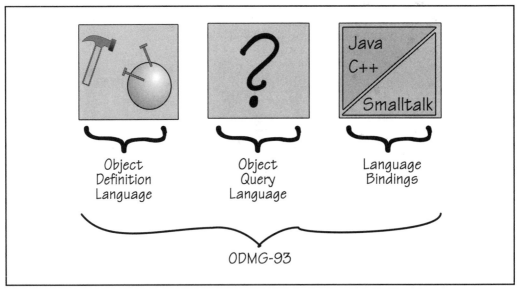

Figure 12-12. ODMG-93 Components.

provides interface and data definition portability across languages and ODBMS vendor platforms.

■ *Object Query Language (OQL)*—ODMG-93 defines an SQL-like declarative language for querying and updating database objects. It supports the most commonly used SQL SELECT structures, including joins; it does not support SQL INSERT, UPDATE, or DELETE (it uses C++ or Smalltalk extensions for this). ODMG-93 purposely did not use the SQL3 semantics for objects because of "limitations in its data model and because of its historical baggage." However, as you will read in the next chapter, OQL and SQL3 may converge. The OMG Query Service tries to bring the best of both worlds together. OQL provides high-level primitives to query different collections of objects—including *sets*, which means unordered collections with no duplicates; *bags*, which means unordered collections with duplicates; and *lists*, which are ordered collections. OQL also supports structures in queries—a very powerful construct.

■ *C++, Smalltalk, and Java language bindings*—ODMG-93 defines how to write portable C++, Java, or Smalltalk code that manipulates persistent objects. The standard defines C++ *Object Manipulation Language (OML)* extensions. The C++ OML includes language extensions for OQL, iterations for navigating through containers, and transaction support. The ODMG-93 people do not believe exclusively in a "universal" Data Manipulation Language (à la SQL). Instead, they propose "a unified object model for sharing data across programming languages, as well as a common query language." According to ODI's Tom Atwood, "The OML should respect the syntax of the base language into which it is being inserted. This enables programmers to feel they are writing in a single integrated programming language that supports persistence." In theory, it should be possible to read and write the same ODBMS from Smalltalk, Java, and C++, as long as the programmer stays within the common subset of supported data types.

Figure 12-13 shows the steps involved in using an ODMG-compliant ODBMS. The process is very similar to the CORBA IDL, except that the stub bindings are for an ODBMS and the OO language application that manipulates persistent objects. Your C++, Java, or Smalltalk applications can directly manipulate data that is either *persistent* or *transient*. The ODBMS updates the persistent data on transaction boundaries. Generally, every object that is reachable from a persistent object is also made persistent. This is called persistence by *reachability*. ODMG also lets you name any object or collection. You can then retrieve a named object, operate on it, or navigate to other objects by following a relationship link. You do all this from within your familiar language environment.

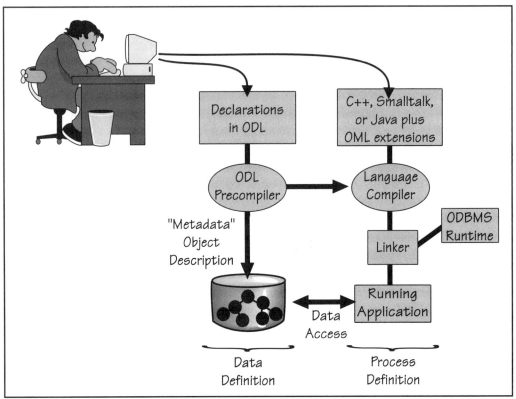

Figure 12-13. The ODMG-93 Process.

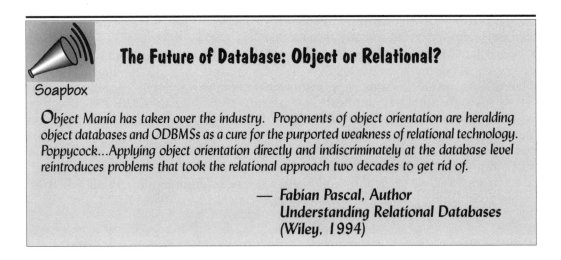

The Future of Database: Object or Relational?

Soapbox

Object Mania has taken over the industry. Proponents of object orientation are heralding object databases and ODBMSs as a cure for the purported weakness of relational technology. Poppycock...Applying object orientation directly and indiscriminately at the database level reintroduces problems that took the relational approach two decades to get rid of.

— *Fabian Pascal, Author*
Understanding Relational Databases
(Wiley, 1994)

Among users, few doubts remain that ODBMS will ultimately be the successor to RDBMS...In the imagery of the poet William Blake, the young god of revolution Orc has begun to age into the icy tyrant Urizen—keeper of the law and standards.

> — *Thomas Atwood, Chairman*
> *Object Design*

We can have our cake and eat it, too! The point is to marry the two technologies instead of throwing mud at each other...It would be a great shame to walk away from the experience gained from more than 20 years of solid relational research and development.

> — *Chris Date*

Date and Pascal both acknowledge that current SQL database implementations have weaknesses; however, they both feel the relational model per se can handle the problems that ODBMSs solve. The power of ODBMS can be approximated in the relational world using nested relations, domains (or user-defined encapsulated data types) and a more powerful set-oriented language than SQL. These features can do the job without chasing after object pointers or manipulating low-level, language-specific record structures. We don't have to mitigate the associative powers of relational theory. Developers won't have to resort to manual methods to maximize and reoptimize application performance—setting the clock back. Date believes that a domain and an object type are the same; the solution is for relational vendors to extend their systems to include "proper domain support."

Stonebraker notes that pure ODBMSs still lack functionality in the areas of complex search, query optimizers, and server scalability. Furthermore, many ODBMSs run their products in the same address space as user programs. This means that there is no protection barrier between a client application and the ODBMS. In addition, ODBMSs have a minuscule market penetration when compared to relational DBMSs. Finally, object/relational and SQL data-type extenders are filling some of the object needs within an RDBMS context.

The ODBMS people feel that there's more to this than just extending the relational model. In fact, they've rejected the SQL3 extensions as being insufficient (a truce is in the making). ODBMS diehards believe that they're creating better plumbing for a world where information systems will be *totally* object-based. Relational databases are an impedance mismatch in a plumbing consisting of ORBs, object services, OO languages, and the Object Web. A pure ODBMS is exactly what's needed. Why keep extending a legacy foundation like SQL with BLOBs, stored procedures, and user-defined types? They prefer to stick to objects all the way and sometimes borrow a few things from SQL (such as queries). They're also recreating the multiuser robust foundation that includes locking, transactions, recovery, and tools.

Of course, we're talking about David and Goliath here. SQL databases are the current kings of the hill. They have the big development budgets and wide commercial acceptance that ranges from MIS shops to the low end of the client/server market. Will the king of the hill be deposed because ODBMSs do objects better? It remains to be seen. But as Esther Dyson puts it, "Using tables to store objects is like driving your car home and then disassembling it to put it in the garage. It can be assembled again in the morning, but one eventually asks whether this is the most efficient way to park a car." ❑

Chapter 13

CORBA Services: Query and Collections

Distributed objects do not float in space; they are connected to one another.

— *CORBA COSS Specification*
(May, 1996)

In this chapter, we cover two related CORBA services: *Query* and *Collections* (see Figure 13-1). These services let you discover objects and group them into collections. They also let you manipulate multiple objects as a group.

THE CORBA QUERY SERVICE

The CORBA *Object Query Service*—adopted in 1995—is the result of a joint submission by nine vendors—including the major ODBMS vendors, Sybase, IBM, SunSoft, and Taligent. In essence, the service lets you find objects whose attributes meet the search criteria you specify using a query. You should note that queries have no access to an object's internal state. This means they do not violate an object's encapsulation; you can hide your object's internal data structures and expose only what you want the public to see.

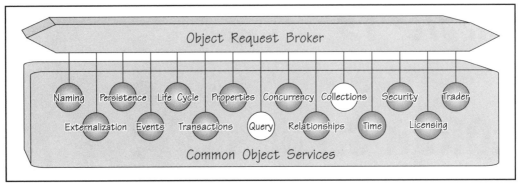

Figure 13-1. CORBA Services: Query and Collections.

You can formulate an object query using one of the following languages: ODMG-93's Object Query Language (OQL), SQL (with object extensions), or a subset of these two languages. The OMG is working with the SQL3 ANSI X3H2 committee and the ODMG to create a single query language for objects.[1] A single query language makes it easier for queries to interoperate across servers; it also gives you a common language for writing queries.

Federated Queries

We designed the Query Service to let you query and manipulate any CORBA object—transient or persistent, concrete or meta, local or remote, individually or in a collection. If there is one object service that can utilize and unify all object services together with the ORB, the Query Service is it.

— *Dan Chang, Object Architect*
IBM

The Query Service can either directly execute a query or delegate it to some other *query evaluator.* For example, the service can use the native query facilities of a relational or object database to execute a nested query. The Query Service combines the query results from all the participating query evaluators and returns the final results to the caller. This means you can use the Query Service to coordinate loose federations of native query managers. The beauty is that each database can use its own optimized search engine while participating in a global search.

---

[1] ODMG's OQL provides full object query capabilities and contains almost all of the SQL-92 query language as a subset. OQL is available today.

Collections for Manipulating Query Results

When you execute a query, the service returns a *collection* of objects that satisfy the search criteria you specify via a *select* operation. Note that CORBA uses the term "query" in its broader connotation. A CORBA query does more than just let you find objects; it also lets you manipulate a *collection* of objects. The collection is returned by the query—it's the result. The Query Service treats the collection itself as an object. It defines operations that let you manipulate and navigate a collection. It also lets you add and remove collection members.

Query Service: The Collection Interfaces

The Query Service provides a "minimalist" collection service to let you manipulate the results of a query (see Figure 13-2). This minimalist service consists of three interfaces:

■ **CollectionFactory** defines a single *create* operation. You invoke this operation to create a new instance of an empty collection.

■ **Collection** defines operations that let you *add, replace, retrieve,* and *remove* members of a collection. You invoke *add_all_elements* to add all the elements from a source collection to your collection. *Insert_element_at* lets you add an

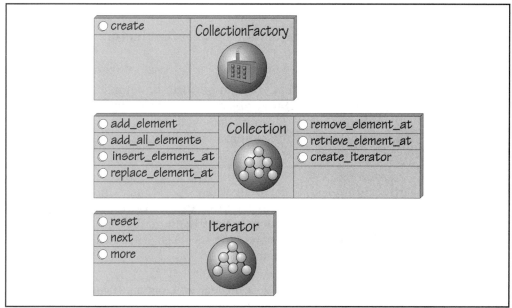

Figure 13-2. Query Service: The Collection Interfaces.

element in a particular position. *Create_iterator* lets you create a movable pointer to navigate the collection.

■ **Iterator** defines three operations that let you traverse a collection. *Reset* points to the start of a collection. *Next* increments the iterator's position. *More* lets you test if there are elements left in the iteration. The method returns true if there are more elements that you can access in a collection; it returns false if you've reached the end of a collection.

These three interfaces can be extended using the CORBA *Collection Service*, which we cover later in this chapter.

Query Service: The Query Interfaces

The Query Service provides a framework consisting of five interfaces for dealing with the preparation and execution of a query (see Figure 13-3).[2] Here's what these interfaces do:

■ **QueryEvaluator** defines an operation to *evaluate* a query. This operation executes the query using the query language you specify (or a default). A database system is an example of a **QueryEvaluator** object; it manages an implicit collection of persistent objects.

■ **QueryManager** is a more powerful form of **QueryEvaluator**. It also lets you *create* a **Query** object.

■ **Query** defines four operations that you can perform on an instance of a query. Every query is represented by a **Query** object. *Prepare* lets you compile a query and prepare it for execution. *Execute* lets you execute a compiled query. *Get_status* lets you determine the preparation/execution status of the query. *Get_result* lets you obtain the result of a query.

■ **QueryableCollection** does not introduce new operations. Instead it inherits its function from the interfaces **QueryEvaluator** and **Collection**. Objects of this class evaluate a query on members of a particular collection. Note that any collection member can itself be an object of this class. This means that you can have an infinite number of nested subqueries.

---

[2] The Query Service also defines an interface called **QueryLanguageType** and six classes derived from it to represent a classification of query languages. These interfaces do not provide any operations. They just use IDL to represent a query language type hierarchy.

You can extend these four interfaces (via inheritance) to provide additional functions. For example, you can extend the **Query** interface to provide a general-purpose result browser that keeps track of successive results. Note that the base Query Service consists of only two interfaces: **QueryEvaluator** and **QueryableCollection**.

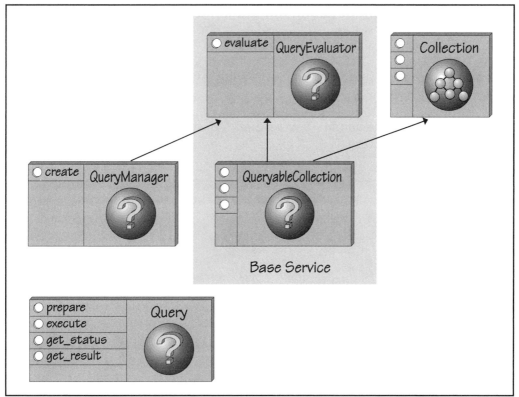

Figure 13-3. Query Service: The Query Interfaces.

A Simple Query Scenario

It's time to go over a couple of scenarios that show how these interfaces play together. We'll start out with the simplest possible query scenario, using an object that implements the **QueryableCollection** interface. Remember, this is an object that knows how to execute a query over a collection of objects it controls. Here are the steps you follow to issue a query and iterate through the result (see Figure 13-4):

1. ***Submit the query.*** You invoke *evaluate* on the **QueryableCollection** object to execute the query. You pass it parameters that include the query statement and the language you used to express the query (OQL or SQL). The target object

executes the query and returns the results in a collection that it controls.

2. ***Create a pointer for navigating the results***. You invoke *create_iterator* to create a new iterator. The iterator is automatically reset to point to the beginning of the collection that contains the query results.

3. ***Read the first element in the collection***. You invoke *retrieve_element_at* to read the object (or a row expressed as a CORBA "any" type) that the iterator is pointing at.

4. ***Point to the next object in the collection***. You invoke *next* to point to the next object or row in the collection.

Loop on the last two steps until you read all the objects that are returned by the query. You're done.

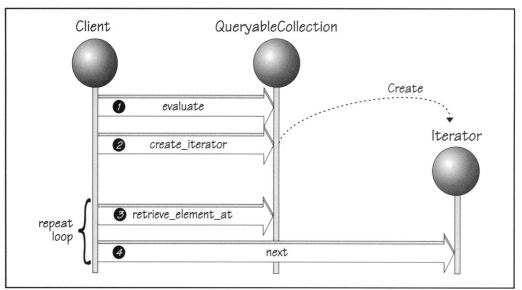

Figure 13-4. A Simple Query Scenario.

A More Complex Query Scenario

Because queries can be complex and resource demanding, there are times when you may want finer control over the processing of a query. In particular, you may want to: 1) use a graphical query picker to construct the query; 2) precompile and save the query to reexecute it at a later time; 3) execute the query asynchronously—this lets you do something else and then come back and check the results of the query later; and 4) check the status of a long-running query to decide whether to continue or abort.

To obtain these finer levels of control, you must use a **QueryManager** object and an associated **Query** object. The **QueryManager** controls a set of collections that you may query. It will assign your query (and the collection against which it executes) to a particular **Query** object. You can interact with this **Query** object to control the execution of your query. The scenario in Figure 13-5 shows the steps you must follow:

1. ***Create a Query object***. You invoke *create* on an object that supports the **QueryManager** interface to create a new **Query** object. The **QueryManager** then creates a new **Query** object and returns its object reference (so that you can call it directly).

2. ***Precompile the query***. You invoke *prepare* on the **Query** object to precompile (and store) the query for later execution. The parameters you pass include the query expression and the language you used to express the query (OQL or SQL).

3. ***Execute the query***. You can execute a precompiled query as many times as you like (perhaps using a different set of search parameters each time). You do this by invoking *execute* on a **Query** object (the object maintains the context

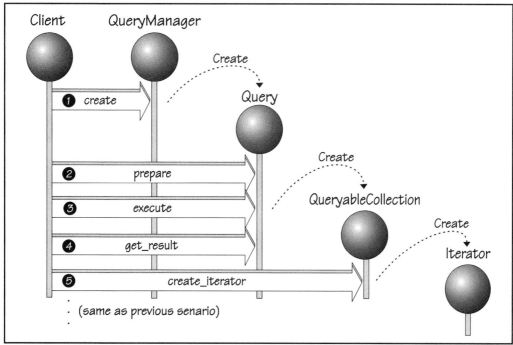

Figure 13-5. A More Complex Query Scenario.

of a query that you previously prepared). In our scenario, the **Query** object places the results of a query in a **QueryableCollection** object. The **QueryManager** typically owns all the collection objects in a domain.

4. ***Obtain the result of the query.*** You invoke *get_result* to make sure the query executed successfully. The call will typically return the object reference of a collection object that contains the results of the query.

5. ***Iterate through the results***. You follow the same steps as in the previous scenario to iterate through the returned collection of objects (or table rows).

This concludes our second query scenario. You should now have a better picture of how these interfaces play together. The trick is to understand that there are different levels of query service available to you. You should also understand how collections can help you process the results of a query.

THE CORBA COLLECTION SERVICE

Collections let you manipulate objects in a group. You typically apply collection operations on groups instead of the individual objects they contain. Examples of collections are *queues, stacks, lists, arrays, trees, sets,* and *bags*. Each of these collection types exhibit behaviors that are specific to the collection. For example, here are some of the operations you can invoke on a set: add a new member, test for equality, test for emptiness, union, intersection, and so on. Some collections are ordered; others use keys to identify the elements. Finally, some collections keep track of object references; others simply collect data types (for example, rows in a table collection).

The CORBA *Collection Service*—passed in mid-1996—provides a uniform way to create and manipulate the most common collections. It defines IDL for these common collection classes. The CORBA Collection Service is based on the Taligent Collection Classes. It's a superset of the ODMG-93 collections, but for distributed objects. We expect that you will be able to acquire multiple substitutable implementations from the supplier community. For example, we expect to see CORBA IDL-ized versions of a variety of collection classes—including the IBM/Taligent C++ collections, the ANSI C++ Standard Template Library (STL), ODMG collections, and Rogue Wave. If this happens, you will never have to reinvent operations for manipulating stacks, queues, sets, and so on.

How does the Collection Service relate to the collection interfaces that were introduced by the Query Service? The Query Service only supports a minimalist collection service. It defines top-level collection interfaces. The Collection Service lets you subclass these interfaces for different types of collections. So you can start using this minimalist collection service now and extend it when you need more function.

Collection Basics

Collections are foundation classes for a broad range of applications. Consequently, they must be able to collect elements of various types. Generally, all elements of a collection instance are of the same type. Collection types differ by the grouping characteristic they expose. For example, an *ordered* collection lets you access its elements positionally. All collections are derived from the base **Collection** interface, which defines operations for adding, replacing, removing, and retrieving elements. It also defines operations for obtaining information on a collection and for creating iterators.

All collections must provide pointers called *iterators*. You use an iterator to navigate the collection and to access elements within a collection. You can use an iterator to retrieve, replace, remove, and add elements. You can test iterators for equality, compare ordered iterators, and clone or assign an iterator. In addition, you can use multiple iterators to point to the same elements in a collection.

Finally, the Collection Service provides a variety of *factories* for creating instances of the most common collection types. Each collection type (or interface) has its own factory. So the CORBA Collection Service defines collections, iterators, and factories that you can use in distributed object environments. You will find that collections are absolutely vital for organizing distributed objects in groups and then iterating through the elements of the group. Collections introduce an iterator-centric programming model that you can use to manipulate groups of arbitrary objects. It's a form of "generic programming."

The CORBA Core Collection Types

The CORBA Object Collection Service defines interfaces for common collection types based on the behavior they exhibit. This behavior is mainly related to the "nature" of the collection instead of the type of the objects it collects. The nature of a CORBA collection can be expressed via the following well-defined properties:

■ ***Ordering of elements:*** A previous or next relationship exists between the elements of an ordered collection. The ordering of a collection can be sequential or sorted. A *sequential* ordering is explicit. A *sorted* ordering is implicit; it is based on a sort criteria that you define.

■ ***Access by key:*** A keyed collection lets you associatively access its elements via a key. A *key* can be computed from an element value via an operation that you define.

■ *Element equality:* An equality collection allows you to test its elements for equality.

■ *Uniqueness of entries*: A collection with unique entries allows exactly one occurrence of an element.

CORBA combines these basic properties to define a variety of collection types. Figure 13-6 shows the different combinations. Each combination maps to an interface that defines a particular collection type—including operations that exploit these properties. The white area in the table represents concrete collections.

		Unordered		Ordered		
				Sorted		Sequential
		Unique	Multiple	Unique	Multiple	Multiple
Key	Element Equality	Map	Relation	Sorted Map	Sorted Relation	
	No Element Equality	KeySet	KeyBag	KeySorted Set	KeySorted Bag	
No Key	Element Equality	Set	Bag	Sorted Set	Sorted Bag	Equality Sequence
	No Element Equality		Heap			Sequence

Figure 13-6. The Collection Property-to-Interface Mapping.

The CORBA Collection Service combines these interfaces via multiple inheritance to form an abstract interface hierarchy (see Figure 13-7). The abstract classes represent the different properties. The leaves of this hierarchy represent concrete collection interfaces that you can instantiate. These concrete interfaces provide a differentiated offering of collection interfaces.

In addition, this division introduces a parallel hierarchy for iterators (see Figure 13-8). The base **Iterator** interface lets you traverse any collection independently of its concrete type. The rest of the iterators are tightly bound with a collection type. For example, **KeyCollection** supports **KeyIterator**. An iterator instance cannot exist independently of the collection for which it was created.

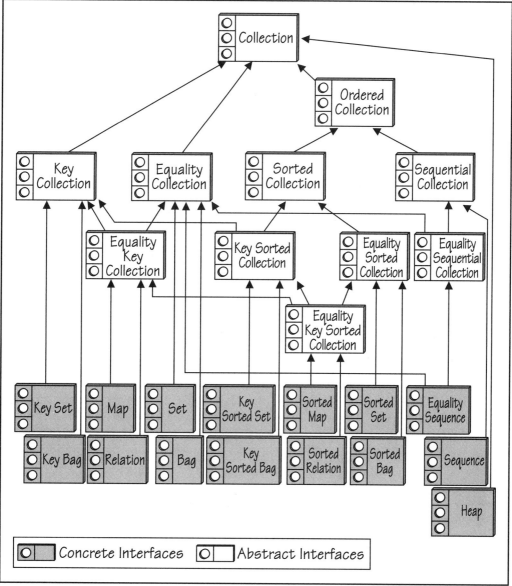

Figure 13-7. CORBA Core Collections: The Collection Interface Hierarchy.

Table 13-1 describes the basic collection types in more detail—including the factories and iterators they support.

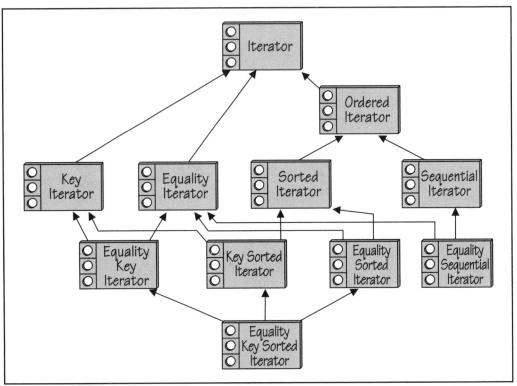

Figure 13-8. CORBA Core Collections: The Iterator Hierarchy.

Table 13-1. The CORBA Basic Collection Types.

Collection interface	Factory/Iterator Interfaces	Description
Bag	BagFactory EqualityIterator	Is an unordered collection of zero or more elements with no key. It supports multiple elements as well as element equality.
SortedBag	SortedBagFactory EqualitySortedIterator	Is a **Bag** that also exposes and maintains a sorted order of elements based on a user-defined element comparison.
KeyBag	KeyBagFactory KeyIterator	Is an unordered collection of zero or more elements that have a key. Multiple keys are supported. It does not support element equality.
KeySortedBag	KeySortedBagFactory KeySortedIterator	Is a **KeyBag** that is also sorted by key.

Table 13-1. The CORBA Basic Collection Types. (Continued)

Collection interface	Factory/Iterator Interfaces	Description
Heap	CollectionFactory Iterator	Is an unordered collection of zero or more elements with no key. It supports multiple elements. It does not support element equality.
Map	MapFactory EqualityKeyIterator	Is an unordered collection with zero or more elements with unique keys. It does not support element equality.
SortedMap	SortedMapFactory EqualityKeySortedIterator	Is a **Map** that is also sorted by key.
Relation	RelationFactory EqualityKeyIterator	Is an unordered collection of zero or more elements with a key. It supports multiple keys as well as equality.
SortedRelation	SortedRelationFactory EqualityKeySortedIterator	Is a **Relation** that is also sorted by key.
Set	SetFactory EqualityIterator	Is an unordered collection for zero or more elements with no key. It supports element equality.
SortedSet	SortedSetFactory EqualitySortedIterator	Is a **Set** that is also sorted by a user-defined element comparison.
KeySet	KeySetFactory KeyIterator	Is an unordered collection with zero or more elements with a key. It does not support element equality.
KeySortedSet	KeySortedSetFactory KeySortedIterator	Is a **KeySet** that is also sorted by key.
Sequence	SequenceFactory SequentialIterator	Is an ordered collection of elements with no key. There is a first and a last element. Each element except the last one has a next element. And each element except the first one has a previous element. It does not support element equality. Multiples may occur.
EqualitySequence	EqualitySequenceFactory EqualitySequentialIterator	Is a **Sequence** that also supports element equality.

Restricted-Access Collections

In addition to the core collections, CORBA defines four restricted-access collection types: **Queue**, **PriorityQueue**, **Dequeue**, and **Stack** (see Figure 13-9). You can think of these collections as restricted access variants of **Sequence** or **KeySortedBag**. The restricted access interfaces form their own hierarchy. They are not incorporated into the hierarchy of combined properties. Here's a description of these interfaces:

- **Queue** is a restricted-access **Sequence**. You can only add (or *enque*) a last element to a **Queue**. And, you can only remove (or *deque*) the first element. It's first-in, first-out.

- **Deque**—or double-ended queue—is a restricted-access **Sequence**; it only lets you add or remove a first or last element.

- **PriorityQueue** is a restricted-access **KeySortedBag**. You can add an element relative to the ordering relation defined for its keys. You can remove only the first element (the one with highest priority).

- **Stack** is a restricted-access **Sequence**. You can only add (or *push*) an element as the last element—meaning at the top. You can only remove (or *pop*) the last element from the top of the **Stack**. It's last-in, first-out.

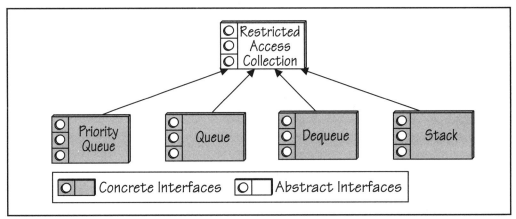

Figure 13-9. The CORBA Restricted Access Collections.

CONCLUSION

This concludes another two CORBA services—the tally is now eleven down and four more to go. CORBA is an extremely ambitious undertaking; it covers the entire field of distributed object computing. The two services we presented in this chapter are extremely important in their own right. We could write an entire book describing the fun things you could do with just these two services. The marriage of object queries with collections is absolute dynamite. But we've got to move on.

Chapter 14

CORBA Services: Object Relationships and Time

In this chapter, we cover two non-related CORBA services: *Relationships* and *Time* (see Figure 14-1). The Relationship Service lets you dynamically create relations between objects that know nothing of each other. The Time Service provides CORBA interfaces for synchronizing distributed time. It also lets you create time-activated triggers.

THE CORBA RELATIONSHIP SERVICE

Applications are built out of existing objects that are connected together.

— CORBA COSS Specification

Real-world objects never exist in isolation. They form a myriad of relationships with other objects. These relationships come and go. Relationships can be static, spontaneous, dynamic, and ad hoc. Distributed objects (and components) must be able to model their real-world counterparts. You should be able to dynamically create and keep track of relationships between objects that are not relationship-aware. You should be able to do this without changing or recompiling objects when they are brought into new relationships.

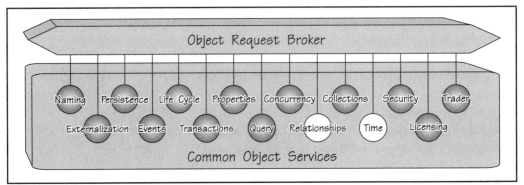

Figure 14-1. CORBA Services: Relationships and Time.

The CORBA *Relationship Service* allows components and objects that know nothing of each other to be related. It lets you do this without changing existing objects or requiring that they add new interfaces. In other words, the service lets you create dynamic relationships between immutable objects. The service keeps track of the relationships between objects; the related objects are not even aware that they are part of a relationship.

Why a Relationship Service?

Without a relationship service, your objects would have to keep track of their relationships using ad hoc pointers. For example, an object could maintain a collection of references to all its related objects. It would need to keep track of the type of the relationship and its attributes.

This ad hoc solution—using object references—is not very appealing or useful. Object references are unidirectional. It is very difficult to navigate a relationship that's maintained by a set of ad hoc pointers. You can't easily export your ad hoc pointers to other objects that need to understand and navigate the relationship. For example, you may need to pass to a deep copy service an object relationship graph so that it can understand which related objects it must copy or move. Most importantly, without a Relationship Service, you cannot create relationships between objects "on-the-fly." Hardcoded relationships between objects won't get you very far in a dynamic component environment. The bottom line is that you need a Relationship Service.

What Exactly Is a Relationship?

Real-world objects are always involved in relationships. For example, consider the book you're reading. Here are some of the relationships in which it is involved (see Figure 14-2):

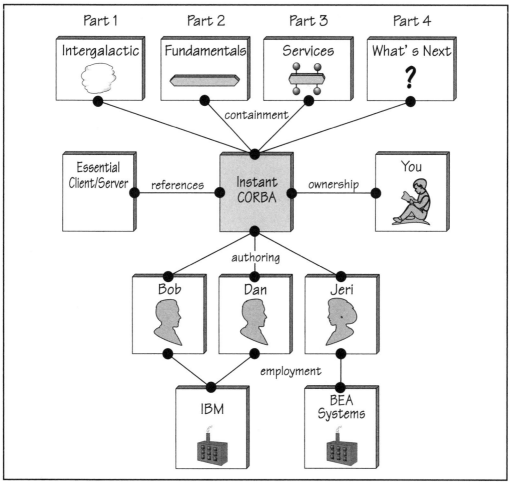

Figure 14-2. A Graph of Related Objects.

- **Ownership relationships** between people and books. A person *owns* a book; a book is *owned* by one or more persons. In the ownership relationship instance shown, you own this book (and we thank you for it).

- **Containment relationships** between books and parts. A book *contains* parts; a part is *contained in* a book. In the containment relationship instance shown, this book contains four parts.

- **Reference relationships** between books. A book *references* other books; a book is *referenced by* one or more books. In the reference relationship instance shown, this book references our other book, **The Essential Client/Server Survival Guide, Second Edition**—what braggarts we are!

■ *Authoring relationships* between books and authors. A book is *written by* one or more authors; an author *writes* a book. In the authoring relationship instance shown, this book was authored by Bob, Dan, and Jeri.

■ *Employment relationships* between companies and people. A company *employs* one or more persons; a person is *employed* by one or more companies. In the relationship instance shown, Jeri works for BEA Systems; Dan and Bob work for IBM (when they're not writing books).

A *relationship* is defined by a set of *roles* that two or more objects play (roles are denoted by the dark bubbles). For example, in an employment relationship, a company plays an *employer* role and a person plays an *employee* role. A single object can play different roles in different relationships. For example, Jeri is an employee and an author. A *degree* refers to the number of required roles in a relationship. All the relationships we've shown in the figure are *binary*—they are of degree two. *Cardinality* defines the maximum number of relationships in which a role is involved. For example, a book has a many-to-one containment relationship with parts (the cardinality is unbounded); but a part is contained in only one book (its cardinality is one).

A relationship can have one or more *attributes*. For example, we could add a *job_title* attribute to the employment relationship. A relationship can also support method invocations that return information. Note that the attributes and methods of a relationship are totally independent of the objects they represent. You can think of the relationship as introducing its own independent semantics. A set of related objects form a *graph*. The objects themselves are *nodes* in the graph; the relationships form the *edges*. Figure 14-2 shows a graph of related objects (each object is a node in the graph).

Levels of Relationship Service

The Relationship Service defines generic interfaces that let you associate roles and relationships with existing CORBA objects. You can then traverse them (in any direction) using very sophisticated graph interfaces. The service maintains the relationships between the related objects. It also defines two specific relationships: *containment* and *references*. The service lets you create relationships of arbitrary degree and cardinality; it will enforce the degree and cardinality constraints and detect violations. The service treats relations, roles, and graphs as first-class CORBA objects. As a result, you can extend their function by subclassing. You can also pass around graphs that describe related objects to interested parties.

The beauty of the CORBA Relationship Service is that it lets you create arbitrary relations between objects that are totally unaware of relationships. You can do this without changing the implementation of the existing objects. The service lets you

223

surround existing objects with a web of relationship objects that you put together piece by piece. The service defines interfaces that let you construct and navigate these relationship webs (node by node). The interfaces of the Relationship Service are grouped into three categories: *base*, *graph*, and *specific*. We go over these three categories in the next three sections.

Relationship Service: The Base Interfaces

The base relations interfaces define operations that let you create **Role** and **Relationship** objects and navigate the relationships in which a role participates (see Figure 14-3). We also show them inheriting from an **IdentifiableObject** interface that lets you test two CORBA object references for equality. This is a very generic object service that should have been part of the ORB interface; instead, it ended up in the Relationship Service (at least you know where to find it). The interfaces are grouped into two modules called *CosObjectIdentity* and *CosRelationships*. Here's what these interfaces do:

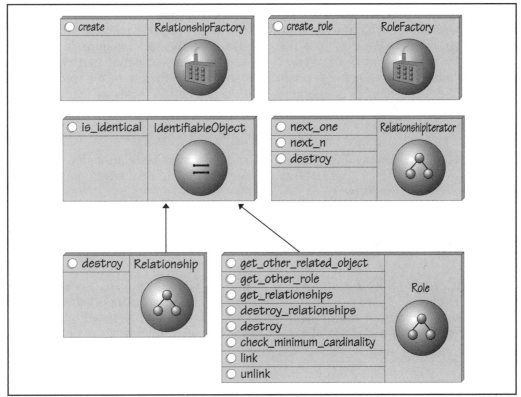

Figure 14-3. Relationship Service: The Base Interfaces.

■ **IdentifiableObject** provides a single operation *is_identical* that returns true if two CORBA objects are identical. The Relationship Service requires this object identity operation for the objects it defines.

■ **RelationshipFactory** defines a *create* operation that lets you create an instance of a relationship. You pass the factory a sequence of named roles that represent the related objects in the newly created relationship. The factory, in turn, informs each of the **Role** objects of the newly created relation by invoking their *link* operation.

■ **RoleFactory** defines a *create_role* operation that lets you associate a role with a CORBA object you pass as a parameter.

■ **Relationship** defines a single operation that lets you *destroy* a relationship. The roles are *unlinked* by the operation before the relationship is destroyed.

■ **Role** defines operations that let you navigate relationships in which a role participates and to link a role to a relationship. You invoke *get_other_role* to get to the related role in a relation; you invoke *get_other_related_object* to get the related object at the other end. You invoke *get_relationships* to obtain the relationships in which a role participates (see next bullet). You invoke *destroy_relationships* to free the role from all the relationships in which it participates. You invoke *destroy* to destroy a role that is not participating in any relationships. *Check_minimum_cardinality* returns true if a role satisfies its minimum cardinality constraints. *Link* is used by factories to link a role into a relationship. *Unlink* is used by the *destroy* operation to remove a role from a relationship.

■ **RelationshipIterator** lets you iterate through additional relationships in which a **Role** participates. An iterator object is returned when you invoke *Role::get_relationships*.

Relationship Service: Graphs of Related Objects

As we explained earlier, a graph is a set of nodes and edges. The *nodes* are the related objects; the *edges* are the relationships. A node can support one or more roles. The graph interfaces let you describe and traverse graphs (see Figure 14-4). Most of these interfaces are self-explanatory, but let's quickly go over the most important ones:

■ **Node** associates an object with its roles. It provides operations that let you add and remove roles. The *roles_of_type* operation lets you query for roles of a particular type.

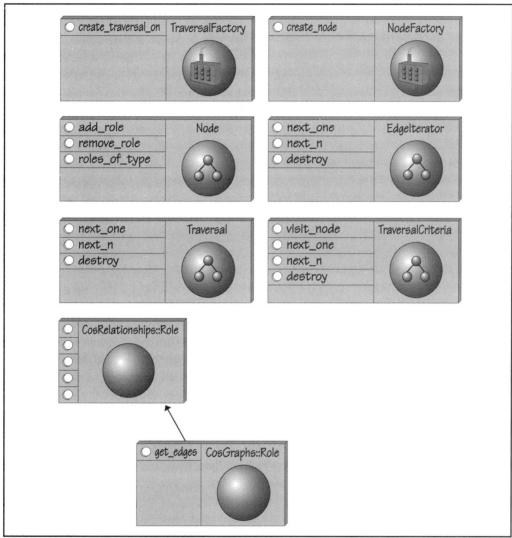

Figure 14-4. Relationship Service: The Graph Interfaces.

- **Traversal** lets you navigate through a graph of related objects starting at a **Node** object that you specify.

- **TraversalCriteria** lets you associate rules in the form of callback functions to determine what relationship/node should be visited next. The operations of this object are invoked by the **Traversal** object.

- **Role** is derived from **CosRelationships::Role**. It provides a new operation called *get_edges*. This operation returns a role's view of its relationships either in the form of a structure or an iterator of type **EdgeIterator**.

- **EdgeIterator** provides two operations that let you iterate through the relationships associated with a role. It also provides a self-destructing operation called *destroy*. You create and obtain an **EdgeIterator** object when you invoke *Role::get_edges*.

As you can see, these graph interface objects can be very useful. For example, you can use them to describe all the objects (and relationships) shown in Figure 14-2. You can then ship a graph object that describes these objects (as well as the objects themselves) to a remote destination where the relationships can be recreated and traversed. You do all this without modifying the related objects or their attributes. They're not in the least way aware that they are part of a graph of related objects. It's magic! The graph interfaces are used by the Life Cycle Service to implement deep copies and moves. They are also used by the Externalization Service to stream a group of related objects.

We anticipate that system integrators and IS shops will be the primary users of this service. Relationships offer them a standard way to define ad hoc ensembles made of multiple components. They will be able to attach roles to different components and connect them via graphs. This is one way for them to assemble a component suite (or ensemble).

Relationship Service: The Containment and Reference Relationships

Containment and *reference* are very common relationships. Consequently, the Relationship Service provides a standardized set of interfaces for both these relationships (see Figure 14-5). You can use these interfaces as a model for how to create your own relationships (for example, authoring, employment, family, friends, and so on).

Notice in the figure that these two relationships do not introduce any new operations. They are simply derived from the existing Relationship Service interfaces. These derived interfaces define CORBA IDL types for all the roles and relationships that are specific to containment and reference. The derived attributes let you define the degree of each relation. The containment relation defines a *ContainsRole* and a *ContainedInRole*. Likewise, the references relation defines a *ReferencesRole* and a *ReferencedByRole*. Both these relations are binary (of degree 2). The factories will enforce these constraints when you create new instances of these relationships.

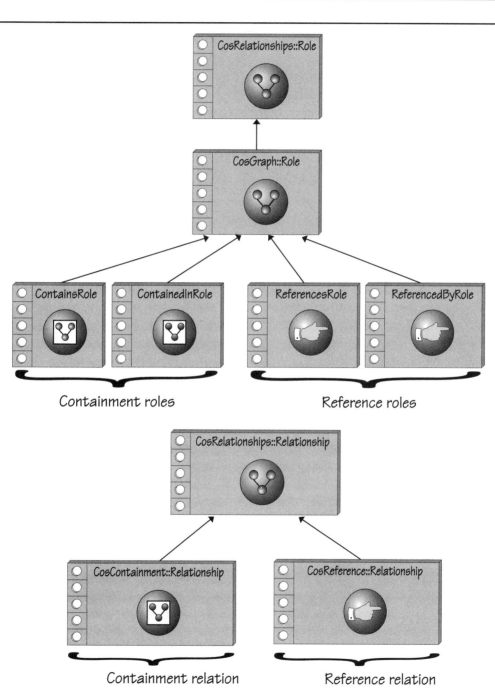

Figure 14-5. Relationship Service: The Containment and Reference Relationships.

THE CORBA OBJECT TIME SERVICE

Maintaining a single notion of time is important for ordering events that occur in distributed object systems. So how does an ORB keep the clocks on different machines synchronized? How does it compensate for the unequal drift rates between synchronizations? How does it create a single-system illusion that makes all the different machine clocks tick to the same time? The *Object Time Service* is the obvious answer.

The Time Service—adopted by OMG in mid-1996—provides interfaces that let you:

■ Obtain current time together with an estimate of error associated with it

■ Ascertain the order in which events occur

■ Generate time-based events based on timers and alarms

■ Compute the interval between two events

These interfaces can work with a variety of time synchronization mechanisms. For example, the underlying time can be obtained via a Cesium clock attached to each node or via some hardware/software time synchronization method (see the next Briefing box). CORBA does not try to reinvent things that have already been invented. It simply defines object interfaces for them.

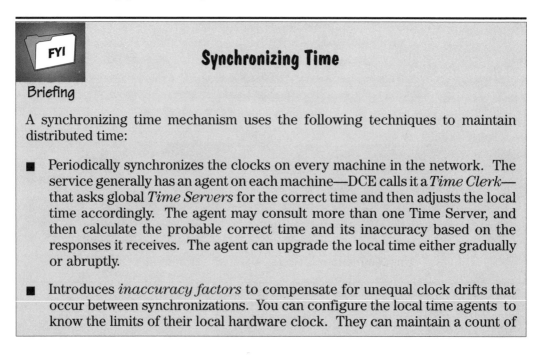

FYI

Synchronizing Time

Briefing

A synchronizing time mechanism uses the following techniques to maintain distributed time:

■ Periodically synchronizes the clocks on every machine in the network. The service generally has an agent on each machine—DCE calls it a *Time Clerk*—that asks global *Time Servers* for the correct time and then adjusts the local time accordingly. The agent may consult more than one Time Server, and then calculate the probable correct time and its inaccuracy based on the responses it receives. The agent can upgrade the local time either gradually or abruptly.

■ Introduces *inaccuracy factors* to compensate for unequal clock drifts that occur between synchronizations. You can configure the local time agents to know the limits of their local hardware clock. They can maintain a count of the inaccuracy factor and return it to an invocation that asks for the time. The time agent requests a resynchronization after the local clock drifts past an inaccuracy threshold.

■ Introduces *time server* objects that answer queries about the time. Following the DCE model, an ORB could provide at least three time servers; one (or more) must be connected to an external time provider. The time servers query one another to adjust their clocks. The external time provider may be a hardware device that receives time from a radio or a telephone source. If no such source is available, the system administrator's watch may suffice.

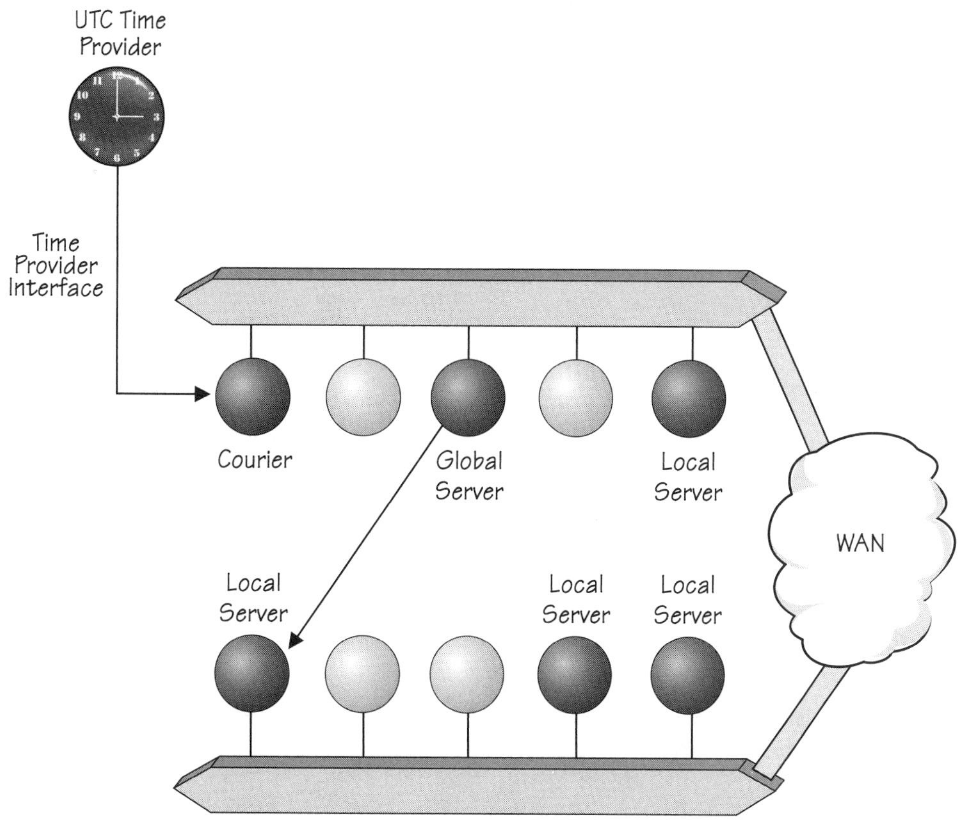

Figure 14-6. A Distributed Time Service.

UTC Time

The Object Time Service uses the *Universal Time Coordinated (UTC)* representation of time from the X/Open DCE Time Service. This makes it easy to work with global clock synchronization time sources—for example, UTC signals broadcast by the WWV radio station of the National Bureau of Standards. UTC time is defined in number of 100-nanosecond time units elapsed since the beginning of the Gregorian calendar—October 15, 1582. It is the industry's most commonly used time base.

UTC time is adjusted using the Greenwich time zone differential factor—for example, -5 hours in New York City. The UTC time in the CORBA specification always refers to time in the Greenwich time zone. This makes the corresponding binary representations of relative time the same as for absolute time. UTC makes it easy for CORBA time to interoperate with time from existing systems—including the *X/Open DCE Time Service*.

The Time Service Interfaces

The Object Time Service consists of five interfaces; three of them—**UTO**, **TIO**, and **TimerEventHandler**—represent instances of basic time objects (see Figure 14-7). The other two interfaces—**TimeService** and **TimerEventService**—define operations that let you create and manage these basic objects. Let's quickly go over these interfaces:

■ The **UTO** interface represents a *Universal Time Object (UTO)*. Each **UTO** object represents a UTC time value and its inaccuracy factor (see the previous Briefing box). The interface defines methods that let you read and manipulate the UTC time contained in the object. For example, you invoke *compare_time*

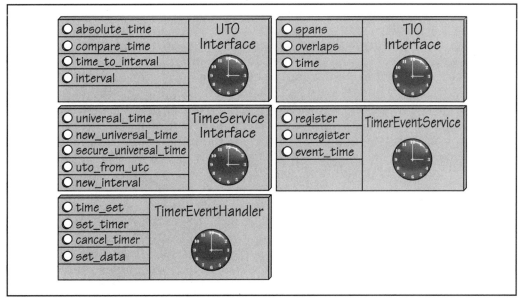

Figure 14-7. The CORBA Time Service Interfaces.

to compare the time in the object with a **UTO** that you pass as a parameter. You invoke *interval* to obtain a time interval object that represents the inaccuracy factor of this **UTO**. You invoke *compare_time* to compare the time in the object with a **UTO** that you pass as a parameter. You invoke *time_to_interval* to obtain a time interval object that represents the difference between the time in the object and a **UTO** that you pass as a parameter. You should note that a **UTO** is immutable. You can pass around references to it, read its value, and compare it with the value of other objects. However, you cannot modify the time in the object.

■ The **TIO** interface represents a *Time Interval Object (TIO)*. The interface defines operations relevant to time intervals. For example, *spans* returns the overlap between the interval in the object (interval A) and a **UTO** object that you pass as a parameter (interval B); Figure 14-8 shows the four possible outcomes. The *overlaps* operation does the same, but for a **TIO** object that you pass as a parameter. Finally, the *time* operation returns a **UTO** in which the inaccuracy interval is equal to the time interval in the **TIO**.

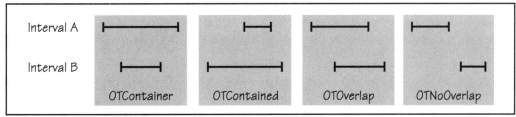

Figure 14-8. Time Interval Overlap.

- The **TimeService** interface defines operations that let you construct **UTO**s and **ITO**s. You invoke *universal_time* to create a **UTO** with the current time and an estimate of its inaccuracy. You invoke *secure_universal_time* to create a **UTO** with the current time obtained from a secure time source; you typically use this operation to create a "trusted" timestamp. You invoke *new_universal_time* to construct a new **UTO** from the values you specify for each attribute; you typically invoke this operation to specify the time for an event to fire. You invoke *uto_from_utc* to create a **UTO** from a UTC time parameter that you pass; you typically invoke this operation to convert a UTC time value you receive over the wire into a **UTO**. Finally, you invoke *new_interval* to construct a new **ITO** with the upper and lower bounds you specify.

- The **TimerEventHandler** interface represents an object that holds information about a timed event—including the time when the event is to be triggered and the action to be taken. You invoke *set_timer* to specify the event trigger time in the form of a **UTO** object that you pass; you can specify the time to be either periodic or relative. You invoke *cancel_timer* to reset a timed event that has not yet triggered. You invoke *set_data* to specify or change the event data that is passed by the *push*. The only thing that you cannot change is the event channel that is associated with this object. Finally, you invoke *time_set* to determine if this event is triggered.

- The **TimerEventService** interface defines operations that let you create **TimerEventHandler** objects and then register and unregister these objects with event channels. The interface only supports the push event model. You invoke *register* to construct a **TimerEventHandler** object. You must specify the event data and a **PushConsumer** object. This is the object that invokes the *push* method when the event fires. You invoke *unregister* to destroy this **TimerEventHandler** object.

A Timer-Based Event Trigger Scenario

It's time for a scenario that shows how these interfaces play together. The scenario in Figure 14-9 walks you through the set up and firing of a timer-based event. Here are the steps:

1. ***Obtain a push consumer object from the event channel***. Invoke *obtain_-push_consumer* on the event channel's **SupplierAdmin** to obtain the reference to a **ProxyPushConsumer** object.

2. ***Register it with the TimerEventService***. Invoke the *register* method on the **TimerEventService**, passing it the reference to the **ProxyPushConsumer**. You also pass it the event data—meaning data the channel will *push* to its subscribers when the event triggers.

3. ***Construct a UTO with the relative trigger time.*** Invoke *new_universal_-time* on the **TimeService** to construct a **UTO** from the values you specify for each attribute. In this scenario, the **UTO** contains the relative time for this event to fire.

4. ***Set the relative trigger time.*** Invoke *set_timer* on the **TimerEventHandler** to specify the event trigger time; you must pass it a reference to the **UTO** object with the relative trigger time. The event handler object is now primed. You can now sit back and wait for the event to trigger.

5. ***The event triggers.*** The event fires at the time you specify. The channel will then invoke *push* methods on all the subscribers to this push consumer proxy. It will pass the event data as a parameter.

6. ***Unregister the event handler.*** Invoke *unregister* on the **TimerEventService** to release the resources of an event handler object. You must pass it the object reference of the **TimerEventHandler** object that you want to unregister.

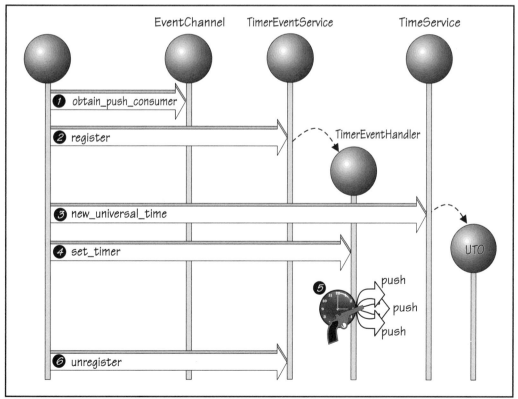

Figure 14-9. A Timer-Based Event Trigger Scenario.

CONCLUSION

This concludes another two CORBA services—the tally is now thirteen down and two more to go. You can use the Relationship Service in countless situations involving independently developed components. For example, you could use that service to create workflows, enforce referential integrity, describe compound documents, and create object containers of all types. The Time Service is also quite useful—especially for ordering events and setting time-triggered events.

Chapter 15

CORBA Services: Licensing and Properties

In this chapter, we introduce the last two CORBA Services: *Properties* and *Licensing* (see Figure 15-1). Again, these are very useful foundation services for a distributed component infrastructure. Properties let you dynamically associate attributes with shrink-wrapped components at run time. You can then manage these attributes independently from the objects they describe. Licensing is very dear to the heart of all component providers. We cannot earn a living without it.

THE CORBA OBJECT LICENSING SERVICE

> As desktop networking increases, control of component usage becomes more difficult. Components will "leak" into organizations from external sources and be propagated quickly via networks and "sneakernet."
>
> — *Gartner Group*
> *(February, 1995)*

For the component market to evolve in a manageable fashion, license management software will have to grow to include component licensing. And components will have to be written to automatically register with license managers. The CORBA *Licensing Service*—originally from Gradient, Digital, and IBM—meets these

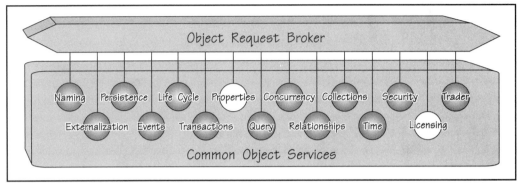

Figure 15-1. CORBA Object Services: Properties and Licensing.

requirements. As we said earlier, it should be dear to the heart of all component providers. The service lets you meter the use of your components and charge accordingly. Traditional licensing mechanisms—for example, site licensing and node-locked licensing—do not play well in the world of distributed ORB-based components. We need more flexible mechanisms for metering the use of our components and charging for their usage.

What Does the Licensing Service Do?

The Licensing Service lets you enforce a wide range of licensing options to fit your business needs. For example, you can provide a grace period to let potential new users test-drive your components, you can ensure that a license is always available to high-priority customers, you can allow multiple components to be used with a single license, and so on. The Licensing Service separates the "I want to be controlled" requirements of a component from the "how am I to be controlled" requirements that deal with policy. A component notifies the service when it wishes to be controlled without getting into the details of how the control is enforced.

The Licensing Service can collect component usage metrics. This helps you determine which components are "shelfware" and which are actively being used. All licenses must have start/duration and expiration dates. You should also be able to assign some licenses to specific users, collections of users, or organizations. The service makes sure that when a licensed component is being used, the component and the licensing server are continuously aware of each other's existence. Finally, the Licensing Service must be a secured server resource. You don't want a Trojan horse (or an imposter licensing system) to give away free licenses to your components. You also don't want to let outsiders tamper with the usage database.

Licensing Service Interfaces

A *component market must protect itself from copying and distribution of good components without reimbursement.*

> — Dr. Ivar Jacobson, Author
> *Object-Oriented Software Engineering*
> *(Addison-Wesley, 1993)*

The Licensing Service consists of two interfaces (see Figure 15-2) that provide all the operations a component needs to license-protect itself. The component uses these interfaces to let the service monitor know when it's being used (including by whom and for how long). Let's go over these two interfaces and explain what they do:

■ **LicenseServiceManager** is like a minibroker for locating license services that implement specific policies. It will connect you with a service that's suitable for your component. The interface supports a single operation with a very long name: *obtain_producer_specific_license_service*. This operation returns an object reference for a particular license service. Note that a "producer" is your licensed component. It's the intellectual property you produced and for which you want to be compensated.

■ **ProducerSpecificLicenseService** provides three operations that do all the work. Your licensed component invokes *start_use* when it's first used. You must

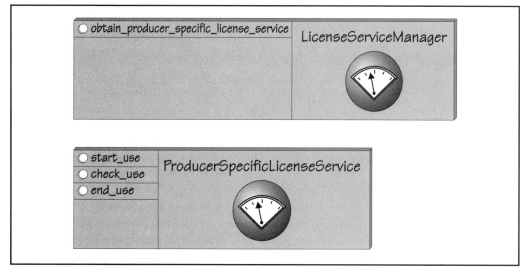

Figure 15-2. The Licensing Service Interfaces.

pass in a parameter all the necessary information associated with the user of the component. The component invokes *end_use* when it stops being used. It invokes *check_use* periodically when it's being used to let the service know the connection with the customer is still live. The service may check for license expiration time and return a message to that effect. How does the component know when to invoke a *check_use*? It knows by either polling at an interval specified by the server, or by asynchronously receiving an event notification from the server telling it to issue a *check_use*.

All the operations between the component and the service are protected by a poor man's authentication mechanism called a *challenge* (it's an in/out parameter that serves as an authentication key in the message). The license server must return the proper challenge result to authenticate itself to the licensed component. We expect these challenges to be replaced by the CORBA Security Service when it becomes widely available.

A Licensing Scenario

The scenario in Figure 15-3 demonstrates how a license-protected component interacts with the Licensing Service. Let's walk through the steps:

1. ***Obtain an object reference for a licensing service***. Every license-protected component must obtain an object reference to a licensing service that imple-

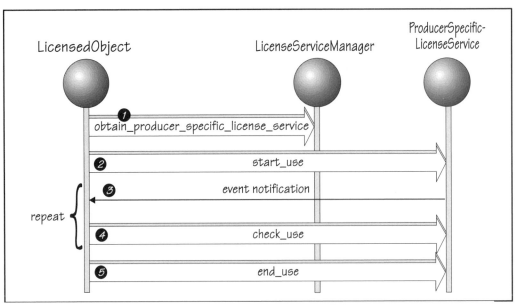

Figure 15-3. Scenario: How A License-Protected Component Interacts With the Licensing Service.

ments a policy that suits the component provider. You do this by invoking *obtain_producer_specific_license_service* on the **LicenseServiceManager**.

2. ***Notify the licensing service when a client starts using your component***. You must determine what it means to use your component and how you want to get paid for it. At one extreme, you may want to charge for each method invocation. At the other extreme, you may want to charge for a connection to a collection of objects. In any case, you invoke *start_use* to tell the licensing service that your component is being used. You must pass it the name of your component, its version, and the object reference for a callback event notification. In addition, you must pass it a user context that is used by the service to determine how to deal with the user of your component—for example, you might want to ask these two important questions: Is the user's license still valid? How should the user be charged for the use of your component? You will receive from the service instructions on how to proceed in the *action_to_be_taken* returned parameter.

3. ***Licensing service sends your component an event notification***. The licensing service tells your component that it's time to perform a *check_use*. It does this using the CORBA Event Service. Alternatively, the component could have issued *check_uses* at server-specified checking intervals.

4. ***Issue a check_use***. You invoke *check_use* to tell the licensing service that your component is still being used. The call returns instructions from the licensing service. You must issue *check_use*—either when requested to do so via an event or at regular intervals. This is how the licensing server and your component are continuously made aware of each other's existence when the component is in use.

5. ***Inform the licensing service when your component is no longer being used***. You invoke *end_use* to tell the licensing service the user (or client) stopped using your component. This is how the meter gets turned off.

In summary, your component must inform the service when it is first used, when it is still in use, and when it stops being used.

THE CORBA OBJECT PROPERTY SERVICE

The *Property Service*—originally from Taligent, SunSoft, and IBM—lets you dynamically associate named attributes with a shrink-wrapped component. You can define these dynamic attributes (or *properties*) at run time without using IDL. Then you can associate them with an object that already exists. Once you define these properties, you can give them names, get and set their values, set their access modes, and delete them. In contrast, you can only get and set an IDL-defined attribute. You cannot create an attribute "on the fly", set its mode, or delete it.

Properties are essentially typed named values that you can dynamically associate with an object outside the IDL type system. For example, you should be able to add an archive property to an existing document at run time and mark the document as ready to be archived. The archive information is associated with the object, but it's not part of the object's type.

Property Service Interfaces

The Property Service consists of six interfaces; four of these are factories and iterators. The two main interfaces are **PropertySet** and **PropertySetDef** (see Figure 15-4). **PropertySetDef** is a subclass of **PropertySet**; it provides additional operations that let you manipulate and control a property's mode.

The Property Service defines four mutually exclusive property *modes*: 1) *normal* means there are no restrictions to the property; 2) *read-only* means clients can read and delete the property but not update it; 3) *fixed-normal* means the property can be modified but not deleted; and 4) *fixed-readonly* means the property can only be read. You can think of these modes as metadata that define the constraints on a property. Every object that supports the Property Service must implement either the **PropertySet** or **PropertySetDef** interfaces. Let's go over the operations these two interfaces define:

- **PropertySet** defines ten operations that let you define, delete, enumerate, and check for the existence of properties. It provides *get* operations for reading property values and their metadata. It also provides "batch" operations that let you deal with sets of properties as a whole. These are the operations whose names end in "s". Note that a property consists of a name (a string), a value (of type any), and a mode.

- **PropertySetDef** defines eight operations that let you control and modify the property modes. You can manipulate these modes either individually or in batches.

It's easy to associate a property with an object and then manipulate it either individually or in a batch. The experience with SNMP and CMIP has taught the industry that it's important to be able to manipulate properties in groups, especially in distributed environments. The Property Service lets you do this very well; it also provides interfaces to iterate through groups of properties.

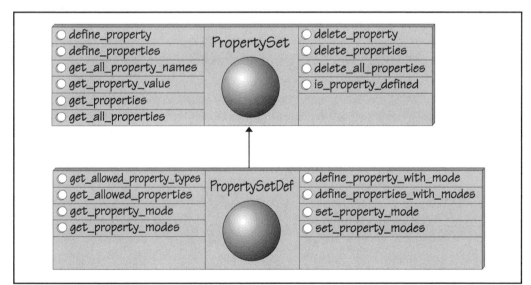

Figure 15-4. The Two Key Property Service Interfaces.

Conclusion

This concludes our presentation of the CORBA services. The tally is fifteen down with no more to go. The message we want to leave you with is that CORBA services represent the cutting edge of distributed object technology and client/server middleware. Most of this technology comes from advanced research projects from SunSoft, Taligent, IBM, HP, Digital, Oracle, ICL, Tandem, Novell, Groupe Bull, AT&T,

and Siemens. In addition, it represents the work of small but highly innovative companies such as Tivoli, Gradient, Iona, Visigenic, Expersoft, Visual Edge, and many others. Some people may call it "design by committee." However, we see it as the most ambitious cross-company effort ever attempted. This is what it takes to create the next generation of intergalactic middleware. No company alone can ever hope to duplicate this effort.

Part 4
CORBA:
What's Next?

An Introduction to Part 4

In Part 4, we first look at the state of CORBA today—including the good, the bad, and the ugly. Then we tell you what's coming down the near-term pipe. We conclude this book with the *Object Web II*—the final destination.

Here's what we will be covering in Part 4:

■ *Chapter 16* is about the state of CORBA today. We start by presenting a vendor scorecard for the CORBA functions that are implemented in commercial ORBs today. After all, you buy products, not standards. So CORBA is only as good as its ORB implementations. Next, we tell you about the good, the bad, and the ugly in CORBA today. We conclude by answering these two key questions: Can you use CORBA and Java today to deploy a new generation of Web-based client/server applications? Is the technology really ready for mission-critical prime time?

■ *Chapter 17* is about CORBA—the next generation. We look at the near-term technologies that will most likely make it into CORBA 3.0 (due in mid-1997). The ORB itself will be enhanced with several new features—including messaging (MOM), support for *composite objects* with multiple interfaces, server-side portable frameworks, and pass-by-value. These features have been under construction for over a year. At a higher level, CORBA will be augmented with a Common Facility for *Mobile Agents* and a *Business Object Framework*.

■ *Chapter 18* is about the *Object Web II*. We explain what remains to be done and where we go from here. As you will see, the Object Web must also be augmented with compound documents and components. Why? Because compound documents can literally provide magic on the Web, especially when combined with Java. Compound document frameworks—like OLE and CORBA's OpenDoc—provide two key technologies: 1) a visual component foundation for creating open Web browsers, and 2) the container technology for distributing, viewing, caching, and storing groups of related components and their data— meaning *shippable places*.

Part 4 covers the new frontiers of distributed object technology. Yes, CORBA is growing up. It is now starting to tackle distributed object issues that go much beyond simple interoperability. The new frontier encompasses server-side frame-works, MOM-based messaging, mobile agents, compound documents, business objects, object TP monitors, and industry-specific frameworks. We call this the *componentization* of distributed objects. The Object Web II is the longer-term vision of how these pieces play together.

Chapter 16

CORBA ORBs: The State of the Union

In this chapter, we look at the state of CORBA today. We start by presenting a scorecard for the CORBA functions that are implemented in commercial ORBs. After all, you buy products, not standards. So CORBA is only as good as its implementations. Next, we tell you about the good, the bad, and the ugly in CORBA today. These observations are based on work we did in our CORBA/Java lab and on the benchmarks we ran in our CORBA/Java programming book. They're also based on feedback we got from large customers, users, and graduate students. We conclude by trying to answer these two key questions: Can you use CORBA and Java today to deploy a new generation of Web-based client/server applications? Is the technology really ready for mission-critical prime time?

THE VENDOR SCORECARD

Table 16-1 compares the features in the top 8 commercial CORBA ORBs. This table is a preview from a much larger study by the Standish Group.[1] The full report should be available by the time you read this. In a nutshell, the story is that most ORB vendors will have implemented the full IIOP CORBA 2.0 protocol by the time you read this. However, they all seem to be struggling to keep up with the Object Services. We will continue this discussion in the next section.

---

[1] Source: Standish Group, *CORBA ORBs* (February, 1997).

Table 16-1. The Commercial ORB Scorecard (Source: Standish Group, February, 1997).

Features	ORBs							
	Digital Object-Broker	Visigenic VisiBroker	IBM SOM	Sun Joe/NEO	HP Orb Plus	IONA Orbix	Expersoft Power-Broker	ICL DAIS
IIOP	✔	✔	✔	✔	✔	✔	✔	✔
IR	✔	✔	✔	✔	'97	✔	✔	✔
Static	✔	✔	✔	✔	✔	✔	✔	✔
Dynamic	✔	✔	✔	✔	'97	✔	✔	✔
Language Bindings								
C	✔		✔	✔	'97	'97		✔
C++	✔	✔	✔	✔	✔	✔	✔	✔
Java	'97	✔	'97	✔	'97	✔	✔	✔
Smalltalk	'97	✔ (via DNS)	✔		✔ (via Parc-Place)	✔		
Cobol		'98	✔			✔		'97
Ada						✔		
CORBAservices								
Naming	✔	✔	✔	✔	✔	✔	✔	'97
Events	'97	✔	'97	✔	✔	✔	'97	✔
Life Cycle	'98	✔	'97	✔	✔	'97	✔	'98
Trader	'97	'97	'97		'97	'97	'97	✔
Transactions	'97	✔ (via third party)	'97	'97	'98	✔ (via third party)	'97	'97
Concurrency	'98	'97	'97	'97	'98	'97	'98	
Security	'97	'97	✔	'97	'97	'97	'97	✔
Persistence	'98		'97	✔	'98	✔	✔	'97
Externalization	'98		✔		'98	'97	'97	
Query	'98	'98	'98	✔		'97	'98	'98
Collections	'98	'98	'98			'97	'98	
Relationships	'98		'97	✔		'97	'97	
Time	'98	'97	'98			'97	'98	'98
Licensing	'98		'98			'97	'98	'98
Properties	'98		'98	✔		'97	'97	'98

247

CORBA ORBS: THE GOOD, THE BAD, AND THE UGLY

In this section, we summarize our experience with developing 3-tier client/server applications using CORBA and Java. We go over the good, the bad, and the ugly. In a sense, this section is one big Soapbox.

CORBA ORBs: The Good

We don't want to turn this section into a diatribe on why ORBs are wonderful. Instead, we will give you our top-ten list of the CORBA benefits that we experienced first-hand in our programs. Here they are, in no particular order:

- **A solid distributed object foundation:** A CORBA *object reference* is a very powerful unit of distributed service negotiation. It points to an object interface, which is a set of related methods that operate on an individual object. In contrast, an RPC only returns a reference to a single function. Furthermore, you can aggregate CORBA interfaces via multiple inheritance. And, CORBA objects are polymorphic—the same call behaves differently depending on the object type that receives it. Of course, RPCs don't support inheritance, polymorphism, or unique objects with state. The bottom line is that a CORBA object reference provides scalpel-like precision; it lets you invoke a set of methods on a specific object. Unique object references are the most efficient way to obtain remote services on the intergalactic network.

- **Callbacks:** We were able to use CORBA callbacks very effectively to control clients from the server side. You can also use callbacks to create client applications (and applets) that dynamically receive content, state, news, status, alerts, and instructions from their servers.

- **Excellent CORBA/Java integration:** We were pleasantly surprised by how well CORBA integrates with Java. CORBA *interfaces* map nicely to their Java counterparts. In addition, Netscape/Visigenic's *Caffeine* makes CORBA totally seamless to Java programmers. We also like the way some Java ORBs are able to seamlessly take advantage of Java threads on the server side. It shows good synergy between CORBA's object activation services and Java's threads. TP Monitors for objects will be able to do wonders in this new environment.

- **Excellent Java ORB performance:** Our benchmarks show that pure Java ORBs are able to hold their ground against their more seasoned C++ counterparts. The JIT compilers helped a lot.

- ***Interoperability with C++ objects:*** We were delighted by the seamless interoperation of Java objects with their C++ counterparts using IIOP. It's the cleanest way for Java objects to talk to existing code on the enterprise, and vice versa. CORBA's language-independent and OS-independent foundation makes it a natural player in the heterogeneous world of Java and the Internet.

- ***Dynamic discovery and introspection:*** CORBA objects are self-describing and introspective. CORBA's dynamic facilities—including the Trader Service, DII, and Interface Repository—provide a solid foundation for the dynamic discovery and invocation of services on the intergalactic network. They let you create very flexible and agile systems.

- ***A modern 3-tier client/server foundation:*** CORBA objects make ideal server objects in a 3-tier (or n-tier) distributed architecture.

- ***Local/remote transparency:*** A CORBA ORB can run in standalone mode on a laptop, or it can be interconnected with every other ORB in the universe via IIOP's intergalactic services. An ORB can broker interobject calls within a single process, multiple processes running within the same machine, or multiple processes running across networks and operating systems. This is all done in a manner that's transparent to your objects.

- ***A versatile server-to-server infrastructure:*** CORBA provides a middle-tier, object-to-object infrastructure that you can use to encapsulate data from multiple sources. In addition, you can use CORBA IDL to encapsulate existing systems and connect them to the ORB. Finally, you can create pools of server objects. Each pool can be managed by an *instance manager* that understands the requirements of an object class and provides the appropriate run-time environment. These instance managers are really *TP Monitors* for objects. They should be able to manage an object's state on transaction boundaries as well as provide load-balancing and smart activation services with object caching. Object TP Monitors can use the CORBA bus to coordinate server-side components and to provide fault-tolerance and load balancing. In addition, they can use IIOP's built-in *Object Transaction Service* to coordinate transactions across components and to manage state at transaction boundaries. You can use this server-to-server bus for intercomponent coordination. For example, you can use it to do publish-and-subscribe, workflow, or to create task forces of cooperating objects.

- ***An open standard:*** CORBA is not controlled by a single vendor. Consequently, you will always be able to obtain your ORBs from more than one vendor. Finally, CORBA is not platform-specific; it runs on all the major hardware platforms and operating systems. Yes, freedom of choice is wonderful! So, it's important for an intergalactic middleware foundation to be open.

We could go on, but we promised to stop after the top ten. Let's go after the bad and the ugly.

CORBA ORBs: The Bad

We did not encounter major problems with CORBA/Java. The bad reads more like a list of what's missing in CORBA ORBs. Here goes:

■ **Where are the CORBA Services?** We need a complete set of CORBA Services implemented in Java. If the ORB vendors need help getting these services out in a hurry, they should contact our graduate students.[2]

■ **Where's MOM?** MOM stands for *Message-Oriented Middleware*. It provides asynchronous message queues on both the client and server sides. MOM allows clients and servers to function at their own designated times and speeds without necessarily being simultaneously active. ORBs must provide MOM services to support mobile users and to facilitate communications in heterogeneous environments. We need to be able to pass objects by value; we also need to ship CORBA/Java agents using these queues.

We have additional esoteric items on our wish list. For example, we would like to see *semantic-level* extensions to the CORBA IDL. The idea is that components should be able to interact with each other at the semantic level. To do so, they need *ontologies* that you can use to create common vocabularies. A good example of this technology is Apple's *Project X*. The good news is that most of these concerns are being addressed by CORBA 3.0 (see the next chapter).

CORBA ORBs: The Ugly

After five years in gestation, most of the ugly has been squeezed out of the CORBA ORBs. There aren't too many nasty little secrets left. In the bad old days, we could always depend on a memory leak somewhere to bring a C++ ORB to its knees. It's becoming harder to do so, especially with Java ORBs.

So what makes an ugly ORB? In our book, it's a server platform that leaves a lot of the infrastructure as an exercise for the customer. This means that we have to reinvent the infrastructure instead of developing our business applications. We think the ORB vendors created a problem by selling ORBs without understanding

---

[2] As their class project, our students were able to build the CORBA *Trader Service* in Java in less than a semester.

the mission-critical requirements of the server side. You just can't shift all the burden to your customers. Most of the early CORBA users spent a lot of time and energy trying to get the server side to scale. We were hoping the ORB vendors could help us, but they didn't come through. Yes, ORBs are wonderful, but someone's got to provide servers that scale. The next time we write a book, we hope to point you to off-the-shelf commercial products that provide these functions.[3]

For the last four years, our perennial questions to the ORB vendors have been (and still are):

- *How do you scale the server side?* We're still looking for an ORB that can manage millions of server objects and their state.

- *Where's the load balancing?* We're still looking for an ORB that can distribute server loads across multiple processors and provide a single system image to the clients. The ORB should be able to prestart server objects and cache their state.[4]

- *Where's the fault-tolerance?* We're still looking for an ORB that provides automatic switchover during failure to an object replica.

In other words, how do you put the server side of the ORB on par with TP Monitors, ODBMSs, and RDBMSs? Four years later, it finally dawned on us that we were barking up the wrong tree. The ORB vendors are simply communications middle-ware providers. And, middleware communications providers do not normally deal with these issues. You don't normally purchase a mission-critical server framework from your TCP/IP stack vendor.

So who's going to provide this mission-critical stuff? In our programming book, we created our own poor man's TP Monitor: the *Object Dispenser*. However, it appears that the TP Monitor vendors have finally taken on this challenge (see the next section). In the meantime, use our Object Dispenser.

TP MONITORS MEET ORBS

TP Monitors are competing with distributed objects to become the application platform of choice for 3-tier client/server computing. So it should come as no

---

[3] Note that the alternatives aren't any better. DCOM is still in terrible shape; *Viper* will help. Today, the only alternative to an ORB that also scales is a procedural-based TP Monitor.

[4] We understand that Digital's *ObjectBroker* was deployed in an application that is able to handle 10,000 clients doing 750,000 method invocations daily. Source: Cushing Group, *Distributed Object Technology at Wells Fargo* (see http://www.cushing.com). This is good news, but it still does not address all the issues we've raised here.

surprise that *Object Request Brokers (ORBs)*—like CORBA and DCOM—are being considered the next generation TP Monitors. In fact, some of the key TP Monitor vendors are about ready to introduce a new generation of TP Monitors built on ORBs. We know of three major projects that are creating ORB-based TP Monitors: IBM's *Business Object Server Solution (BOSS)*, BEA Systems' Tuxedo-based *ObjectWare*, and Microsoft's *Viper*. Of course, Viper is only for DCOM objects.

So what do TP Monitors do for ORBs? In pure CORBA and DCOM implementations, objects can appear anywhere at any time. However, under the control of a TP Monitor, objects can be managed in a *predictable* manner. For example, a TP Monitor can prestart objects, manage their life cycle, and provide transaction-level authorization. TP Monitors do not like to be surprised. They like to be in control of their environment (see the next Briefing box). In contrast, pure objects are totally anarchistic. The marriage of objects and TP Monitors will create some interesting new patterns.

So what do ORBs do for TP Monitors? Objects allow TP Monitors to work with transactional middleware provided by standard off-the-shelf ORBs. The ORBs will be incorporated into commodity desktop operating systems such as NT, OS/2 Warp, Windows 95, and Macintosh. In addition, ORBs will be distributed freely with Web browsers where they will be used to provide a distributed object foundation for Java and intranets. For the first time, TP Monitor vendors will not be providing the transactional middleware themselves—both CORBA and DCOM include transaction services. Better yet, TP Monitors will work with mainstream middleware on both clients and servers. In addition, the distributed object infrastructure provides TP Monitors with myriads of standard services—including metadata, dynamic invocations, persistence, relationships, events, naming, component factories, licensing, security, collections, and many others. These are services TP Monitor vendors will not have to recreate.

Objects also make it easier for TP Monitors to create and manage rich transaction models—such as nested transactions and long-lived transactions (or workflow). TP Monitors will become frameworks for managing very smart components. Once TP Monitors and ORBs figure out how to play together, they can literally perform magic. TP Monitors will become the coordinators of distributed components on the Internet and Intranets. Instead of managing procedural server classes, TP Monitors will manage Java Server Beans, Oracle Cartridges, CORBA Business Objects, and Viperized ActiveXs (see Figure 16-1). TP Monitors will prestart components, manage their persistent state, and coordinate their interactions across networks. TP Monitors will provide a broad array of mission-critical services—including long-lived transactions, transactional workflow, load-balancing, transactional queues, fault-tolerance, and life cycle management. TP Monitors will make ORBs mission-critical. In return, ORBs will bring TP Monitors to the client/server mainstream—they will become the orchestrators of the Object Web.

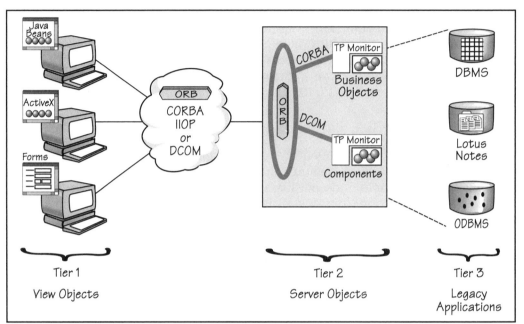

Figure 16-1. The Morphing of TP Monitors With ORBs.

FYI

OLTP Etiquette: The Five Commandments

Briefing

Online Transaction Processing (OLTP) systems have a 30-year tradition of squeezing every ounce of performance out of system resources. They're the masters of scale. Most of the world's largest client/server systems follow the OLTP discipline. They are typically synchronized by a *TP Monitor*. To play in an OLTP system, your programs must abide by these commandments:

■ ***Thou shalt not covet a system resource for too long***. You must never hog a system resource—including database connections, locks, communication sessions, server objects, and file handles. Clients should never hold state on the server for too long.

■ ***Thou shalt use transactions to clean up your messes***. You must use transactions to let the outside world know when you're committing your work. TP Monitors, SQL Databases, and ODBMSs use transaction boundaries to schedule and release the resources you use. Transactions are also used to synchronize the actions of OLTP server-side objects. Finally, transactions provide ACID properties that are used to clean up messes. For example, a resource manager can undo the effects of a failed transaction.

- ***Thou shalt reuse resources across clients*.** Servers must prestart pools of resources and allocate them to a client on an as-needed basis. When the client commits (or releases a resource), the server can assign it to another client. System resources are scarce; they must be recycled and shared.

- ***Thou shalt come in, do your work, and get out*.** Pat Helland—the *Viper* architect from Microsoft—calls it the "surgical strike approach." Servers must provide granular services; clients must come in, use the service, and get out.

- ***Thou shalt deal with large numbers of small things.*** This typically means that you must componentize your software. TP Monitors were the first to introduce a server component discipline. However, the components are procedural. ORBs and a new generation of Object TP Monitors—BOSS from IBM, Viper from Microsoft, and ObjectWare from BEA Systems—will be used to orchestrate server objects.

These five deceptively simple rules capture the folklore OLTP architects have successfully used to create some of the world's most complex distributed systems. Most of these rules apply to server-side CORBA objects. The good news is that OLTP only uses five commandments. This could mean that distributed systems are less complicated than their Biblical counterparts. ❑

IS CORBA READY FOR CLIENT/SEVER PRIME TIME?

There are two messages we want to leave you with. First, CORBA/Java have brought the fun back to client/server computing. It's a great time to be a programmer. Second, this is an unfinished story. The *Object Web* is just starting to take off. Java and CORBA are the two foundation technologies for the Object Web. However, Java and CORBA are not enough. We cover what remains to be done in the next two chapters.

So does this mean that Java and CORBA are not ready for client/server prime time? Absolutely not! The key message you should get from our books is that you can start now. Even in its current incarnation, CORBA/Java provides the best platform for creating Web-based client/server applications today.

In addition, CORBA/Java objects have a long shelf life, so you won't be throwing away code. The distributed object foundation only gets better with time. It's like writing SQL applications today when you know that SQL3 is on its way. Your applications should be upwardly compatible. This is the beauty of a standards-based approach.

Figure 16-2 shows the CORBA feature cycle. It is very typical of new client/server technologies. In the early years, the emphasis is on new functions. The mission-critical features come later. CORBA is starting to become mission-critical.

ORB vendors are getting tons of feedback from their bleeding-edge customers. As a result, they're starting to make their ORBs more robust. By 1998, we expect ORBs to be as robust as TP Monitors are today.

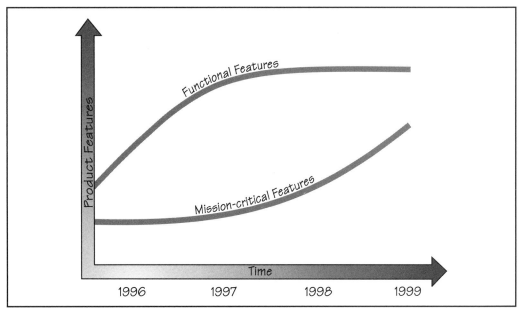

Figure 16-2. The Feature-Introduction Curves of CORBA.

Our final advice is that you should develop your first CORBA client/server application using *stateless server* objects. They're much easier to manage, and they scale well. You can then move to objects with state when Object TP Monitors (with help from ODBMSs) become available as off-the-shelf solutions. Trust us, this is one infrastructure you don't want to build yourself.

Chapter 17

CORBA: The Next Generation

CORBA seems to be perpetually under construction. It is now moving at bullet-train speeds just to keep up with the requirements of the Object Web. CORBA must also maintain its two-year headstart over DCOM—the ORB alternative from Microsoft. So, there's no slowing down. In this chapter, we will look at the features that will most likely make it into CORBA 3.0 (due in mid-1997). In the next chapter, we look at the longer-term requirements of the Object Web.

CORBA 3.0 is the umbrella name for the next-generation ORB technology. The ORB itself will be enhanced with several "cool" new features—including messaging, multiple interfaces, server-side portable frameworks, and pass-by-value. These features have been under construction for over a year. At a higher level, CORBA will be augmented with a Common Facility for *Mobile Agents* and a *Business Object Framework*. In addition, CORBA's Common Facilities include the OpenDoc-based *Compound Document* framework. OpenDoc is now commercially available on multiple platforms—including Windows 95, Mac OS, OS/2, and AIX. It is also being integrated with Java Beans.

At the domain level, we expect to see industry-specific frameworks for Manufacturing, Electronic Commerce, Transportation, Telecom, Healthcare, Finance, and the Internet. Figure 17-1 shows how CORBA is evolving. Yes, it's a moving target. There's a ton of new stuff coming down the object pipe. Some ORB vendors (and book authors) are complaining that they can't keep up with the pace of innovation. But there's no stopping in this fast-moving industry. For vendors, it's either stay ahead of this fast-moving train or get out of this business.

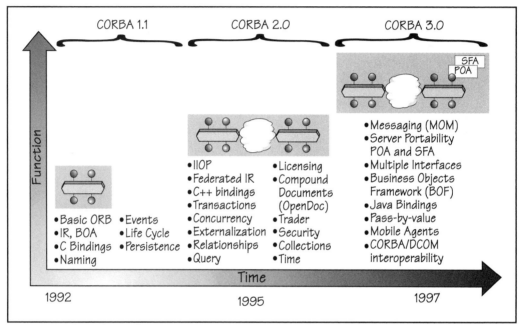

Figure 17-1. The Evolution of CORBA.

CORBA 3.0: THE NEXT-GENERATION ORB

In this section, we give you a snapshot of the following CORBA 3.0 ORB-related technologies: messaging, multiple interfaces, server-side portable frameworks, and pass-by-value. Most of these technologies are in the merger phase, which means that multiple vendor submissions are being molded into a final specification. So we don't have the final details. This section is based on the current state of these submissions, which is very fluid. However, all these specifications will be finalized by mid-1997—in time for CORBA 3.0.

CORBA 3.0 MESSAGING: ORB MEETS MOM

The CORBA *Messaging Service* promises to turn ORBs into full-fledged MOMs. To be more precise, the ORB will subsume the functions of *Message Oriented Middleware (MOM)*. As we go to press, the OMG has received seven strong submissions to its *Messaging RFP*. The submitters include ORB vendors such as

ExperSoft and Iona, as well as major MOM players like Tibco, Digital, IBM, Nortel, and PeerLogic. It seems that MOM needs CORBA, and vice versa.

What Does CORBA Do for MOM?

CORBA provides MOM with a common object model, which includes IDL and a strong architectural framework on which to build applications. Here's a short list of what CORBA does for MOM:

■ *Provides uniform object-based interfaces.* Currently, each MOM product provides its own non-standard API. Most of these APIs are procedural. CORBA offers a standard object interface for MOMs. It also offers IDL support and a complete distributed object infrastructure.

■ *Provides technology for describing the message content.* Currently, the contents of messages are opaque to the MOM. Users must reinvent techniques for describing the contents of their messages, including the data types. CORBA allows MOM messages to be typed via IDL; it also provides generic data types.

■ *Defines endpoints for a message exchange.* Currently, each MOM has its own model of what constitutes an endpoint. Depending on the product, an *endpoint* can be either a queue, a process, or an object. In CORBA, an endpoint is a unique object reference.

■ *Provides interoperable middleware.* Currently, each MOM vendor must define its own proprietary wire-level protocols. None of these products interoperate. CORBA IIOP defines wire protocols that allow products from multiple vendors to interoperate. IIOP also supports transactions and security. Consequently, MOMs built on top of IIOP will interoperate.

■ *Provides an Internet foundation.* CORBA IIOP is becoming a standard Internet protocol. This means CORBA will have well-known ports, URL mappings, and standard proxies for firewalls. MOMs—without CORBA—would have to individually recreate all this infrastructure.

In summary, CORBA provides MOMs with standard interfaces and a strong object foundation. CORBA will allow you to write—for the first time—portable and interoperable MOM applications.

What Does MOM Do for CORBA?

By and large, CORBA is a synchronous *request-reply* protocol. You invoke a method and wait until it completes. If you don't want to wait, you must run each invocation in its own thread. Currently, CORBA provides three mechanisms to circumvent this limitation: 1) you can declare a method to be *oneway* (or *datagram*), 2) you can use the DII's *deferred synchronous* mode, and 3) you can use the CORBA *Event Service*.

These three point solutions fall short of what a full-fledged MOM provides. OMG's solution is to extend CORBA to support the semantics of MOM. In addition to request-reply, your objects should be able to communicate over IIOP ORBs by simply putting messages in queues and getting messages from queues (see Figure 17-2). You should be able to invoke the same method using either MOM or request-reply semantics. The ORB should be able to determine—at run time—the invocation style based on the *Quality of Service (QoS)* you specify.

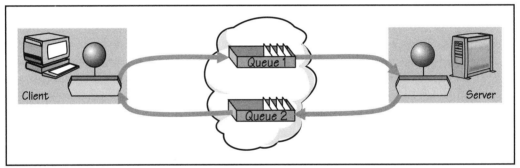

Figure 17-2. CORBA/MOM: Two-Way Message Queuing.

Before we dive into the implementation details, here's a more detailed list of what MOM does for CORBA:

■ ***Allows clients to make non-blocking requests***. MOMs allow objects to make asynchronous requests that do not block the client's execution thread. This means that your clients do not have to be multithreaded. Consequently, they can be simpler to write and maintain.

■ ***Allows clients and servers to run at different times***. Clients can make requests that do not complete during the lifetime of the client object—they simply "fire and forget." This model is useful in loosely-coupled, inter-enterprise situations—the two sides do not have to be up for a transaction to complete. Note that the rising popularity of the Internet mitigates the need for asynchronous-coupling across enterprises. On the Internet, all servers must be up and running all the time. Yes, the Internet never goes to sleep; it's a bit like New York City.

■ ***Supports nomadic clients***. CORBA will be able to provide *time-independent*, queued services for nomadic clients. Disconnected clients will be able to accumulate outgoing transactions in queues and then do a bulk upload when a connection is established with a server (see Figure 17-3). MOMs allow either the client or the server to be unavailable.

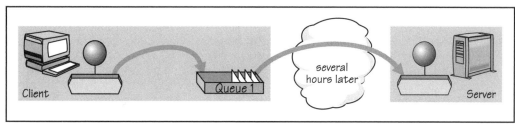

Figure 17-3. CORBA/MOM: Save Your Messages Until You Connect With a Server.

■ *Allows servers to determine when to retrieve messages off their queues.* Server objects—CORBA now calls them *servants*—can pick messages off the queue either on a first-in/first-out basis or according to some priority or load-balancing scheme—for example, multiple server instances can pick messages off the same queue (see Figure 17-4). The servers can also use message filters to throw away the messages they don't want to process, or they can pass them on to other servers. Queues can either be *persistent* (logged on disk) or *non-persistent* (in memory). The type of queue will depend on the QoS you specify.

MOM-style communications will make CORBA more flexible and time-tolerant. However, MOM also introduces some complications, which we cover in the next section.

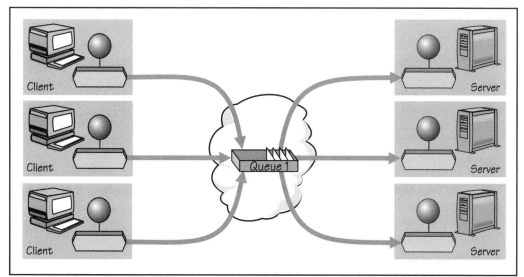

Figure 17-4. CORBA/MOM: Load-Balancing via a Many-to-Many Queue.

When to Use CORBA, MOM-Style

Comparing the request-reply and messaging paradigms is like doing business via a telephone call versus exchanging letters or faxes (see Figure 17-5). An interaction using a telephone call is immediate—both parties talk to each other directly to conduct their business. At the end of the phone conversation, a unit of work is concluded. In contrast, conducting business via mail allows you to stage work, prioritize it, and do it when you're ready for it. You're in control of the workflow, not that ringing phone. On the other hand, it may be frustrating on the client side not to receive immediate feedback.

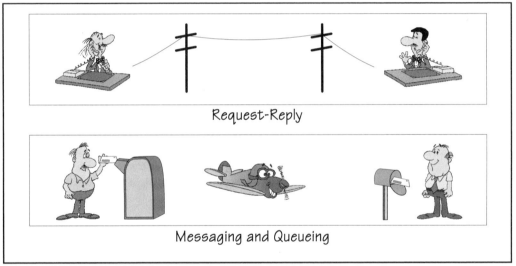

Request-Reply

Messaging and Queueing

Figure 17-5. MOM Versus RPC: Do You Like the Post Office or Telephones?

Table 17-1 compares the messaging and request-reply models. Messaging is, of course, more flexible, loosely-coupled, and time-tolerant than request-reply. However, messaging only skews things in time and may create its own level of complications. In the telephone analogy (request-reply), you complete the work as it arrives; you don't have to manage stacks of incoming letters (or faxes). Your clients are happy to get immediate service. When you close shop at the end of the day, you're all done with your work. In the mail analogy, letters may start to pile up, and clients may be polling their incoming mailboxes continuously, waiting for a response. We may have made life easier for the server at the expense of the client. On the other hand, messaging does free clients from being synchronized to their servers; this can be very liberating for mobile users.

Messaging encourages an event-driven model of communications. You can send off multiple requests to multiple servers and then accept the responses as they come

Table 17-1. Comparing MOM and Request-Reply.

Feature	MOM: Messaging and Queuing	Request-Reply
Metaphor	Post office-like.	Telephone-like.
Client/Server time relationship	Asynchronous. Clients and servers may operate at different times and speeds.	Synchronous. Clients and servers must run concurrently. Servers must keep up with clients.
Client/Server sequencing	No fixed sequence.	Servers must first come up before clients can talk to them.
Style	Queued.	Call-Return.
Partner needs to be available	No.	Yes.
Load-balancing	Single queue can be used to implement FIFO or priority-based policy.	Requires a separate Object TP Monitor (or Smart POA).
Transactional support	Yes (to and from MOM).	Yes (end-to-end).
Message filtering	Yes.	No.
Performance	Slow. An intermediate hop is required.	Fast.

back. Your application doesn't block waiting for the responses. Instead, responses are treated like events. They just happen. Of course, you must be prepared to deal with them when they happen. Request-reply systems can mimic this type of asynchronous, loosely coupled, event-driven behavior using threads.

In summary, a modern ORB should support both MOM and request-reply styles of communication. Each distinctive style presents its own paradigm for conducting business. You'll end up choosing—perhaps via a QoS parameter—the style that provides the best fit for your particular needs.

How Will CORBA Do MOM?

As we go to press, it's still too early to tell how CORBA will do MOM. So, we came up with the following composite based on the seven submissions OMG received:

■ *Either side can specify the message style via a QoS attribute*. The QoS attribute allows both clients and servers to specify the style of a request or response. The QoS may include the following attributes: *acknowledgment-level, time-to-live, priority, cost, reliability, routing, transaction-support,* and *persistence-level.*

- *Clients will be able to set the QoS on an individual call basis*. The client may use the **Current** pseudo-object to control the QoS on a per-call (or per-session) basis. Of course, administrators can also set a default QoS. You may remember that the **Current** object is used to control transactions and security, so this would just be an extension for the messaging QoS. After it specifies the QoS, the client does a regular CORBA invocation.

- *Clients specify a callback object to handle responses.* The deferred response is sent to a callback object—typically, this is an object that manages a persistent queue either on the client or on a networked server. The IDL compiler may automatically generate the stubs for the callback object. Trust us; this is code you do not want to write yourself.

- *Queue-aware servers must provide a MOA*. The server must provide a *Message Object Adapter (MOA)* derived from POA (see next section). The MOA allows a queue-aware server to control the order in which it processes the requests it receives.

- *Messages can be objects*. Eventually, the message itself may be an object. You will then be able to store, query, retrieve, and pass these messages around using CORBA 3.0's pass-by-value and object services such as Query and Persistence.

CORBA MOMs will most likely be built on top of IIOP, but will provide gateways to existing MOM products—such as IBM's *MQSeries*, Digital's *MessageQ*, PeerLogic's *Pipes*, Covia's *Integrator*, and Tibco's *TibNet*.

The bottom line is that the marriage of MOM with CORBA is dynamite. It opens up a ton of new possibilities for distributed objects. For example, MOMs can be integrated with CORBA Services—such as Events, Query, and Trader—to provide very powerful publish-and-subscribe systems for the Object Web.

CORBA 3.0: THE PORTABLE SERVER

As you know, the client side of CORBA is very portable, but the server side isn't. The problem is that the original BOA was underspecified. Consequently, every ORB vendor introduced their own BOA extensions to fill-in-the-blanks. In June 1995, OMG issued an RFP for a *Portable Server-Side ORB*. As we go to press, five submissions for server-side portability are being merged into one. In this section, we summarize the direction this submission is taking. However, you should be warned that it's still very fluid.

Is It Goodbye BOA?

The CORBA designers had two choices: 1) they could fix the BOA, or 2) they could toss it away and start from scratch. They picked the second approach. Why? It turns out that the vendor BOA extensions were too diverse to reconcile. Consequently, fixing the existing BOA would have led to incompatibilities with existing ORBs. Instead of creating a gigantic migration problem, the CORBA designers chose not to touch the existing BOA—it continues to live "as is." But the designers are also defining two new object adapters: the *Portable Object Adapter (POA)* and the higher-level *Server Framework Adapters (SFAs)*.

So what does this do to your existing applications? The good news is that you won't have to rewrite your existing server objects; you only have to rewrite the code that interfaces to the ORB. In addition, most vendors will continue to maintain their BOA (alongside the POA) for many years to come. Remember that ORBs are designed to support multiple object adapters. The bottom line is that BOA is here to stay, but CORBA 3.0 will also introduce a POA and multiple SFAs.

What Is POA?

The POA is simply the BOA done right. Its design incorporates several years of experience by ORB vendors and users. Like BOA, the POA deals with the transparent activation of objects (remember the big conspiracy). Like BOA, POA can start: 1) a server program for each method, 2) a separate program for each object, and 3) a shared program for all instances of an object type. An implementation can also specify its own activation technique. Like BOA, the POA will support both static skeletons and DSI.

POA supports objects that are either *transient* or *persistent*. Transient objects only live within the process that creates them. Persistent objects typically have state; their life extends beyond the process that creates them.

POA also introduces some new concepts. You must now supply an *instance manager* for each implementation of an object interface (or *implementation type*). The instance manager creates *servants*—or running instances of a particular implementation. The POA invokes operations on instance managers to create servants on demand. It also invokes operations on the instance manager to deactivate the servant.

You must register your instance managers with the POA so that it can create instances of your objects. The POA maintains a map of active instance managers; it also maintains a map of the IDs of all active objects (or servants). An active object is identified by its object reference that in turn encapsulates an object ID. As usual, the client only sees the object reference.

Finally, without turning this into a Soapbox, we hope the term "servant" doesn't make it into the final standard. Implementation instance (or object) is just fine with us.

What Are SFAs?

The *Server Framework Adapters (SFAs)* are language-specific frameworks for the server-side of CORBA. It's very likely that CORBA 3.0 will include the following SFAs: SFA/C, SFA/C++, and SFA/Java (other languages will come later). SFAs provide language-specific interfaces that mask the POA; they also define a framework for running your objects. SFAs are designed to make the server-side of CORBA appear natural to C++, Java, or Smalltalk programmers. SFAs provide seamless interfaces to the ORB (and distributed objects) from within a language. For example, SFA servants simply become instances of a language class. Of course, the class must implement IDL-defined interfaces. SFAs create new objects by invoking language constructors instead of CORBA operations (or factories). For languages that are not object-oriented, SFAs define an object-like run-time environment.

Figure 17-6 shows the server-side of CORBA 3.0—the shaded box is portable across ORBs. POA and SFA each deal with a different level of abstraction. POA lets you intimately control the server environment; SFAs make it easier to use. Your application must use either SFA or POA; you can't use both at the same time. In addition, you can still use BOA, but it will lock you into a particular vendor's implementation. We recommend that you move your code to the new SFA frameworks as soon as they become commercially available—perhaps by late 1997. This move shouldn't be too traumatic. For the most part, the implementation of your objects will not change. The change will mostly be in the server code that starts and stops your objects.

CORBA 3.0: MULTIPLE INTERFACES AND VERSIONING

The CORBA 3.0 object model will support multiple interfaces as well as the versioning of interfaces. Currently, CORBA objects only support multiple interfaces via inheritance. In the new model, a *composite object* will be able to dynamically manage multiple independent interfaces—even if they're not related through inheritance. Each interface type represents a logically distinct service (defined in IDL).

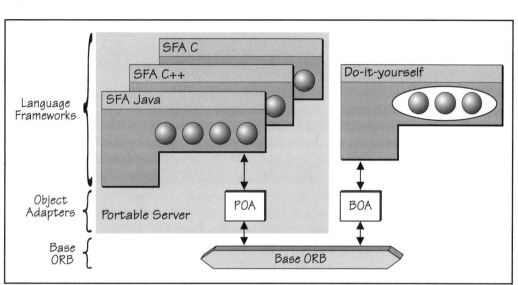

Figure 17-6. CORBA 3.0: The New Server-Side CORBA.

The CORBA IDL will be extended to define the multiple interfaces of a composite object. In addition, the IDL will support multiple versions of the same interface.

The Composite Object

The composite model allows an object to expose multiple interfaces that a client can then discover at run time. Each interface presents a view of the capabilities of the object. The idea is that a single component can provide a set of related services that it manages as a unit. In addition, all the interfaces operate on a shared state.

The client typically binds to the object's *principal interface*. However—with the proper credentials—the client should be able to bind to any of the IDL-defined interfaces an object supports. In addition, the client can determine at run time if an object supports a given interface. It does this either by asking the object itself via a *request_interfaces* method or by querying the Interface Repository.

To make all this work, the CORBA IDL must also be extended to support the definition of a composite object. Figure 17-7 is a composite of the different OMG submissions on this topic. The idea is that you can define via IDL the multiple interfaces an object *supports*. You should also be able to specify the *initial* (or principal) interface. The object must support a *request_interfaces* method that lets a client dynamically discover the interfaces an object supports and other metadata. Finally, the object must provide a factory that knows how to create this composite object.

If you know DCOM or ActiveX, composite objects should be second nature. A composite CORBA object is very similar to an ActiveX. However, one of the key differences is that composite CORBA objects have state and object references. In addition, they can be composed via multiple inheritance. These are very significant differences.

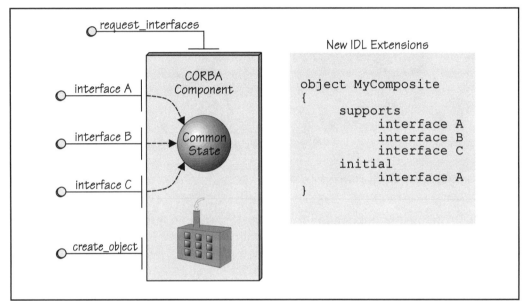

Figure 17-7. A Composite CORBA Object.

Interface Versioning

Interface versioning is another function that should be dear to the heart of component providers. It lets you track different versions of your components (and their interfaces) as they evolve; it also maintains their evolution history. CORBA 3.0 may include a change management service that ensures an object instance uses a consistent implementation version.[1] For example, an old version of an object instance may use an old implementation version, and so on. The version may even be directly encoded in an object reference. This will let you invoke several versions of the same object at the same time. A version may also have context associated with it—for example, demo, test, and release. The default is always the latest version.

Interfaces will be tracked by the IDL and Interface Repository. You should be able to create new versions explicitly—for example, by invoking *CreateVersion* or

---

[1] As we go to press, it's still unclear if this function will make it into CORBA 3.0.

implicitly—for example, when a long transaction commits. The service should be able to track snapshots of a mutually consistent collection of components. It could also maintain change reasons as well as backward and forward deltas from a periodic baseline. Finally, the service should be able to let you *checkout* a version of a component, *checkin* a modified version, and so on.

CORBA 3.0: PASS-BY-VALUE

You may recall that CORBA 2.0 only supports pass-by-value for non-object types. This means that CORBA copies the values of *in* parameters from the client to the server; it copies the values of *out* parameters from the server to the client—as part of a reply. Finally, it copies *inout* parameters in both directions—during the invocation and the reply. However, if a type is an object, CORBA 2.0 only passes its reference. This means it does not copy the state of the object. CORBA 2.0 builds on the idea that all objects are remotable. Consequently, they can be accessed via their object reference. So you just pass object references in a call, not the object itself.

CORBA 3.0 extends this coverage to also support pass-by-value for objects. This means that the actual state of the object is copied in the call. So why is this important? Pass-by-value has become an important issue in the support of remote Java interfaces. In Java, a parameter can be a local object. Consequently, this object's state must be copied as part of the remote invocation. Currently, Netscape/Visigenic's *Caffeine* supports pass-by-value over an IIOP ORB. It does this by flattening the state of an object and all its ancestors. The objects are then transported using normal IIOP encodings. CORBA 3.0 will standardize this process.

COMMON FACILITIES: COMPOUND DOCUMENTS AND MOBILE AGENTS

In this section, we start moving up the object food chain by looking at two very important CORBAfacilities—*Compound Documents* and *Mobile Agents*. As you may recall from Chapter 1, *Common Facilities* provide horizontal end-user-oriented frameworks that are applicable to most domains. Like everything else in CORBA, Common Facilities are defined in IDL. The adopted OMG Common Facilities are collectively called *CORBAfacilities*. In 1996, OMG adopted its first Common Facility—the OpenDoc-based *Distributed Document Component Facility (DDCF)* for Compound Documents. As we go to press, OMG is working on a merged specification for *Mobile Agents*. These are applet-like CORBA components that carry their state and itinerary. Warning: This specification is still under construction.

CORBA Mobile Agents

A *mobile agent* is a CORBA object that can move its code and state across an IIOP network. The agent autonomously starts executing its code when it reaches a destination. You can move an agent to where it can best perform its tasks. These mobile agents can be particularly useful in applications like distributed system management and workflow. Unlike a Java applet (or Bean), an agent also moves its state and context. In addition, it has an *itinerary*—or travel plan—that tells it where to go next. So an agent is an autonomous, self-contained object (or *mobile component*). It knows what to do and where to go. Each agent has a globally unique identifier (a URL), that stays with it throughout its lifetime.

Agents move—via a CORBA ORB—between named hosts; each host is known by its URL. An *Agent Transfer Manager (ATManager)* must be present on every host. This is the element that knows how to externalize, transport, internalize, and run an agent. CORBA also defines interfaces that allow agents to exchange either synchronous or asynchronous messages. In addition, an agent can exchange messages with its *dispatcher* (it's like a control tower for agents). Finally, a CORBA agent executes within an *agent context*; it is used to protect hosts from malicious agents.

What Does a CORBA Agent Look Like?

So, what exactly is an agent? It is simply a CORBA object that supports the **Agent** interface. Here's a sampling of the operations it provides: *dispatch, run, clone,*

dispose, set_itinerary, get_itinerary, handle_message, after_creation, after_arrival, before_disposing, get_property, and *set_property.*

An **Agent** object has an identifier and a codebase that identifies the location of its execution code. Each agent executes within an **AgentContext** object. Here's a sampling of the operations it provides: *create_agent, receive_agent,* and *revert_agent.*

The Agent Execution Environment

The **ATManager** interface handles agent transfer requests and responses. It provides a generic interface that can accommodate any agent system. There must be at least one running **ATManager** object on each of the hosts an agent may visit. The **AgentWriter** and **AgentReader** interfaces support the marshaling and unmarshaling of an agent's code and data.

The **AgentClass** interface encapsulates an agent's execution code. It has a name as well as an associated **AgentClassLoader**. The **AgentClassManager** manages **AgentClassLoader** objects. It knows where to find the agent's codebase. The code itself is represented as a sequence of octets. The facility also includes various helper interfaces to encapsulate URLs, messages, requests, responses, future replies, itineraries, proxies, and streams. It's a very complete system.

Agents are CORBA objects. Consequently, you can discover them at run time using the CORBA Naming, Query, or Trader Services. Of course, mobile agents are always on the move. So they must keep these services informed of their whereabouts.

The Mobile Agent Framework is a good example of how CORBA complements Java, and vice versa. In this case, it would be natural to implement the agents and their framework in Java. CORBA provides the intergalactic facilities to dispatch, locate, and remotely control these agents. Depending on your perspective, an agent is either a mobile CORBA object or a Java applet (or Bean) with state. In either case, it's a marriage made in heaven.

CORBA Meets Compound Documents

In March 1996, OMG adopted OpenDoc as the basis for its compound document technology (see the next Briefing box). This means that CORBA now has a consistent architecture for both the client and the server. In addition, OpenDoc makes it possible for CORBA clients and servers to exchange components via mobile document containers. OpenDoc enables CORBA to get into the mobile object business in a big way. It also makes it possible for CORBA to play on both the client and server sides of the Internet and Intranets. So the news is that CORBA is no longer just middleware and server technology; it can now play on clients as well. This chapter gives you a birds' eye view of OpenDoc and how it plays in the CORBA world. It also explains the OpenDoc compound document model.

FYI

Compound Documents: Why All The Fuss?

Briefing

A *compound document* is nothing more than a metaphor for organizing collections of components—both visually and through containment relationships. It's an integration *framework* for visual components. The document is essentially a collection site for components and data that can come from a variety of sources. Because documents are so familiar, they create a very natural paradigm for the large-scale introduction of objects "for the masses." For most users, their first interaction with objects will be through these compound documents.

The Borderless Desktop

Compound documents are "places" where components live. The desktop itself is in the process of becoming a giant compound document that integrates in a "borderless" manner applications and operating system services. So the modern desktop simply becomes a giant container of components; some of these components are containers of other components, and so on. Components can be moved via drag-and-drop from the desktop to any visual container (and vice versa) to fit a user's needs for working "space." But isn't that the same as moving files into desktop folders? Yes, except that the visual components that are being moved around are more intelligent than anything that lives on today's desktops. In addition, they know how to collaborate with other components to share visual real estate and storage. Instead of seeing boxes within boxes, you will see something that looks more like a visual tapestry. It's really a self-organizing tapestry made up of intelligent components.

Documents Come in All Shapes

A compound document is primarily a visual container of components. With newer compound document technologies—such as OpenDoc—these components can have irregular shapes. With irregular shapes, we can create container/component combinations that are bounded only by the imagination. For example, it's easy to imagine containers that look like airplane bodies, stadiums, garden plots, cities, shopping malls, and so on. You will be able to create applications by dragging components from palettes and dropping them into containers. It's just like a game of *SimCity*, except that each of these components is live and can directly interact with a user (see Figure 17-8). The beauty is that these components can be supplied by different vendors that know nothing of each other. Note that containers themselves are also components—they too can be embedded inside other components. So everything is very recursive.

Figure 17-8. If SimCity Were a Compound Document.

A Home for All Data Types

Compound document data is more than the vanilla text of spreadsheets and paper documents. Data can be anything—including movies, sounds, animation, controls, networked calendars, and virtual folders. Each new kind of medium that is developed—video, sound, animation, simulation, and so on—can be represented by a component in a document. Database access components can feed visual information to users and to other components. For example, using scripts you can feed the data to a spell-checker component or a data-trend analysis component. Of course, all these components must have agreed-upon data structures.

Compound documents can accept new kinds of data at run time because the data content is managed by the component that owns the data. In contrast, a traditional application restricts the types of data that can go into a document to the data types that are known by the application at compile time. If a new type of content becomes available, the application has no way to incorporate it into a document. You must modify and recompile a traditional application to incorporate new data types.

In-Place Editing

Switching among visual components within a document or across documents is much less intrusive than switching between conventional applications. You can immediately edit any content *in-place* without having to launch and execute different applications to create and assemble data. In-place editing allows the component to bring its editing tools to the container—including menus, toolbars, adornments, and small child windows. Instead of the user going to the program that manipulates data, the program comes to the container.

You no longer need to manually manage the various file formats that make up a compound document—all the pieces are now held in one place. The software that manipulates the document is hidden. You're manipulating parts of a document instead of switching between applications. The compound document either contains the data for its components or maintains links to data that's stored elsewhere. So you never have to visually leave the document—everything is right there.

Visual Frameworks

Of course, the price of living within a framework is that you must accept the constraints (and rules of engagement) that it imposes to accrue the benefits. It's an all-or-nothing proposition. The constraints imposed by a compound document framework include its protocols for sharing a common file, negotiating for visual real estate, and exchanging information with the outside world. Components are no longer free-standing. They live within the document. And they also use the container as an intermediary to receive events, share resources, and communicate with each other. In return, components achieve higher levels of visual collaboration and can be distributed via mass market channels. It's a classic trade-off.

Compound documents are also a key technology for enterprise client/server systems and for the Internet and Intranets. Servers can ship flexible front-ends (for example, a storefront) for their services using compound documents. In addition, you can use compound documents to package and ship across networks all types of self-contained components—including roaming agents, mobile components, and workflow. We call this technology *shippable places*. So welcome to this brave new world. We cover shippable places in the next chapter. ❑

What Is OpenDoc?

OpenDoc is a component software architecture implemented as a set of cross-platform classes and services. The component model is a pure rendition of the compound document paradigm. Components in the OpenDoc world are called *parts*. Parts live within compound documents. You can't have free-floating OpenDoc components. All OpenDoc components must be associated with a compound document. An OpenDoc part consists of data stored in compound documents—including text, graphics, spreadsheets, and video—plus a *part editor* that manipulates this data. An OpenDoc document is a user-organized collection of parts.

OpenDoc defines the rules of engagement for parts to coexist in compound documents and to share visual real estate. It also provides an elaborate scripting model that lets parts collaborate via scripts. The OpenDoc runtime—packaged as IDL-defined CORBA classes—provides a cross-language and cross-platform compound document environment.

If you come from the world of CORBA, an OpenDoc part is nothing more than a CORBA object with desktop smarts. OpenDoc extends the CORBA ORB to the desktop. Parts within a desktop can use a CORBA ORB to collaborate with other desktop parts and to access server objects wherever they reside. The ORB provides transparent access to remote components and CORBA services such as security, transactions, and naming. But before we get into these client/server collaborations, let's first go over the OpenDoc component model and see how it complements and extends CORBA.

OpenDoc's Constituent Technologies

OpenDoc defines the rules of engagement for parts to: 1) seamlessly share screen real estate within a window; 2) store their data within a single container file; 3) exchange information with other parts via links, clipboards, and drag-and-drop; 4) coordinate their actions via scripts, semantic events, and CORBA method invocations; and 5) interoperate with other desktop component models—for example, ActiveXs and Java Beans. Figure 17-9 shows OpenDoc's constituent technologies and how they relate. The CORBA-compliant *System Object Model (SOM)* is from IBM. The rest of the technologies—including *Bento, Uniform Data Transfer, Compound Document Management*, and the *Open Scripting Architecture (OSA)*—are from Apple. In addition, IBM is distributing *ComponentGlue*, an interface and library that provides seamless interoperability between OLE and OpenDoc for Windows. In addition, a portable version of OpenDoc is being written entirely in Java.

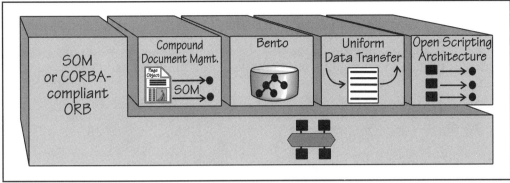

Figure 17-9. OpenDoc's Constituent Technologies.

Client/Server, OpenDoc-Style

From a client/server viewpoint, an OpenDoc document acts as a central integration point for multiple sources of data that reside on different servers (see Figure 17-10). Parts can be linked to corporate databases, workflow managers, image repositories, e-mail, or the local spreadsheet. The document is the client/server application. It acts as a repository of client/server relationships—or "links" to external data sources and remote functions. End-users can assemble these applications by simply opening an OpenDoc container document and dragging parts into it. They can lay out live parts within a visual document just like we do today with page layout programs. Creating an application becomes a paste and layout job—no programming is required. Power users, IS shops, and system integrators

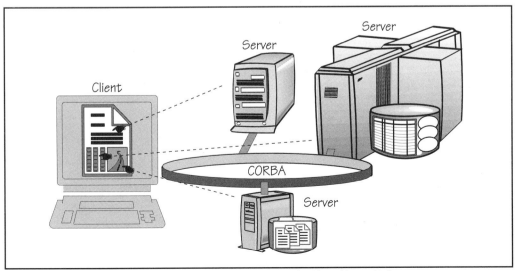

Figure 17-10. OpenDoc Document as a Central Integration Point for Client/Server Links.

can create more sophisticated client/server systems by writing OpenDoc scripts that orchestrate complex interpart collaborations.

It's easy to imagine other metaphors for visual containers into which parts can be dragged, dropped, rearranged, and manipulated to suit a user's needs. Examples of OpenDoc containers are business forms, airplanes, database front-ends, floor plans, desktops, garden plots, and any visual representation that you can use as a container of parts. We anticipate that software providers will provide "designer containers" to complement the parts business; parts and containers will work together "hand in glove." For example, an airline container can be populated with parts representing seats, passengers, crew, luggage, and so on.

Live OpenDoc documents can be saved, shipped across networks to different platforms, and reopened later with the same client/server links. Remember that we're talking about live multimedia documents with application intelligence and links to external data sources. You can move these roaming compound documents—via a workflow manager—from place to place to reflect a business process within and across enterprises. Finally, OpenDoc's market acceptance will depend on how well it integrates with Java Beans. For example, OpenDoc may become the container of choice for Beans.

THE CORBA BUSINESS OBJECT FRAMEWORK

The *Business Object Facility (BOF)* could provide the "magic bullet" that brings CORBA to the programming masses. Most of this book describes the infrastructure of distributed objects. We deal with the ORB and system objects. However, many application developers would prefer not to deal with this system-level stuff (see Figure 17-11). They simply want to write their intergalactic components using a

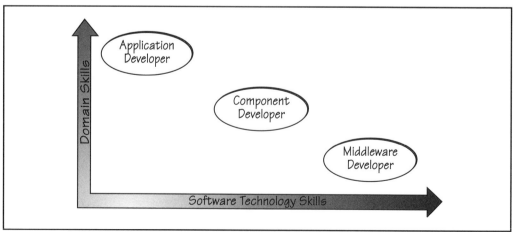

Figure 17-11. The Great Divide: Which Side Are You On?

minimal *surface area*—meaning the number of things they must understand to create a component. One way to greatly reduce the surface area is to hide the underlying CORBA system interfaces.

So instead of turning everyone into a CORBA programmer, it may make more sense to embed CORBA within industry-specific frameworks that expose domain-level objects. To get there, OMG members are currently specifying domain frameworks for Manufacturing, Electronic Commerce, Transportation, Telecom, Healthcare, Finance, and others. But, what do these frameworks build on? You may have guessed it: They build on another framework—the BOF. To be more exact, the BOF defines a generic CORBA component—or *business object*. It is the root object of all domain-specific business objects—they inherit all the CORBA functionality from this object (see Figure 17-12).

The Elements of BOF

As we go to press, OMG has received six strong submissions for the BOF. We will provide a brief description that combines elements from all these submissions. Warning: It's very speculative. The BOF introduces the following new CORBA elements:

- *A base CORBA business object.* This is an interoperable CORBA object that incorporates a variety of CORBA services such as Transactions, Life Cycle, Events, Externalization, and Licensing. It hides most of these services from the application programmer. Domain-specific business objects are derived from this base object (or component). It's the root of all business objects.

- *A component definition language.* This is a superset of the CORBA IDL; it describes the semantics of a CORBA business object—including its properties, views, state, behavior, relationships, events, rules, roles, policies, triggers, persistence, initializers, constraints, and pre- and post conditions.

- *The business object framework.* These are add-on services to support business objects. These services implement the IDL semantic extensions for components. They also provide containers for managing the Quality of Service of groups of objects. Finally, the framework should allow you to add objects to CORBA Collections and then query them via the Query Service.

- *Semantic messaging.* Business objects communicate via self-describing messages. The message is passed as a parameter in a regular CORBA method invocation. The data within the message is semantically tagged with names and values that are meaningful to an application. One of the BOF submissions calls these application-level messages *Semantic Data Objects (SDOs)*.

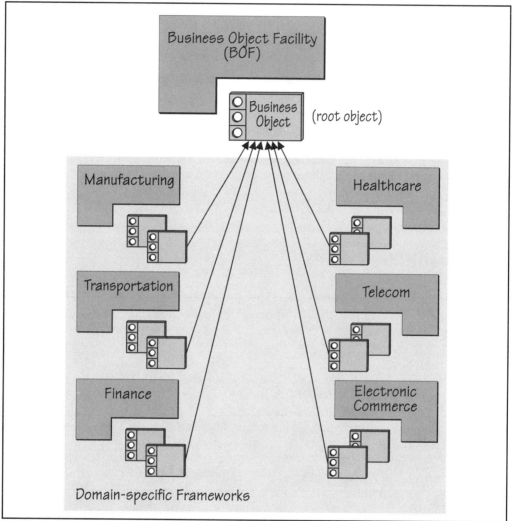

Figure 17-12. The Root Business Object.

The central idea behind BOF is that you should be able to easily create and integrate CORBA components by describing their business semantics, not their system-level behavior. The BOF provides an integrated interface to the CORBA Object Services. You can think of BOF as a 4-GL for describing and assembling CORBA components. The BOF IDL extensions make it easy for a tool to provide visual interfaces for wiring and assembling components. BOF enables the dynamic integration of independently-developed components at run time. For example, you should be able to assemble components into applications via drag-and-drop.

A CORBA component should provide ad hoc notifications—via events—to its subscribers. An *event* encapsulates an interesting occurrence in the life of an object. For example, the component could notify its subscribers whenever a property or relation changes. Note that changes to components must only be applied within the context of a transaction.

The Component Assembly Line

A visual tool should let you set a component's properties (including its state, rules, and relationships) via a property editor. A *rule* represents things that must be done or validated when a change is made to a component. Note that you can dynamically add rules to an existing object without changing its code. You should also be able to dynamically assign a role to any eligible component—for example, you can assign the role of U.S. President to objects that represent U.S. citizens.

The tool should also let you click on any component to discover its inputs (its methods and attributes) and its outputs (the events it emits). You should then be able to drag a line (or wire) from the output of one component to the input of another. This causes the method to be invoked when the event fires. So, welcome to the CORBA component assembly line. Do you believe in silver bullets?

CONCLUSION

This chapter provided a glimpse into CORBA's near-term future. As you can see, CORBA is growing up. OMG is now starting to tackle distributed object issues that transcend simple interoperability. The new distributed object frontier encompasses server-side frameworks, MOM-based messaging, mobile agents, compound documents, business objects, and industry-specific frameworks. We call this the componentization phase of distributed objects. In the next chapter, we present a longer-term vision of how these pieces play together on the *Object Web II*.

Chapter 18

The Object Web II Vision

In our other books, we paint a vision of an *Object Web*. Java and CORBA are a good first step towards creating the Object Web, but they're not enough. The Object Web must also be augmented with compound documents and components. Why? Because compound documents can literally provide magic on the Web, especially when combined with Java. Compound document frameworks—like OLE and OpenDoc—provide two key technologies: 1) a visual component foundation for creating open Web browsers, and 2) the container technology for distributing, viewing, caching, and storing groups of related components and their data— meaning *shippable places*. In this chapter, we give you a quick overview of how the *Object Web II* pieces are coming together.

Compound Documents as Open Web Browsers

Imagine a Web browser built entirely from components. In addition, imagine that the Web browser itself is a visual container of components. This means that it's a component that also lets you embed other components. For example, the Web browser can be built as an OpenDoc or OLE container. So what can you do with such a thing?

For starters, this new kind of browser can provide an integrated visual experience unlike anything you've seen to date. Components and Java applets will be able to seamlessly share the visual real estate within a browser's window. You will be able to edit the contents of any component *in-place*, regardless of how deeply embedded it is within other components. You will also be able to drag-and-drop components within the browser as well as between the browser and the surrounding desktop. This means that you should be able to embed components within other components and then move them around at will across documents, desktops, and networks.

In today's browsers, components own a static rectangular area within a page. In a compound document browser, components can take any shape, and you can move them around and embed them at will. You should be able to resize components within a browser, zoom in on their contents, and visually rearrange the contents of the page in any way you want. The components will automatically share the document's menu, clipboard, and palette. Everything will look very seamless.

Unlike today's browsers, the visual components will be able to interact with each other in many unpredictable ways. For example, you'll be able to drag a URL that represents a CORBA object, and then drop it on a button to create an active pushbutton. It will invoke a remote CORBA method when you click on it. You'll be able to shop by dragging merchandise and dropping it in an electronic shopping cart. You'll pay with e-cash that you pull out of an electronic wallet and drop on an invoice. And you will be able to drag an electronic signature and drop it on a message to seal a deal. The imagination is really at the controls in terms of what you can do with this marriage of Internet technology, CORBA, and components.

The Desktop Is the Browser

The next generation Internet browser will consist of a set of components and the compound document containers in which they play. In addition to Web pages, you'll be able to download containers of components called *shippable places*. So where do you find one of these component-based Web browsers? It turns out that both the OLE and OpenDoc camps are developing component suites and frameworks for the Internet.

The OpenDoc suite—called *Cyberdog*—is the more advanced of the two. Cyberdog from Apple (and possibly Netscape) is an extendable suite of OpenDoc parts and containers for the Internet. The OLE suite—called *Sweeper*—is a component toolkit for creating Internet applications. It builds on top of an OLE document extension called *DocObjects*. This is a visual container that looks like the Office 95 three-ring binder. Microsoft's Internet Explorer 4.X—code named *Striker*—will be built entirely from OLE ActiveX components.

Compound Documents as Portable Component Stores

Most of today's Web pages are simply files that get transmitted out of the file system or the Web server and sent down the wire to the client. But increasingly, as information becomes richer and more finely honed, you want to pull it from other sources. According to Microsoft's Paul Maritz, "Over time most information that gets sent over the Internet will not come out of file systems, but will come out of structured stores."

One of the key pieces of a compound document technology are the portable *structured files*. You use them to store and distribute components. The two best-known examples of such containers are OpenDoc's *Bento* file system and OLE's *compound files* (also known as *DocFiles*). Both systems provide a "file system within a file." Both let components store their data in self-describing, navigatable data streams (also see the next Briefing Box). So what can these structured containers do for the Object Web?

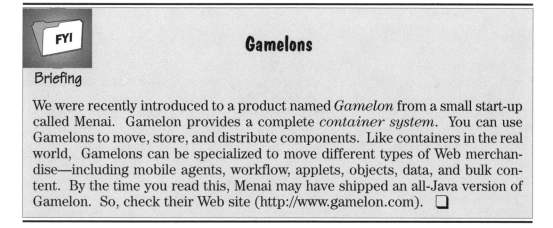

FYI

Gamelons

Briefing

We were recently introduced to a product named *Gamelon* from a small start-up called Menai. Gamelon provides a complete *container system*. You can use Gamelons to move, store, and distribute components. Like containers in the real world, Gamelons can be specialized to move different types of Web merchandise—including mobile agents, workflow, applets, objects, data, and bulk content. By the time you read this, Menai may have shipped an all-Java version of Gamelon. So, check their Web site (http://www.gamelon.com). ❏

Simply put, structured containers allow us to store multiple components in a single document, move them as a single unit across networks, cache them where it makes most sense, and store them in document databases. The component store also becomes a unit of defense for an entire set of components. For example, OpenDoc's Bento lets you selectively encrypt a set of components. Finally, the containers can also persistently store a document's context and act accordingly. For example, you can store in a Bento file—along with a set of components—a user's preferences, login state, and the most current visual layout of the document. Bento also lets you store the previous snapshots of the documents in the form of drafts.

In summary, components need component stores so that you can move them around the Web at will. Structured containers are lightweight, shippable object databases that were designed specifically to store, manage, and transport components. We can think of hundreds of ways these structured component containers can be used to create a smarter Object Web. The next section looks at one such example— *shippable places*.

What Is a Shippable Place?

A *place* is a visual ensemble of related components. A *shippable place* is a mobile container of components; it's a place that can be shipped over the Net. Today's user interfaces are centered around a primitive place that represents a desktop. In contrast, shippable places let you interact with multiple places that represent collaborative environments based on real-world models. A place is a mini *virtual world*. For example, we can have places for 12-year olds, lawyers, or accountants. A place is typically used to display components that represent people and things.

For example, places can represent meeting rooms, libraries, offices, homes, stadiums, shopping malls, museums, parks, and auditoriums. People live, work, shop, and visit these places. *Things* are tools that help us communicate, interact, and work within these places.

A *place* is implemented as a collection of components stored in a structured file container. You assemble a place by dragging components and dropping them within a visual container, which you then store in a structured file. You should be able to connect to a place via its URL and then download it just like any ordinary Web page. Of course, a place will have a digital signature that guarantees it came from a trusted server. The client will also have to authenticate itself before it can use the downloaded place.

Once the place is secured on your desktop, it will serve as a visual front-end for all kinds of specialized Internet services and business objects. The components within a place will typically communicate with their back-end counterparts using a CORBA ORB. A place is a dynamic assembly of ever-changing data, video feeds, and other live content. The place provides an anchor point on the client that servers can invoke via CORBA callbacks.

You will probably keep the place on your desktop for weeks or months at a time, occasionally refreshing it with newer versions of the components it contains. The place is really one of many alternate desktops. You can also customize a place to reflect your preferences and needs. So, a place is a mobile document that you will store and access over time. In contrast, a Web page is more transient; it comes and then goes. With Web pages, screen updates are wholesale page replacements that destroy a user's context. In addition, there is no easy way for servers to tell clients that something has changed. Places fix these problems. Note that Marimba's *Castanet* provides some of the elements of shippable places. But it's still a far cry from being a virtual world. To get there, Marimba needs to be augmented with compound documents, portable containers, CORBA callbacks, and Java Beans.

Figure 18-1 shows the evolution of shippable client front-ends. Web technology made it possible for servers to ship HTML pages to clients where they are displayed in GUI format. The Web then evolved to support HTML-based forms that let clients send data to their servers. With Java, servers can now embed code—in the form of applets—within HTML pages; Java makes Web pages active and smart. Finally, we have shippable places. Like a page, a place can contain Java components. But unlike a page, a place can live on your desktop for as long as you need it. A place also has its own storage, so it can remember your preferences and maintain links to the outside world.

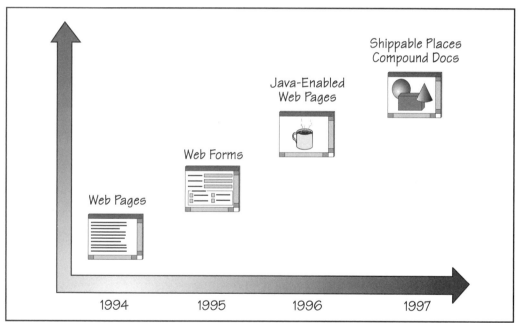

Figure 18-1. From Web Pages to Shippable Places.

The Future Web Client

Figure 18-2 shows three client models for the Web. In the first model, the browser is the desktop; it assumes that people live within their browsers. This is the current Netscape model of the world. In the second model, everything on the desktop is Web-enabled; the idea is that you will be able to access the Web from within any application or component without starting a browser. This is the Cyberdog model of the world; Microsoft will also support this model in Windows 97. The third model is shippable places; it lets you access the Web from within your places. A place can have multiple concurrent sessions with Web object servers. In addition, multiple

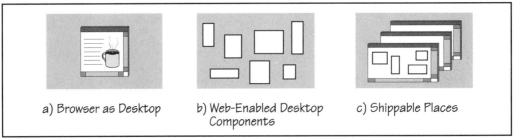

a) Browser as Desktop b) Web-Enabled Desktop Components c) Shippable Places

Figure 18-2. The Evolving Web Client Model.

places can be concurrently active on the same desktop. The Object Web may end up supporting all three models.

In summary, compound document frameworks—like OpenDoc and OLE—were built to transport and display components. They will now allow us to display Web pages made up of components. And they will componentize the Web browser itself. Compound documents will allow us to create, assemble, and distribute an infinite variety of dynamic Web content. Both OpenDoc and OLE will support distributed components on top of their respective ORBs—CORBA and DCOM.

The Object Web II

Figure 18-3 shows a more detailed vision of the Object Web. It's the CORBA/Java Object Web from Part 1 augmented with shippable places, component coordinators, object stores, and mobile containers. We call it the *Object Web II*. As usual, the first tier belongs to the client. In this case, the client belongs to Java Beans, ActiveXs, OpenDoc compound documents, and shippable places.[1]

Clients will be able to access the Internet via componentized browsers—for example, Cyberdog or a future version of Netscape. In addition to ordinary HTML pages, the browser will be able to play compound document titles. A *title* is a shippable place; it will be able to contain Java Beans, ActiveXs, OpenDoc parts, Java applets, and regular HTML content. Titles will be played within browsers as well as within other containers—for example, an OpenDoc or OLE-enabled desktop. Remember, OpenDoc parts can play in OLE containers; they can also contain OLE ActiveXs. So, in theory, everything can play within everything else.

The second tier will be provided by any server that can service both HTTP and CORBA clients. CORBA objects act as a middle tier; they encapsulate the application's

---

[1] Microsoft also has a version of the Object Web; it is based on DCOM, Viper, OLE compound documents, and ActiveX. We describe the Microsoft Object Web in our book, **The Essential Client/Server Survival Guide, Second Edition** (Wiley, 1996).

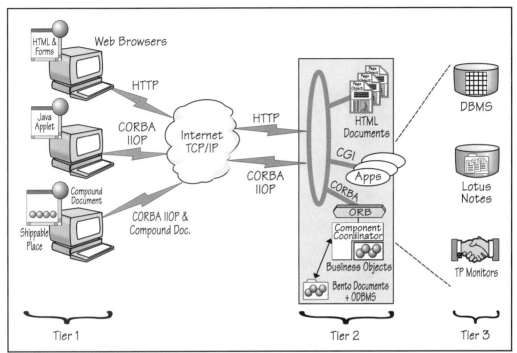

Figure 18-3. The CORBA/Java Object Web.

business logic. They interact with client components via any CORBA ORB that can run IIOP over the Internet. Of course, the CORBA objects on the server can interact with each other using a CORBA ORB. They can also talk to existing server applications in the third tier using SQL or any other form of middleware. The third tier is almost anything a CORBA object can talk to. This includes TP Monitors, MOMs, DBMSs, ODBMSs, Lotus Notes, and e-mail.

In a CORBA/Java Object Web, the second tier also acts as a store of component titles and shippable places. These can be stored in shippable compound files—for example, Bentos, Gamelons, or Java Jars—that are managed by an ODBMS or DBMS. ODBMSs are better suited for the task. An ODBMS can treat a compound file as just another user-defined data type; an SQL database must support object extenders to provide the same kind of service. An ODBMS could transparently cache active compound document files in memory. So when a client requests a shippable place or component Web page, the ODBMS can service the request almost instantaneously by shipping a compound file that's in-memory.

The second-tier must also provide a server-side component coordinator (or Object TP Monitor). We described these critters at length earlier in Chapter 16. But what is a *server-side component*? It's a CORBA server object that also implements a minimum set of component services. Examples of CORBA server components are

Oracle's *Cartridges*, JavaSoft's *Enterprise Beans*, and OMG's *Business Objects*. These are named CORBA objects that are also transactional, secure, and capable of emitting events.

It's Time To Say Good-Bye

The future is bright, fruitful, and positive.

— Bob Marley

Two important pieces of the Object Web are here today: CORBA and Java. This book provides a snapshot of CORBA technology at this particular time. The Object Web offers our best hope for creating—in record time—new client/server applications that can go where no other applications have gone before. Yes, CORBA's future, is "bright, fruitful, and positive." But to unleash the true power of this wonderful technology, we need better tools and more mission-critical ORBs.

If you're ready for this journey, you may want to check our companion book, **Client/Server Programming with Java and CORBA** (Wiley, 1997). It starts out where this one leaves off. We show you how to write complete 3-tier client/server applications in CORBA and Java. For our departing readers, it's time to say good-bye. We thank you for letting us be your guide. For our readers who are making the connection, we will meet again on the next leg of this journey.

Where to Go for More Information

We compiled the following list of resources to help you find more information on the topics we covered in this book.

CORBA

CORBA: The OMG Publications

OMG publishes three books on the CORBA standard that come in three ring binders to make them easier to update:

- **CORBA: Architecture and Specification** (OMG, 1996). This book covers the CORBA 2.0 ORB, IDL, Interface Repository, and inter-ORB communications. It sells for $68 ($199 with an update subscription service).

- **CORBAservices** (OMG, 1996). This book covers the CORBA services. It sells for $68 ($199 with an update subscription service).

- **CORBAfacilities** (OMG, 1996). This book covers the CORBA Common Facilities Architecture. It sells for $68 ($199 with an update subscription service).

In addition, OMG publishes a bi-monthly 28-page news magazine called FIRST CLASS. A one-year subscription costs $50. Call the OMG at 1-508-820-4300 to order any of the above.

Updates on the CORBA Standard

The OMG meets every two months—usually in attractive locations—to continue its standards work. If you can't attend, the best way to find out what's happening is to visit the OMG Web site at http://www.omg.org.

Books on CORBA

- Thomas Mowbray and Ron Zahavi, **The Essential CORBA: Systems Integration Using Distributed Objects** (Wiley, 1995). This book is on object methodology and design using CORBA. Tom Mowbray is the current chair of the CORBA Common Facilities Task Force. So you will get a dose of valuable CORBA insights from reading this book.

- Roger Sessions, **Object Persistence** (Prentice Hall, 1996). This book contains everything you need to know about CORBA's Persistent Object Service (POS). Roger Sessions was one of POS's key architects.

- Jon Siegel, et al., **CORBA Fundamentals and Programming** (Wiley, 1996). This book is a CORBA programmer's Bible; it covers multivendor C++ and Smalltalk CORBA ORBs.

- Randy Otte, et al., **Understanding CORBA** (Prentice Hall, 1995). This well-written book covers CORBA 1.1. You may find some helpful insights.

- Thomas Mowbray and Raphael Malveau, **CORBA Design Patterns** (Wiley, 1997). This useful book uses design patterns to explain CORBA programming techniques. The patterns are documented in CORBA IDL. As far as we know, this is the first design patterns book to cover distributed systems.

- Robert Orfali and Dan Harkey, **Client/Server Programming with Java and CORBA** (Wiley, 1997). This book by your authors shows you how to program 3-tier client/server solutions using CORBA, Java, and JDBC. It can also serve as a gentle introduction to CORBA programming in Java.

Distributed Objects

There are tons of books on object-oriented methodologies and languages. However, very few of these books deal with distributed objects. Here are a few that you may find helpful:

- David Taylor, **Object-Oriented Information Systems** (Wiley, 1992). This book is a very approachable introduction to objects.

- Grady Booch, **Object-Oriented Analysis and Design (Second Edition)** (Benjamin-Cummings, 1994). This second edition of Booch's book is superb reading. It's also an introduction but with more emphasis on language constructs, methodology, and notation.

- Rick Cattell, **The Object Database Standard: ODMG-93** (Morgan Kaufmann). This is the published ODMG standard. To get more information on the Object Database Management Group (ODMG) contact http://www.odmg.org.

- Oliver Sims, **Business Objects** (McGraw-Hill, 1994). This book provides a general introduction to client/server business objects. Oliver Sims is the principal architect of Newi and an early pioneer of business objects. You should read this book, even if you have no interest in Newi.

■ Orfali et al., **The Essential Distributed Objects Survival Guide** (Wiley, 1996). This book is a gentle introduction to distributed objects and components. It covers CORBA 2.0, OpenDoc, OLE, OpenStep, Newi, and a variety of other topics.

Client/Server

This is a huge topic in its own right. The best place to get started is with our book— **The Essential Client/Server Survival Guide, Second Edition** (Wiley, 1996). This gentle introduction covers all of client/server from the NOS to TP Monitors, ORBs, and the Internet. We also recommend:

■ Jim Gray and Andreas Reuter, **Transaction Processing Concepts and Techniques** (Morgan Kaufmann, 1993). This book is the Bible of transaction processing.

■ David Vaskevitch, **Client/Server Strategies, Second Edition** (IDG, 1995). Vaskevitch is Microsoft's VP of enterprise computing. This book provides an insider's view of Viper and Microsoft's client/server directions. Most of the meat is in the last part. The rest of the book is mostly about the business aspects of client/server technology. It's worth a read.

CORBA ORB Vendors

We provide a list of the top 8 CORBA ORB vendors. We also throw in some comments that you should treat as Soapbox material (it's simply an opinion):

■ *Digital Equipment Corp*
ORB name: ObjectBroker
http://www.digital.com/info/objectbroker/
Comments: This is the first and most seasoned ORB on the market. It runs on dozens of platforms and scales well. As we go to press, rumor has it that ObjectBroker is being acquired by BEA Systems (http://www.beasys.com), the makers of Tuxedo. If this happens, it may lead to a big marriage of ORBs and TP Monitors.

■ *Expersoft*
ORB name: PowerBroker
http://www.expersoft.com/
Comments: PowerBroker was picked as the Anderson Consulting ORB in a much publicized bake-off. It is one of the best C++ ORBs on the market. Expersoft (spelled without a "t") is a very innovative startup; it is staking out the high-end of the ORB market.

- *HP*

  ORB name: ORB Plus

  http://www-dmo.external.hp.com/gsy/orbplus.html

  Comments: HP was very influential in the development of the CORBA specification. ORB Plus is a solid ORB that supports both DCE and IIOP on the HP platform.

- *IBM*

  ORB name: SOM

  http://www.software.ibm.com/objects/somobjects/

  Comments: SOM 3 is a service-rich ORB; it is a precursor to the much-awaited SOM 4 that is intended to support IBM's CORBA-based Object TP Monitor—the Business Object Server Solution (BOSS).

- *ICL*

  ORB name: DAIS

  http://www.icl.co.uk/products/dais/home.html

  Comments: This is a mission-critical ORB by the UK-based company, International Computer Limited (ICL). It has few features, but it scales well.

- *IONA*

  ORB name: Orbix

  http://www.iona.ie/

  Comments: Iona is a leading provider of CORBA technology. Its C++ Orbix ORB now runs on 20 operating systems—including twelve Unix variants, OS/2, NT, Windows 95, Macintosh System 7.5, OpenVMS, and MVS. Iona is also releasing OrbixWeb V2—one of the industry's first all-Java ORBs.

- *SUN*

  ORB name: NEO/Joe

  http://www.sun.com/sunsoft/neo/

  Comments: NEO is a very robust and service-rich ORB for Sun platforms. Joe—now packaged with NEO—is Sun's all-Java multiplatform ORB. Currently, Joe only provides client-side support. Joe may eventually get bundled with the Java JDK.

- *Visigenic*

  ORB name: VisiBroker

  http://www.visigenic.com/prod

  Comments: VisiBroker for Java started life as PostModern's BlackWidow ORB. It was the first CORBA ORB to support both client and server Java objects. VisiBroker for C++ is a very fast IIOP-based C++ ORB that runs on multiple platforms. In August 1996, Netscape chose VisiBroker as its ORB; it will be incorporated in all the Netscape browsers and servers. In February 1997, Oracle chose VisiBroker as its NCA ORB. So VisiBroker is becoming ubiquitous through its OEM partnerships.

Index

A

absolute_time method 231
Abstract classes 96, 98
Access control 18, 171
Access decision 171
Access identity 159
Access policy 159
access_allowed method 171
AccessDecision interface 159, 170–171
AccessPolicy interface 175
ACID (Atomicity, Consistency, Isolation, and
    Durability) 198
ACL (Access Control List) 158–159
Action timestamp 162
Activation 263
ActiveX 42, 282, 286
Ada 5
ADB MATISSE 195
add_all_elements method 207
add_element method 207
add_link method 130
add_object method 187
add_role method 224
add_type method 132–133
Adjudicator 162
Administration 153, 165, 175
After method call 20
Agent context 268
Agent interface 269
AgentClass interface 269
AgentClassLoader interface 269
AgentClassManager interface 269
AgentReader interface 269
Agents 38, 268
    Roaming 26
Agile systems 85
AIX 255
Alexander, Christopher 105
ANSI 206
Apple 2, 6, 41–42, 282
    Project X 249
    Semantic metadata 249
    Semantic networks 249
Applets 34, 62, 268
Application events 160
Application frameworks 26

assign_PID method 187
assign_PID_relative method 187
Asynchronous requests 258
AT&T 242
ATManager (Agent Transfer Manager) 268
ATManager interface 269
Attributes 222, 239
Atwood, Thomas 201, 203
Audit 173
Audit log 160–161, 173
Audit policies 160–161
Audit trail 160–161, 173
audit_needed method 171, 173
audit_write method 171, 173
AuditChannel interface 171, 173
AuditDecision interface 171, 173
AuditPolicy interface 176
authenticate method 169
Authenticated ID 155
Authentication 18, 151–178
Authorization 158–159

B

B2 security 154
Bag
    Defined 201
Bag interface 215, 217
BagFactory interface 217
Bancilhon, Francois 198
BEA Systems 2, 189, 251, 253
Beans 42, 255, 268, 270, 285–286, 288
before method call 20
begin method 141
begin_context method 190
Bento 180, 184, 274, 283–285, 287
Bernstein, Barbara 135
bind method 108
bind_context method 108
bind_new_context method 108
Binding 107
BindingIterator interface 108
Black Widow 44, 47–48
Blake, William 203
BLOBs (Binary Large Objects) 203

BOA (Basic Object Adapter) 13, 200, 263–264
  Activation policy 79
  Defined 78
  Persistent server 81
  Server-per-method 81
  Shared server 79
  Unshared server 80
BOA::change_implementation method 77
BOA::create method 77
BOA::deactivate_impl method 77, 79–80, 82,
    84
BOA::deactivate_obj method 77, 79–80, 82, 84
BOA::dispose method 77
BOA::get_id method 77
BOA::get_principal method 77
BOA::impl_is_ready method 77, 79–80, 82, 84
BOA::obj_is_ready method 77, 79–80, 82, 84
BOA::set_exception method 77
BOF (Business Object Facility) 277
Booch, Grady 22
BOSS (Business Object Server Solution) 189,
    251, 253
Business object framework 244, 255
Business objects 19, 21–26, 34, 277, 288

C

C++ 195–196, 201, 264
C2 security 154
CAD (Computer Aided Design) 198
Caffeine 37, 101, 247, 268
Callbacks 45, 48, 53–59, 247, 262, 284
cancel_timer method 231–232
Capability list 158
Cartridges 32, 41–42, 288
CASE (Computer Aided Software
    Engineering) 195
Cassell, Jonathan 195
Castanet 285
Cattell, Rick 183, 194
CDR (Common Data Representation) 15
Cell Directory Service (CDS) 106
CGI (Common Gateway Interface) 2, 30–31, 34,
    43
  Bottleneck 34
Chang, Dan 185, 206
change_mode method 148
Check in 198
Check out 198
check_minimum_cardinality method 223
check_use method 237

CI Labs 42
Class
  Skeleton 57
  Stubs 57
Class object 264
clear_audit_selectors method 176
CLI (Callable Level Interface) 184, 187
Client stubs 57
Client/server
  3-tier 27, 31, 248, 286–287
  Agile Systems 85
  And OpenDoc 276
  And the Web 253
  CORBA/Java-Style 29–42, 43–50
  Post-scarcity 40
  Security 152
Cobb, Ed 136, 149
COBOL 5
Collection interface 207–208, 214
CollectionFactory interface 207, 217
Collections 212
Collections Service 18, 212–218
COMlets 30
commit method 141
commit_one_phase method 141
commit_subtransaction method 141
Common Facilities 255, 268–270, 274, 276
compare_time method 231
Component assembly 278
Component Coordinator 32, 42, 189, 251, 254,
    288
Component licensing 236
Components 38, 42, 244, 251, 281–282
  And business objects 26
  And compound documents 271
  And CORBA 282–283
  And Web browsers 282–283
  Defined 7
  Infrastructure 26
  Server-side 32, 288
  Suites 26
  Supersmart 26
  System services 26
Composite credentials 173
Composite delegation 157
Composite object 265–266
Compound documents 38, 244, 255, 270–271,
    274, 276, 281–282, 286–287
  And components 271
  Containers 271
  Defined 271
  In-place editing 273

Index

CompuServe 40
Concurrency control service 17
Configuration 198
connect method 186–187
connect_push_consumer method 121
connect_push_supplier method 121
Connection interface 187
Constraints 129, 277
ConsumerAdmin interface 121
ContainedInRole interface 226
Containers 195–196, 201, 271, 283–285
Containment 226
Containment relationship 221
ContainsRole interface 226
continue_authentication method 169
Control attributes 159
Controller 23–24
Coordinated Universal Time 229
Coordinator interface 141
copy method 113–114, 169
copy_node method 114
copy_relationship method 114
copy_role method 114
CORBA (Common Object Request Broker
      Architecture) 3–28, 57, 200
  Access control 157
  Access identity 159
  And components 282–283
  And compound documents 282–283
  And DCE 17
  And Internet 16, 31–32, 34, 38
  And Java 2, 34–35, 288
  And MOM 124
  And ODBMS 186, 200
  And OpenDoc 274
  And Relational Databases 187
  And shippable places 282–283
  And SQL 184, 187
  Any type 89
  AttributeDef interface 94
  Attributes 88, 90, 94, 239
  Audit trail 160–161
  Authentication 155–156
  Authorization 158–159
  Basic types 89
  BindingIterator interface 108
  BOA 13
  BOA_Init 75
  Business objects 21–25
  Callbacks 53–59, 247
  Change management 235–242, 245–254
  Classes 88, 90

CORBA (Common Object Request Broker
      Architecture) *(continued)*
  Collection Interface 208
  CollectionFactory Interface 207
  Collections Service 205, 207–208, 212–218
  Common Data Representation (CDR) 15
  Compound Life Cycle 114
  Concurrency Service 136, 146–148, 150
  Conspiracy 183, 186
  ConstantDef interface 94
  Constants 94
  Constructed types 89
  Contained interface 96, 98
  Container interface 96, 98
  content_type 92
  Context objects 143
  Control interface 142
  Coordinator interface 142, 144, 146
  CORBAfacilities 19
  CORBAservices 17
  Credentials 155–156
  Current interface 142, 144, 146
  Data types 89
  Datastore_CLI 184–185, 188
  Datastores 184
  DCE format 99
  DCE/ESIOP 17
  Deadlocks 147
  describe_interface 98
  DII 33, 61–72, 248
  Direct Access (DA) 185
  Direct Attribute (DA) 183
  Domain 163–164
  DSI 13
  Dynamic Data Object (DDO) 183, 185
  Dynamic discovery 248
  Dynamic interface 54
  Dynamic method invocation 8, 11, 54
  EdgeIterator Interface 226
  Encryption 163
  ESIOP 14, 17
  Event channel 116
  Event Service 49, 105, 116, 119, 124
  Eventchannel interface 119
  Events 116
  ExceptionDef interface 94
  Exceptions 88, 94
  Externalization 37
  Externalization Service 185, 190, 192
  FactoryFinder interface 114
  FileStreamFactory 190
  General Inter-ORB Protocol (GIOP) 15

CORBA (Common Object Request Broker
    Architecture) *(continued)*
  GenericFactory interface 114
  get_implementation 46, 56
  get_interface 46, 56, 98
  ID pragma 100
  IdentifiableObject Interface 224
  Identifier 88
  IDL 4–6, 8–9, 19, 22, 85–102, 119, 248
  IDL grammar 87
  IDL precompiler 87, 100
  IDL structure 87
  IIOP 248
  Implementation Repository 13, 46, 56–57
  Initialization 73–84
  Interface Repository 9, 13, 46, 56, 62, 75,
    85–102
  Interface Repository Federations 99
  InterfaceDef interface 94
  Interfaces 88, 90, 94
  Internet Inter-ORB Protocol (IIOP) 16
  Interoperable Object References (IORs) 17
  Inter-ORB 16
  Introduction 3–28
  Introspection 248
  IRObject interface 96, 98
  is_nil 46, 56
  Iterator Interface 208
  Java ORBs 43–50, 247
  Language bindings 5, 8
  LicenseServiceManager Interface 237
  Licensing Service 236, 238–239
  Life cycle 37, 105–124
  LifeCycle interface 115
  LifeCycleObject interface 114
  list_initial_services 75
  Lock modes 147
  LockCoordinator interface 148
  Locks 147
  Lockset 147–148
  Lockset interface 148
  LocksetFactory interface 148
  Messaging 257
  Metadata 9, 85–102
  Method signature 89, 93
  Methods 90
  Module 88, 90, 94
  ModuleDef interface 94
  Multithreading 53–59
  Name binding 107
  Namespace 94, 106
  Naming context 106

CORBA (Common Object Request Broker
    Architecture) *(continued)*
  Naming Service 61, 75, 105–124, 125
  NamingContext 111
  NamingContext interface 108
  Nested locks 148
  Nested transactions 142, 146–148
  Next generation 255, 268, 279
  Node 114
  Node interface 114, 224
  Non-repudiation 162–163
  Object 82
  Object adapter 13, 75, 200
  Object reference 13, 17, 46, 54, 56, 106, 247
  Object Services 205–218, 219–234, 235–242,
    245–254
  object_to_string 46, 56
  ODMG-93 183, 185
  Open platform 248
  OperationDef interface 94
  Operations 88–90, 94
  OperationsFactory interface 114
  ORB federations 93
  ORB interface 56
  ORB_init 74
  ORBlet 30
  OTS (Object Transaction Service) 49
  ParameterDef interface 94
  Parameters 89, 94, 268
  Pass-by-value 268
  PDS interface 185, 187
  Persistence Object Service (POS) 179–201
  Persistent Data Services (PDSs) 183
  Persistent Identifier (PID) 183
  Persistent Object (PO) 183
  Persistent Object ID (PID) 186
  Persistent Object Manager (POM) 183
  PID interface 186
  PIDFactory interface 186
  PO interface 183–184, 187
  POFactory interface 186
  POM interface 185, 187
  Pragmas 100
  Prefix pragma 100
  Principal 155–156
  Privilege delegation 157
  Properties Service 106, 239–241
  Protocol 183, 185
  Pseudo-object 74–75, 77, 142, 144
  Query Interface 208
  Query Service 187, 205–209, 211–212
  QueryableCollection Interface 208

CORBA (Common Object Request Broker
 Architecture) *(continued)*
 QueryEvaluator Interface 208
 QueryManager Interface 208
 Recoverable object 140, 144
 Recoverable resource 144
 Recoverable server 140
 Relationship 114, 192
 Relationship interface 114, 224
 Relationship Service 114, 218, 220, 222–
  224, 226, 234
 RelationshipFactory Interface 224
 RelationshipIterator Interface 224
 Repository ID 92, 98–100
 Repository interface 94
 resolve_initial_references 75
 Resource interface 142, 144
 Role 114
 Role interface 114, 224, 226
 RoleFactory interface 224
 Scoped name 88, 99
 Security 9, 151–178
 Security domains 163–164
 Select/cursor 187
 Self-describing data 91
 Sequence 89
 Server-side 250
 Skeleton 13
 SQL CLI 187
 SQL schema mappers 185
 Static interface 54
 Static invocation 11
 Static method invocation 8, 53–59
 Streamable 191
 StreamFactory 190
 StreamIO 191
 Streams 185, 190
 string_to_object 46, 56
 Stubs 54
 System Management 235–242, 245–254
 Tagged profiles 17
 The Bad 249–250
 The Good 54, 247–248
 The Ugly 249–250
 Time Service 228–229
 Trader Service 61–62, 105, 125–134
 Transaction 135–150
 Transaction context 140, 142–143
 Transaction coordinator 140
 Transaction Service 135–150
 Transactional client 140
 Transactional locks 147

CORBA (Common Object Request Broker
 Architecture) *(continued)*
 Transactional server 140
 TransactionalLockset interface 148
 TransactionalObject interface 143–144
 Transactions 9
 Traversal Interface 225
 TraversalCriteria Interface 225
 Two-phase commit 140, 142, 146
 Type codes 91
 TypeCode interface 92
 Typed events 119
 TypeDef interface 94
 Typedefs 89, 94
 Types 85–102, 268
 Unique prefixes 99
 Version 1.1 7, 14
 Version 1.2 92
 Version 2.0 7, 50, 85–102
 Version pragma 100
 Versus RPC 54, 247
 Well-known objects 75
CORBA 3.0 19, 255–258, 262–268
CORBA interfaces
 AccessDecision 159, 170–171
 AccessPolicy 175
 Agent 269
 AgentClass 269
 AgentClassLoader 269
 AgentClassManager 269
 AgentWriter 269
 ATManager 269
 AuditChannel 161, 171, 173
 AuditDecision 161, 171, 173
 AuditPolicy 161, 176
 Bag 215, 217
 BagFactory 217
 BindingIterator 108
 Collection 207–208, 214
 CollectionFactory 207, 217
 Connection 187
 ConsumerAdmin 121
 ContainedInRole 226
 ContainsRole 226
 Coordinator 141
 CORBA::BOA 77, 166
 CORBA::Current 167–168
 CORBA::DomainManager 167
 CORBA::Object 102, 168
 CORBA::ORB 166
 CosContainment::Relationship 226
 CosGraph::Role 226

CORBA interfaces *(continued)*
  CosGraphs::Role 224
  CosReference::Relationship 226
  CosRelationships::Relationship 226
  CosRelationships::Role 224, 226
  Credentials 155, 168–169, 171–173
  Current 141, 155–156, 164, 171–173, 262
  Cursor 187
  CursorFactory 187
  Datastore_CLI 187
  DelegationPolicy 176
  Deque 218
  DomainAccessPolicy 175
  DynamicPropEval 131
  EdgeIterator 224
  EqualityIterator 215, 217
  EqualityKeyIterator 215, 217
  EqualityKeySortedIterator 215, 217
  EqualitySequence 215, 217
  EqualitySequenceFactory 217
  EqualitySequentialIterator 215, 217
  EqualitySortedIterator 215, 217
  EventChannel 121
  FactoryFinder 113
  FileStreamFactory 190
  form_complete_evidence 174
  GenericFactory 113
  Heap 215, 217
  IdentifiableNamingContext 110
  IdentifiableObject 223
  ImplementationDef 102
  InterfaceDef 62, 66, 68–69, 102
  Iterator 207, 214–215, 217
  KeyBag 215, 217
  KeyBagFactory 217
  KeyIterator 215, 217
  KeySet 215, 217
  KeySetFactory 217
  KeySortedBag 215, 217
  KeySortedBagFactory 217
  KeySortedIterator 215, 217
  KeySortedSet 215, 217
  KeySortedSetFactory 217
  LicenseServiceManager 237
  LifeCycleObject 113
  Link 130
  LockCoordinator 148
  Lockset 148
  LocksetFactory 148
  Lookup 130, 134
  Map 215, 217
  MapFactory 217

CORBA interfaces *(continued)*
  NamingContext 108, 110
  Node 114, 224
  NodeFactory 224
  NRCredentials 163, 171, 174
  NRPolicy 174, 177
  NVList 63, 65–66, 68
  Object 62–64, 66–69, 102
  OfferIterator 130
  OperationDef 68, 70
  Operations 114
  OperationsFactory 114
  ORB 13, 63, 66, 74, 102
  PDS 186
  PID 186
  PIDFactory 186
  PO 186
  POFactory 186
  POM 186
  PrincipalAuthenticator 155, 169
  PriorityQueue 218
  ProducerSpecificLicenseService 237
  PropertySet 110, 240
  PropertySetDef 240
  Proxy 130
  ProxyPushConsumer 121
  ProxyPushSupplier 121
  PushConsumer 119, 121
  PushSupplier 119, 121
  QueriableNamingContext 110
  Query 208
  QueryableCollection 208
  QueryEvaluator 110, 208
  QueryManager 208
  Queue 218
  ReferencedByRole 226
  ReferencesRole 226
  Register 130, 133
  Relation 215, 217
  RelationFactory 217
  Relationship 114, 223
  RelationshipFactory 223
  RelationshipIterator 223
  Request 64, 67–68, 70
  RequiredRights 170
  Resource 141
  Role 114, 223
  RoleFactory 223
  SecureInvocationPolicy 176
  SequenceFactory 217
  SequentialIterator 215, 217
  ServiceTypeRepository 132–133

CORBA interfaces *(continued)*
  Set 215, 217
  SetFactory 217
  SortedBag 215, 217
  SortedBagFactory 217
  SortedMap 215, 217
  SortedMapFactory 217
  SortedRelation 215, 217
  SortedRelationFactory 217
  SortedSet 215, 217
  SortedSetFactory 217
  Stack 218
  Stream 190
  Streamable 190
  StreamableFactory 190
  StreamFactory 190
  StreamIO 190
  SubtransactionAwareResource 141
  SupplierAdmin 121
  TimerEventHandler 231–232
  TimerEventService 231–232
  TimeService 231–232
  TIO 231
  TransactionalLockset 148
  Traversal 224
  TraversalCriteria 224
  TraversalFactory 224
  UTO 231
CORBA methods
  _request 63–64, 67, 70
  absolute_time 231
  access_allowed 170–171
  add_all_elements 207
  add_arg 64, 70
  add_element 207
  add_item 63, 65–66
  add_link 130
  add_object 187
  add_role 224
  add_type 132–133
  add_value 65–66, 68
  assign_PID 187
  assign_PID_relative 187
  audit_needed 171, 173
  audit_write 171, 173
  authenticate 169
  begin 141
  begin_context 190
  bind 108
  bind_context 108
  bind_new_context 108
  BOA::change_implementation 77

CORBA methods *(continued)*
  BOA::create 77
  BOA::deactivate_impl 77, 79–80, 82, 84
  BOA::deactivate_obj 77, 79–80, 82, 84
  BOA::dispose 77
  BOA::get_id 77
  BOA::get_principal 77
  BOA::impl_is_ready 77, 79–80, 82, 84
  BOA::obj_is_ready 77, 79–80, 82, 84
  BOA::set_exception 77
  BOA_init 74
  cancel_timer 231–232
  change_mode 148
  check_minimum_cardinality 223
  check_use 237
  clear_audit_selectors 176
  commit 141
  commit_one_phase 141
  commit_subtransaction 141
  compare_time 231
  connect 186–187
  connect_push_consumer 121
  connect_push_supplier 121
  continue_authentication 169
  copy 113–114, 169
  copy_node 114
  copy_relationship 114
  copy_role 114
  create 148, 166, 190, 207–208, 223
  create_compound_operations 114
  create_iterator 207
  create_list 63, 66
  create_node 224
  create_object 113, 187
  create_operation_list 63, 66, 68
  create_PID_from_key 186
  create_PID_from_string 186
  create_PID_from_string_and_key 186
  create_PO 186
  create_related 148
  create_request 63–64, 67–68
  create_role 223
  create_subtransaction 141
  create_transactional 148
  create_transactional_related 148
  create_traversal_on 224
  create_uninitialized 190
  define_index 110
  define_properties 240
  define_properties_with_modes 240
  define_property 240
  define_property_with_mode 240

CORBA methods *(continued)*
delete 64, 67–68, 71, 186
delete_all_properties 240
delete_index 110
delete_object 187
delete_properties 240
delete_property 240
describe 62, 66, 68–69, 130
describe_interface 62, 66, 68–69
describe_link 130
describe_type 132–133
destroy 108, 114, 121, 130, 223–224
destroy_relationships 223
disconnect 186–187
disconnect_push_consumer 119, 121
disconnect_push_supplier 119, 121
drop_locks 148
end_context 190
end_use 237
evalDP 131
evaluate 208
event_time 231–232
execute 187, 208
export 130, 133
externalize 190
externalize_to_stream 190
find_factories 113
flush 190
for_consumers 121
for_suppliers 121
forget 141
form_complete_evidence 171, 174
free 65, 68
free_memory 65
fully_describe_type 132
generate_token 171, 174
get_active_credentials 168
get_all_properties 240
get_all_property_names 240
get_allowed_properties 240
get_allowed_property_types 240
get_association_options 176
get_attributes 156, 167, 169, 171
get_audit_selectors 176
get_control 141
get_coordinator 148
get_count 65
get_credentials 167–168
get_current 167–168
get_delegation_mode 176
get_domain_policy 167
get_edges 224

CORBA methods *(continued)*
get_effective_rights 175
get_implementation 102
get_interface 62, 64, 66, 68–69, 102
get_next_response 66
get_NR_features 171
get_NR_policy_info 174, 177
get_object_type 187
get_option 187
get_other_related_object 223
get_other_role 223
get_parent_status 141
get_PIDString 186
get_policy 167, 173
get_properties 240
get_property_mode 240
get_property_modes 240
get_property_value 240
get_relationships 223
get_required_rights 170
get_response 64
get_result 208
get_rights 175
get_security_features 168–169
get_security_mechanisms 168
get_security_names 168
get_service_information 166, 168
get_status 141, 208
get_token_details 171
get_top_level_status 141
get_transaction_name 141
grant_rights 175
hash 102
hash_top_level_transaction 141
hash_transaction 141
identify_all_occurances 110
identify_any_occurance 110
insert_element_at 207
internalize 190
internalize_from_stream 190
interval 231
invoke 64
is_a 102
is_ancestor_transaction 141
is_descendant_transaction 141
is_equivalent 102
is_identical 223
is_identical_PID 187
is_nil 102
is_property_defined 240
is_related_transaction 141
is_same_transaction 141

CORBA methods *(continued)*
  is_top_level_transaction 141
  is_valid 169
  link 223
  list 108
  list_initial_services 74
  list_links 130
  list_types 132–133
  lock 148
  mask_type 132
  max_left 130
  modify 130
  modify_link 130
  more 207
  move 113–114
  move_node 114
  move_relationship 114
  move_role 114
  new_context 108
  new_interval 231–232
  new_universal_time 231–232
  next 207
  next_n 108, 130, 223–224
  next_one 108, 223–224
  non_existent 102
  object_to_string 102
  obtain_producer_specific_license-
    _service 237
  obtain_pull_consumer 121
  obtain_pull_supplier 121
  obtain_push_consumer 121
  obtain_push_supplier 121
  overlaps 231
  override_default_credentials 168
  override_default_mechanisms 168
  override_default_QOP 168
  poll_next_response 66
  poll_response 64
  prepare 141, 208
  push 119, 121
  query 130, 134
  read_boolean 190
  read_char 190
  read_double 190
  read_float 190
  read_graph 190
  read_long 190
  read_object 190
  read_octet 190
  read_short 190
  read_string 190
  read_unsigned_long 190

CORBA methods *(continued)*
  read_unsigned_short 190
  rebind 108
  rebind_context 108
  received_credentials 167
  refresh 169
  register 231–232
  register_mapping_schema 187
  register_resource 141
  register_subtran_aware 141
  remove 65, 113–114
  remove_element_at 207
  remove_link 130
  remove_node 114
  remove_role 224
  remove_type 132
  replace_audit_selectors 176
  replace_element_at 207
  replace_rights 175
  reset 207
  resolve 108, 130
  resolve_initial_references 74
  restore 186
  resume 141
  retrieve_element_at 207
  retrieve_object 187
  revoke_rights 175
  roles_of_type 224
  rollback 141
  rollback_only 141
  rollback_subtransaction 141
  secure_universal_time 231–232
  select_object 187
  send_deferred 64
  send_multiple_requests_deferred 66
  send_multiple_requests_oneway 66
  send_oneway 64
  set_association_options 176
  set_audit_channel 176
  set_audit_selectors 176
  set_credentials 155, 167, 173
  set_data 231–232
  set_delegation_mode 176
  set_NR_features 171
  set_NR_policy_info 177
  set_option 187
  set_position 187
  set_privileges 169
  set_property_mode 240
  set_property_modes 240
  set_required_rights 170
  set_security_features 168–169

CORBA methods (continued)
  set_timeout 141
  set_timer 231–232
  spans 231
  start_use 237
  store 186
  string_to_object 102
  suspend 141
  time 231
  time_set 231–232
  time_to_interval 231
  transact 187
  try_lock 148
  unbind 108
  unbind_all_occurances 110
  universal_time 231–232
  unlink 223
  unlock 148
  unmask 132
  unregister 231–232
  update_object 187
  uto_from_utc 231–232
  verify_evidence 171, 174
  visit_node 224
  withdraw 130
  withdraw_using_constraint 130
  write_boolean 190
  write_char 190
  write_double 190
  write_float 190
  write_graph 190
  write_long 190
  write_object 190
  write_octet 190
  write_short 190
  write_string 190
  write_unsigned_long 190
  write_unsigned_short 190
CORBA/Java ORB 43–50
CORBA::BOA interface 77, 166
CORBA::Credentials interface 168–169
CORBA::Current interface 167–168
CORBA::DomainManager interface 167
CORBA::NVList 63, 65–66, 68
CORBA::Object 63–64, 67, 102
CORBA::Object interface 102, 168
CORBA::ORB 63, 66, 74
CORBA::ORB interface 102, 166
CORBA::Request 64, 67–68, 70
CORBAfacility 268–270, 274, 276

CORBAservices 17, 249
  Collection 18, 212–218
  Concurrency control 17
  Events 17, 105–124
  Externalization 18
  Licensing 18
  Life cycle 17, 105–124
  Naming 17, 105–124
  Persistence 17
  Properties 18
  Query 18
  Relationship 18
  Security 18, 151–178
  Time 18
  Trader 18, 125–134
  Transactions 17, 167
CosContainment::Relationship interface 226
CosGraph::Role interface 226
CosGraphs::Role interface 224
CosReference::Relationship interface 226
CosRelationships::Relationship interface 226
CosRelationships::Role interface 224, 226
Covia 262
create method 148, 166, 190, 207–208, 223
create_compound_operations method 114
create_iterator method 207
create_node method 224
create_object method 113, 187
create_PID_from_key method 186
create_PID_from_string method 186
create_PID_from_string_and_key method 186
create_PO method 186
create_related method 148
create_role method 223
create_subtransaction method 141
create_transactional method 148
create_transactional_related method 148
create_traversal_on method 224
create_uninitialized method 190
Credentials 154
Credentials interface 155, 171–173
CSI (Common Secure IIOP) 177
Current interface 141, 155–156, 164, 171–173, 262
Cursor interface 187
CursorFactory interface 187
Cushing Group 250
Cyberdog 282, 286

D

DA (Direct Access) 185
DA (Direct Attribute) 183
DAIS 245
Datagram 64, 66, 258
Datastore_CLI interface 187
Date, Chris 203
DCE (Distributed Computing Environment) 12,
    15, 17, 99, 230
  Cell Directory Service (CDS) 106
  Kerberos 17
  Network Data Representation (NDR) 17
DCOM (Distributed Component Object
    Model) 2–3, 42, 249–250, 255, 286
DDCF (Distributed Document Component
    Facility) 268, 270, 274, 276
Declarative language 86
Deferred response 262
Deferred synchronous 64, 258
define_index method 110
define_properties method 240
define_properties_with_modes method 240
define_property method 240
define_property_with_mode method 240
Delegated credentials 159
Delegation 152, 172, 176
DelegationPolicy interface 176
delete method 186
delete_all_properties method 240
delete_index method 110
delete_object method 187
delete_properties method 240
delete_property method 240
Delivery authority 162
Deque interface 218
describe method 130
describe_link method 130
describe_type method 132–133
destroy method 108, 114, 121, 130, 223–224
destroy_relationships method 223
Developer 2000 41
Digital 6, 41, 50, 124, 236, 242, 245, 250,
    257, 262
DII (Dynamic Invocation Interface) 12, 52, 61–
    72
disconnect method 186–187
disconnect_push_consumer method 119, 121
disconnect_push_supplier 119, 121
Dispatcher 268

Distributed objects
  Collections 212–218
  Events 105–124
  Life cycle 105–124
  Naming 105–124
  Security 151–178
  Trader 125–134
Dixon, Graeme 136
DocFiles 283–285
DocObjects 282
Domain 159, 203
Domain frameworks 256, 277
DomainAccessPolicy interface 175
drop_locks method 148
DSI (Dynamic Skeleton Interface) 13
DSOM 4.0 109
Dynamic methods 52
Dynamic properties 127, 131
Dynamically composed class 131
DynamicPropEval interface 131
Dyson, Esther 204

E

ECMA 235 177
EdgeIterator interface 224
Edges 224
Electronic commerce domain 277
Encapsulation 153, 248
Encryption 163, 177
end_context method 190
end_use method 237
Endpoint 257
Enterprise Beans 288
Enterprise Java 44
Equality collections 214
EqualityIterator interface 215, 217
EqualityKeyIterator interface 215, 217
EqualityKeySortedIterator interface 215, 217
EqualitySequence interface 215, 217
EqualitySequenceFactory interface 217
EqualitySequentialIterator interface 215, 217
EqualitySortedIterator interface 215, 217
EqualitySortedIteratorinterface 215, 217
ESIOPs (Environment-Specific Inter-ORB
    Protocols) 14, 17
evalDP method 131
evaluate method 208
Event 173
Event channel 118, 120
Event proxies 119–120

Event Service 17, 105, 124, 249, 262
Event traces 22
event_time method 231–232
EventChannel interface 121
Events 32, 105, 160, 277
Evidence 174
Evidence storage 162
Evidence store 174
execute method 187, 208
Expersoft 41, 50, 242, 245, 257
export method 130, 133
Exporters 125
Externalization service 18
externalize method 190
externalize_to_stream method 190
Extranet 49

F

Factory 76, 213, 265
FactoryFinder interface 113
Fault-tolerance 248
Federated traders 128
FileStreamFactory interface 190
Finance domain 277
find_factories method 113
Fine-grained objects 199
Firewall 257
flush method 190
for_consumers method 121
for_suppliers method 121
forget method 141
form_complete_evidence interface 174
form_complete_evidence method 171, 174
Frameworks 203, 273
fully_describe_type method 132

G

Gamelon 283–285, 287
Gartner Group 235
GemStone 41, 195
General Inter-ORB Protocol (GIOP) 15
General Magic 198
generate_token method 171, 174
GenericFactory interface 113
get_active_credentials method 168
get_all_properties method 240
get_all_property_names method 240
get_allowed_properties method 240

get_allowed_property_types method 240
get_association_options method 176
get_attributes method 156, 167, 169, 171
get_audit_selectors method 176
get_control method 141
get_coordinator method 148
get_credentials method 167–168
get_current method 167–168
get_delegation_mode method 176
get_domain_policy method 167
get_edges method 224
get_effective_rights method 175
get_NR_features method 171
get_NR_policy_info method 174, 177
get_object_type method 187
get_option method 187
get_other_related_object method 223
get_other_role method 223
get_parent_status method 141
get_PIDString method 186
get_policy method 167, 173
get_properties method 240
get_property_mode method 240
get_property_modes method 240
get_property_value method 240
get_relationships method 223
get_required_rights method 170
get_result method 208
get_rights method 175
get_security_features method 168–169
get_security_mechanisms method 168
get_security_names method 168
get_service_information method 166, 168
get_status method 141, 208
get_token_details method 171
get_top_level_status method 141
get_transaction_name method 141
Gradient 236, 242
Graham, Ian 22
grant_rights method 175
Graphs 224
Gray, Jim 28, 136–137
Gregorian calendar 229
Groupe Bull 242
Groupware 39

H

hash_top_level_transaction method 141
hash_transaction method 141
Healthcare domain 277

Heap interface 215, 217
Helland, Pat 253
Hitachi 42
Homan, Pete 136
Houston, Ian 136
HP 2, 6, 41, 50, 242, 245
HTTP (Hypertext Transfer Protocol) 2, 31, 34
   State 34

I

Ibex 195
IBM 2, 6, 40–42, 50, 124, 189, 206, 236, 242,
   245, 251, 253, 257, 262
ICL 242, 245
IDAPI 187
IdentifiableNamingContext interface 110
IdentifiableObject interface 223
identify_all_occurances method 110
identify_any_occurance method 110
IDL (Interface Definition Language) 4–6, 9, 19,
   22, 45, 57, 85–102, 201, 265, 267, 274,
   277
   And C++ 87
   and ODMG-93 201
   Contract 87
   CORBA 4–6
   Format 57
   Notational tool 87
   Precompiler 54, 57, 86–87
IIOP (Internet Inter-ORB Protocol) 14, 32, 34,
   43–46, 48–50, 258
Implementation name 77
Implementation Repository 46, 56–57, 77–78
ImplementationDef interface 102
Importers 125
Information Highway 40
Initialization service 73–84
In-place editing 273, 282–283
insert_element_at method 207
Instance manager 248, 263
Integrator 262
Intelligent office 195
Interaction diagrams 22
Interface 54, 62, 64, 66, 68–69, 102, 247
Interface name 77
Interface Repository 9, 12–13, 46, 56–57, 62,
   77, 85–102
   Defined 93
   Federations 99
   Uses 93

Interface versioning 265–267
InterfaceDef interface 102
InterfaceDef::describe method 62, 66, 68–69
InterfaceDef::describe_interface method 62, 66,
   68–69
InterfaceDef::lookup_name method 62, 66, 68–
   69
Intermediary 172–173
internalize method 190
internalize_from_stream method 190
Internet 16, 40, 258
   And CORBA 31–32, 34, 38
Internet Explorer 4.0 282
Internet Foundation Classes 49
Interoperable Naming 109
Interoperation 165
interval method 231
Introspection 32, 52
Iona 41, 44–47, 49–50, 136, 242, 245, 248
IOR (Interoperable Object Reference) 17, 164
is_ancestor_transaction method 141
is_descendant_transaction method 141
is_identical method 223
is_identical_PID method 187
is_property_defined method 240
is_related_transaction method 141
is_same_transaction method 141
is_top_level_transaction method 141
is_valid method 169
ISAPI (Internet Server API) 31
Iterator 213–214
Iterator interface 207, 214–215, 217
Itinerary 268

J

Jacobson, Ivar 22, 237
Jars 287
Java 5, 253, 264, 268, 288
   And CORBA 2, 34–35, 76, 288
   Applet 34–35, 62
   Beans 38, 101
   Callbacks 53–59
   Mobile code 37
   ORBs 43–50
   The Bad 250
   The Ugly 250
   Threads 80
Java Beans 38, 255, 286
Java Transaction Service 41
Java2IDL 101

Java2IIOP 101
JavaScript 49
JavaSoft 2, 31, 40–42, 44, 288
Joe (Java Objects Everywhere) 41, 44–45, 49, 109, 245
Joint Object Services Submission (JOSS) 106

K

Kerberos 163, 177
KeyBag interface 215, 217
KeyBagFactory interface 217
Keyed collections 213
KeyIterator interface 215, 217
KeySet interface 215, 217
KeySetFactory interface 217
KeySortedBag interface 215, 217
KeySortedBagFactoryinterface 217
KeySortedIterator interface 215, 217
KeySortedSet interface 215, 217
KeySortedSetFactory interface 217

L

Language bindings 57
LDAP (Lightweight Directory Access Protocol) 17
LicenseServiceManager interface 237
Licensing 236, 238–239
Licensing Service 18
Life cycle 18
Life cycle service 17, 105, 124
LifeCycleObject interface 113
Link interface 130
link method 223
List
    Defined 201
list method 108
list_links method 130
list_types method 132–133
LOA (Library Object Adapter) 200
Load-balancing 248, 259
Local/remote transparency 9, 25, 248
lock method 148
LockCoordinator interface 148
Locking 136
Locks 147
Lockset interface 148
LocksetFactory interface 148
Lookup interface 130, 134

Lotus 2

M

Macintosh 255, 271
Manufacturing domain 277
Map interface 215, 217
MapFactory interface 217
Marimba 285
Maritz, Paul 283
Marley, Bob 288
Marshaling 12
mask_type method 132
MATISSE 195
max_left method 130
Menai 283–285
MessageQ 262
Messaging 124, 255, 257–261
Metaclass 20
Metadata 9, 23, 52, 265
MetaWare 9, 100
Method
    Invocation 57
    Signature 12
Microsoft 42, 187, 189, 251, 253, 255, 286
Middleware 8, 13, 20, 150
    And transactions 150
Mission-critical ORBs 254
MIT 177
Mixins 191
MOA (Message Object Adapter) 262
Mobile agents 244, 255, 268–270
Model 23–24
modify method 130
modify_link method 130
MOM (Message-Oriented Middleware) 8, 116, 124, 249, 257–260
more method 207
move method 113–114
move_node method 114
move_relationship method 114
move_role method 114
Mowbray, Thomas 15
MQSeries 262
Multimedia 198
Multiple interfaces 255, 265–266
Multithreading 76, 80
MVC (Model/View/Controller) 23–24

N

Name binding 107
Named Value List 63, 65–66, 68
Namespaces 106
Naming
   IBM/Sun Interoperable Naming 109
Naming Service 17, 61, 125, 249
NamingContext interface 108, 110
NDR (Network Data Representation) 17
NDS (NetWare Directory Service) 17
NEO 41, 44–45, 109, 245
Nested relations 203
Netscape v, 2, 6, 37, 40, 42, 44, 47–49, 101,
   268, 286
   And Cyberdog 282
Netscape ONE (Open Network
   Environment) 47–49
NetWare 287
Network Computing Architecture 31, 41
new_context method 108
new_interval method 231–232
new_universal_time method 231–232
NeXT 31
next method 207
next_n method 108, 130, 223–224
next_one method 108, 223–224
NIS+ 17, 106
Node interface 114, 224
NodeFactory interface 224
Nodes 224
Nomadic clients 259
Non-repudiation 18, 151–178
Non-tampering 163
Nortel 124, 257
Novell 41, 242
NRCredentials interface 163, 171, 174
NRPolicy interface 163, 174, 177
NSAPI (Netscape Server API) 31
NVList::add_item method 63, 65–66
NVList::add_value method 65–66, 68
NVList::free method 65, 68
NVList::free_memory method 65
NVList::get_count method 65
NVList::remove method 65

O

O2 Technology 195, 198

Object
   And TP Monitors 251
   And transactions 135–150
   Change management 235–242, 245–254
   Collections 205, 207–208, 212
   Collections Service 208
   Concurrency 136, 146–148, 150
   Events 105, 116, 119, 124
   Externalizations 190, 192
   Licensing 236, 238–239
   Locking 136, 146–148, 150
   Locks 136, 147
   Naming 105–107, 111
   Persistence 179–201
   Persistence Service 76
   Properties 106, 239–241
   Query Service 205–209, 211–212
   Relationships 114, 218, 220, 222–224, 226,
      234
   Roaming 198
   System management 235–242, 245–254
   Time 228–229
   Trading 105
   Versus RPC 54, 247
   Well-known 75
Object activation 247
Object adapter 58, 78, 200
Object bus 26
Object database 195–196, 198, 200–201, 203–
   204
Object Design 195
Object discovery 125–134
Object dispenser 250
Object extender 287
Object IDs 196
Object Life Cycle Service 113
Object Linking and Embedding (OLE) 271
Object reference 46, 56, 126, 264
   Defined 55
   Operations 46, 56
Object repositories 198
Object Services
   Collections 205, 207, 212
   Concurrency 136, 146–148, 150
   CORBA 205–218, 219–234, 235–242, 245–
      254
   Events 105, 116, 119, 124
   Externalization 190, 192
   Licensing 236, 238–239
   Naming 105–107, 111
   Persistence 179–201
   Properties 106, 239–241

Object Services (continued)
  Query 205–208, 211–212
  Relationships 114, 218, 220, 222–224, 226, 234
  Time 228–229
  Trader 105
  Transactions 135–150
Object TP Monitors 32, 42, 84, 189, 248, 250–251, 254, 288
Object Web 2, 39–40, 42, 62, 253, 255, 281–282, 286–288
Object Web II 244, 279, 286, 288
Object White Pages 125
Object Yellow Pages 125–134
Object::_request method 63–64, 67, 70
Object::create_request method 63–64, 67–68
Object::get_implementation method 102
Object::get_interface method 62, 64, 66, 68–69, 102
Object::hash method 102
Object::is_a method 102
Object::is_equivalent method 102
Object::is_nil method 102
Object::non_existent method 102
ObjectBroker 50, 245, 250
Objective C 5, 264
Objectivity 195, 198
ObjectStore 198
ObjectWare 189, 251, 253
obtain_producer_specific_license_service method 237
obtain_pull_consumer method 121
obtain_pull_supplier method 121
obtain_push_consumer method 121
obtain_push_supplier method 121
ODA (Object Database Adapter) 200
  Defined 200
ODBC 187
ODBMS (Object Database Management System) 17, 41, 180, 182–184, 186, 195–196, 198, 200–201, 203–204, 254, 287
  Architecture 195
  Defined 194
  Features 196
  Object Adapters 78
  Programming 196
  Versus SQL 202–203
ODI (Object Design, Inc.) 41, 195, 201
ODL (Object Definition Language) 195
  Defined 201

ODMG (Object Database Management Group) 18, 205–207, 212
  and OMG 199
ODMG-93 (Object Database Management Group-93) 185, 194–195, 200–201
  and SQL 201
  Components 201
  ODL 201
  OML 201
  OQL 201
OfferId 130
OfferIterator interface 130
Office 95 282
OLE (Object Linking and Embedding) 244, 281–282, 286
  And the Web 30
OLTP (Online Transaction Processing)
  Commandments 252–253
  Etiquette 252–253
  Folklore 253
OMG (Object Management Group) 3, 188, 199, 201, 288
  and ODMG 199
OML (Object Manipulation Language) 195, 201
ONE (Open Network Environment) 31
One-way 64, 258
Ontologies 249
Ontos 195, 198
OO Frameworks 203
OODA (Object Database Adapter)
  Defined 200
OOUI (Object-Oriented User Interface) 203
Open Database Connectivity (ODBC) 187
Open Scripting Architecture (OSA) 274
OpenDoc 30, 38, 244, 255, 268, 270–271, 274, 276, 281–282, 286
  And CORBA 274
  And the Web 30
  Bento 274
  Client/Server 276
  Defined 274
  Open Scripting Architecture (OSA) 274
  Part 274
  SOM 274
Operations interface 114
OperationsFactory interface 114
OQL (Object Query Language) 18, 201, 205–207
Oracle 2, 31–32, 40–42, 288
  Cartridges 32, 288
Oracle Web Server 3.0 41
Oracle8 204

Orange Book 154
ORB (Object Request Broker) 7, 26, 200, 203–204
  IDL precompiler 57
  Implementation Repository 57, 78
  Interface 12
  Language bindings 57
  Security 151–178
  Up-calls 57
  Versus RPC 10
ORB interface 13
  get_implementation 46, 56
  get_interface 46, 56
  is_nil 46, 56
  object_to_string 46, 56
  string_to_object 46, 56
ORB Plus 50
ORB::BOA_init method 74
ORB::create_list method 63, 66
ORB::create_operation_list method 63, 66, 68
ORB::get_next_response method 66
ORB::list_initial_services method 74
ORB::object_to_string method 102
ORB::poll_next_response method 66
ORB::resolve_initial_references method 74
ORB::send_multiple_requests_deferred method 66
ORB::send_multiple_requests_oneway method 66
ORB::string_to_object method 102
Orbix 44–47, 49–50, 245
OrbixWeb 44–47, 49–50, 248
OrbixWeb V1 45
OrbixWeb V2 47
ORBlets 2
  OLE COMlet 30
ORBPlus 245
Ordered collections 213
OS/2 255
OS/2 Warp 40, 271, 287
OSAgent 48
OSF (Open System Foundation) 17
OToole, Annrai 136
OTS (Object Transaction Service) 17, 167, 248
overlaps method 231
override_default_credentials method 168
override_default_mechanisms method 168
override_default_QOP method 168

P

Pascal, Fabian 202–203
Pass-by-value 255, 262, 267–268
PDS interface 186
PDSs (Persistent Data Services) 183
PeerLogic 124, 257, 262
Persistence Service 17, 76
Persistent Object Service 199
Persistent objects 263
Persistent server 82, 84
PID (Persistent Identifier) 77, 183, 194
PID interface 186
PIDFactory interface 186
Pipes 262
Place 284–285
PO (Persistent Object) 183, 201
PO interface 186
POA (Portable Object Adapter) 263–264
Poet 195
POFactory interface 186
Policies 129
Policy 277
Polymorphism 9, 54, 153, 247
POM (Persistent Object Manager) 183
POM interface 186
Portable frameworks 255
Portable server 263
Ports 257
POS (Persistence Object Service) 188
POS 1 188
POS 2 188–189
Post-conditions 277
PostModern 47–48
Postprocessor 101
PowerBroker 50, 245
Pragma 12
Pre-conditions 277
Preferences 129
prepare method 141, 208
Principal 154–155, 159, 161
PrincipalAuthenticator interface 155, 169
PriorityQueue interface 218
Private key 177
Privilege 155
Privilege delegation 157
Privileges 159
ProducerSpecificLicenseService interface 237
Project Spring 44
Project X 249
Proof-of-origin certificate 162

Proof-of-receipt certificate 162
Properties 127
Properties Service 18
Property editor 279
PropertySet interface 110, 240
PropertySetDef interface 240
Proxy 12
Proxy interface 130
ProxyPushConsumer interface 121
ProxyPushSupplier interface 121
Pseudo-object 63–64, 66–67, 74, 77, 102, 166,
    171, 173
Public key 177
Publish-and-subscribe 248, 262
Pull events 119
Push events 119
push method 119, 121
PushConsumer interface 119, 121
PushSupplier interface 119, 121

Q

QOP (Quality of Protection) 168
QOS (Quality of Security) 166
QoS (Quality of Service) 258, 262
QueriableNamingContext interface 110
Query
    Federations 206
    Nested 206
Query interface 208
query method 130, 134
Query Service 18, 262
    Collections interfaces 208
QueryableCollection interface 208
QueryEvaluator interface 110, 208
QueryManager interface 208
Queue 262
Queue interface 218
Queue-aware server 262
Queues 258–259
Queuing 260–261

R

read_boolean method 190
read_char method 190
read_double method 190
read_float method 190
read_graph method 190
read_long method 190

read_object method 190
read_octet method 190
read_short method 190
read_string method 190
read_unsigned_long method 190
read_unsigned_short method 190
rebind method 108
rebind_context method 108
received_credentials method 167
Recoverable resources 140
Reference 226
Reference data 77
Reference ID 77
Reference relationship 221
ReferencedByRole interface 226
ReferencesRole interface 226
Referential integrity 196
refresh method 169
Register interface 130, 133
register method 231–232
register_mapping_schema method 187
register_resource method 141
register_subtran_aware method 141
Relation interface 215, 217
RelationFactory interface 217
Relationship
    Attributes 222
    Cardinality 222
    Containment 221
    Degree 222
    Edges 224
    Graph 222, 224
    Nodes 222, 224
    Role 222
Relationship interface 114, 223
Relationship service 18
RelationshipFactory interface 223
RelationshipIterator interface 223
Remote Procedure Call (RPC) 260–261
remove method 113–114
remove_element_at method 207
remove_link method 130
remove_node method 114
remove_role method 224
remove_type method 132
replace_audit_selectors method 176
replace_element_at method 207
replace_rights method 175
Repository IDs 12
Request::add_arg method 64, 70
Request::delete method 64, 67–68, 71
Request::get_response method 64

Request::invoke method 64, 67–68, 70
Request::poll_response method 64
Request::send_deferred method 64
Request::send_oneway method 64
Request-reply 258
RequiredRights interface 170
reset method 207
resolve method 108, 130
Resource 140, 142
Resource interface 141
restore method 186
resume method 141
retrieve_element_at method 207
retrieve_object method 187
Reuter, Andreas 137
revoke_rights method 175
RFC 1510 177
RFP (Request For Proposal) 11, 19
Rights 159
RMI (Remote Method Invocations) 2
Roaming agents 26
Role 222
Role interface 114, 223
RoleFactory interface 223
Roles 159, 277
roles_of_type method 224
rollback method 141
rollback_only method 141
rollback_subtransaction method 141
RPC (Remote Procedure Call) 8
   Versus ORB 10
RSA 163
Rule 279
Rules 277
Rumbaugh, Jim 22

S

SDO (Semantic Data Object) 277
Secure federations 154
Secure IIOP 164, 166, 171, 173, 177
Secure method 156
secure_universal_time method 231–232
SecureInvocationPolicy interface 176
Security 9
Security authority 164
Security domain 163–164
Security policy 165
Security service 18, 151–178
Security ticket 155
Security-aware application 166, 171

Sedona 41
select_object method 187
Self describing systems 85
Semantic messaging 277
Semantic metadata 249
SequenceFactory interface 217
SequentialIterator interface 215, 217
Servant 259, 263–264
Server-per-method 81
Server-to-server infrastructure 248
Service type 127, 131
ServiceTypeRepository interface 132–133
Servio 195
SESAME 177
Sessions, Roger 179, 185, 189–190
Set
   Defined 201
Set interface 215, 217
set_association_options method 176
set_audit_channel method 176
set_audit_selectors method 176
set_credentials method 155, 167
set_data method 231–232
set_delegation_mode method 176
set_NR_features method 171
set_NR_policy_info method 177
set_option method 187
set_position method 187
set_privileges method 169
set_property_mode method 240
set_property_modes method 240
set_required_rights method 170
set_security_features method 168–169
set_timeout method 141
set_timer method 231–232
SetFactory interface 217
SFA (Server Framework Adapter) 263–264
Shared server 79–80
Shippable places 39, 281–287
Siemens 242
SimCity 271
Simple delegation 157
Sims, Oliver 25
Single-level stores 182
Site licensing 236
Smalltalk 5, 195, 201, 264
Sniffer 152
Snyder, Alan 136
Sockets 2
Solstic 41
SOM (System Object Model) 50, 100, 245, 274
SOM 3.0 245

SOM 4.0 41, 245
SortedBag interface 215, 217
SortedBagFactory interface 217
SortedMap interface 215, 217
SortedMapFactory interface 217
SortedRelation interface 215, 217
SortedRelationFactory interface 217
SortedSet interface 215, 217
SortedSetFactory interface 217
spans method 231
SPKM 177
Spring 44, 242
SQL (Structured Query Language)
   Callable Level Interface (CLI) 184
   CLI 185, 187
   Dynamic 185
   Schema mappers 185
   Versus ODBMS 202–203
SQL Access Group (SAG) 187
SQL databases 180
SQL3 18, 187, 198, 201, 205–207
SSL (Secure Sockets Layer) 163, 177
Stack interface 218
Standard Stream Data Format 193
Standish Group 245
start_use method 237
Stateless objects 254
Static method invocations 52, 53–59
store method 186
Stored procedures 8
Storey, Tony 136
Stream interface 190
Streamable interface 190
StreamableFactory interface 190
StreamFactory interface 190
StreamIO interface 190
Streams 190–191
Striker 282
Stringified object 61
Structured files 283–285
Stub 12–13
Subdomain 164
SubtransactionAwareResource interface 141
Subtransactions 139
Sun 2, 6, 17, 44–45, 245
SunSoft 41, 180, 242
SupplierAdmin interface 121
Surface area 277
suspend method 141
Sweeper 282
Synchronous 64
System administration 153, 165, 175

System events 160
System management 175

T

Taligent 190, 242
Tampering 161
Tandem 6, 41, 242
Tandem NonStop kernel 287
Task scripts 22
Telecom domain 277
Threads 76, 80, 258
Tibbetts, John 135
Tibco 124, 257, 262
TibNet 262
time method 231
Time service 18
time_set method 231–232
time_to_interval method 231
Time-independent queues 259
TimerEventHandler 231–232
TimerEventService interface 231–232
TimeService interface 231–232
TIO (Time Interval Object) 231
TIO interface 231
Tivoli 136, 242
Tokens 154–155, 174
Tools 32, 278
TP Monitors 32, 39, 84, 136, 138, 149–150,
    189, 203, 247–248, 250–251, 254, 288
   And objects 248, 250–251
   And ORBs 250
Trader Service 18, 62, 125–134, 262
transact method 187
Transaction coordinator 140
Transaction Service 17, 167
Transaction state 167
TransactionalLockset interface 148
Transactions 9, 189, 203, 248, 252, 277
   And Objects 135–150
   Defined 137
   Flat 138
   Long-lived 198
   Nested 135, 138–139, 148
   Saga 138
   Top-level 139
   X/Open DTP Standard 139
Transarc 136, 146
Transient objects 263
Transportation domain 277
Traversal interface 224

TraversalCriteria interface 224
TraversalFactory interface 224
Trojan horse 152
Trust domains 154
Trusted domain 164
Trusted ORB 159
try_lock method 148
Tuxedo 41, 189, 251
Two-level stores 182
Two-phase commit 140, 142, 146

U

unbind method 108
unbind_all_occurances method 110
Unique collections 214
UniSQL 195
universal_time method 231–232
unlink method 223
unlock method 148
unmask method 132
unregister method 231–232
Unshared server 80
Up-call interfaces
   Defined 57
update_object method 187
URL (Unified Resource Locator)
   And objects 282–283
Use cases 22
User sponsor 155
User-defined types 196, 203
UTC (Universal Time Coordinated) 229–230
UTO (Universal Time Object) 231
UTO interface 231
uto_from_utc method 231–232
UUID (Universal Unique Identifier) 12, 99

V

verify_evidence method 171
Versant 41, 195
Versioning 198, 265–267
Vetter, Brian 136
View 23–24
Viper 42, 189, 250–251, 253, 286
Virtual world 284–285
VisiBroker 245
   Event Service 249
   Naming Service 249
   Object Transaction Service 249

VisiBroker for C++ 47–48
VisiBroker for Java 40, 44, 47–50, 71
Visigenic 37, 44, 47–48, 101, 245, 249, 268
visit_node method 224
Visual Edge 242
VisualAge 41
VisualAge for C++ 100, 185

W

Web browsers
   And components 282–283
WebObjects 31
WebServer 31
Wells Fargo 250
Windows 271
Windows 95 40, 255
Windows 97 286
withdraw method 130
withdraw_using_constraint method 130
Workflow 248, 251, 276
World Wide Web (Web)
   Objects 30
write_boolean method 190
write_char method 190
write_double method 190
write_float method 190
write_graph method 190
write_long method 190
write_object method 190
write_octet method 190
write_short method 190
write_string method 190
write_unsigned_long method 190
write_unsigned_short method 190

X

X.500 17, 106
X/Open 139, 230
X/Open CLI 184, 187
X3H2 206
XBase 187

Y

Yellow Pages 61

Make the Java/CORBA Connection!

From the authors of the best-selling books: *The Essential Client/Server Survival Guide* and *The Essential Distributed Objects Survival Guide*.

Robert Orfali • Dan Harkey

Client/Server Programming with JAVA and CORBA

Contents at a Glance

Part 1. CORBA Meets Java . . . . 64 Pages
Part 2. Core CORBA/Java . . . . 50 Pages
Part 3. The Dynamic CORBA . . . . 46 Pages
Part 4. CORBA and Its Competitors . . . . .170 Pages
Part 5. The Existential CORBA . . . . 68 Pages
Part 6. JDBC: 2 Tier Versus 3-Tier . . . . 129 Pages
Part 7. The Grand Finale: CORBA/Java Club Med 88 Pages

I highly recommend it!

Whether you're a seasoned Java programmer, a distributed objects expert, or looking to be a little of both, this book gives you the programming know-how you need to combine these two technologies into workable client/server solutions for the Object Web. Full of working code, tutorials, and design tradeoffs, this book:

- Covers everything from simple ORBs to object activation.

- Uses tutorials and client/server benchmarks to compare CORBA and its competitors—including Java/RMI, Java/DCOM, Sockets, and HTTP/CGI.

- Covers in detail Netscape's ORB: VisiBroker for Java and shows you how to use Caffeine to write CORBA/Java applications without IDL.

- Provides a Debit-Credit benchmark for JDBC databases to compare 2-tier vs. 3-tier client/server solutions.

- Includes a Web-based Club Med client/server application using CORBA, Java, JDBC, and applets.

- Shows how to use CORBA's dynamic facilities such as callbacks, dynamic invocations, object introspection, and the interface repository.

- Compares the performance of C++ ORBs with Java ORBs.

- Comes with a CD-ROM containing over 15 Java-based client/server applications.

WILEY

Available at Bookstores Everywhere

For more information visit **http://www.wiley.com/compbooks**

ISBN: 0471-16351-1, 658 pages, 1997, $44.95 US / $62.95 CAN

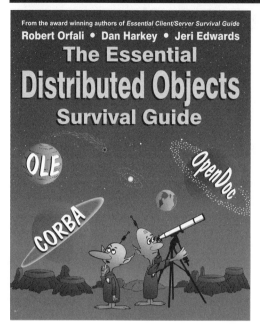

Your Survival Guide to Client/Server!

Robert Orfali • Dan Harkey • Jeri Edwards

The Essential Client/Server Survival Guide

Second Edition

Completely Updated Award-winning Bestseller

Contents at a Glance

Part 1. The Big Picture . . . . 54 Pages
Part 2. Clients, Servers, and Operating Systems 140 Pages
Part 3. Base Middleware: Stacks and NOSs . . . 50 Pages
Part 4. SQL Database Servers . . . . 108 Pages
Part 5. Client/Server Transaction Processing . 66 Pages
Part 6. Client/Server Groupware . . . . 56 Pages
Part 7. Client/Server With Distributed Objects 84 Pages
Part 8. Client/Server and the Internet . . . . . .114 Pages
Part 9. Distributed System Management . . . . . 52 Pages
Part 10. Bringing It All Together . . . . 22 Pages

I highly recommend it!

It's as savvy, informative, and entertaining as anything you are likely to read on the subject. Client/server isn't one technology but many—remote SQL, TP, message-oriented groupware, distributed objects, and so on. Like the proverbial blind men feeling the elephant, most of us have a hard time seeing the whole picture. The authors succeed brilliantly in mapping the elephant.

> — *Jon Udell, BYTE Magazine*

The scope and depth of topics covered in the Guide, with its straightforward and often humorous delivery, make this book required reading for anyone who deals with computers in today's corporate environment.

> — *Bob Gallagher, PC Week*

Absolutely the finest book on client/server on the market today.

> — *Richard Finkelstein*
> *President of Performance Computing*

Charmingly accessible.

> — *Dr. Jim Gray*
> *Author of* Transaction Processing

WILEY

Available at Bookstores Everywhere

For more information visit **http://www.wiley.com/compbooks**

ISBN: 0471-15325-7, 676 pages, 1996, $32.95 US / $46.50 CAN